Athene Series
Feminist Scholarship on Culture and Education

(continued)

PIONEERING DEANS OF WOMEN

More Than Wise and Pious Matrons

JANA NIDIFFER

Foreword by Mary Ann Dzuback

Teachers College, Columbia University
New York and London

Published by Teachers College Press, 1234 Amsterdam Avenue, New York, NY 10027

Library of Congress Cataloging-in-Publication Data

Nidiffer, Jana, 1957–
    Pioneering deans of women : more than wise and pious matrons / Jana Nidiffer.
      p. cm. — (Athene series)
    Includes bibliographical references (p.) and index.
    ISBN 0-8077-3915-4 (cloth : alk. paper) — ISBN 0-8077-3914-6 (paper : alk. paper)
    1. Deans of women—United States—Biography. 2. Women deans (Education)—
    United States—Biography. I. Title. II. Series.
    LC1620.N53 2000
    378.1'12—dc21   99-041290

ISBN 0-8077-3914-6 (paper)
ISBN 0-8077-3915-4 (cloth)

Printed on acid-free paper

Manufactured in the United States of America

07 06 05 04 03 02 01 00   8 7 6 5 4 3 2 1

To Arthur Levine
with grateful appreciation for countless kindnesses

CONTENTS

FOREWORD

Until recently, the majority of scholarship in the history of higher education in the United States either did not deal with gender, or merely alluded to the presence or absence of women. The early exceptions to this narrative line were explorations of women's colleges and, occasionally, coeducational institutions. But the scholarship was preoccupied with the founding and administration of colleges, the development and transformation of research universities, state and national policy in higher education, the impact of academic scholars on intellectual history, and colleges and universities' roles in middle-class formation and professionalization. Because most histories of higher education did not use gender as a category of analysis until the 1980s, it is not surprising that what was considered the academic cultural norm was actually the white masculinization of academe.

The pioneer historians who chose to write about women and women's experiences—Thomas Woody, Jeanne L. Noble, Mabel Newcomer, and the more critical and feminist late 1960s and 1970s studies by Jill Kerr Conway, Patricia Albjerg Graham, Charlotte Conable, Carol Lasser, and Roberta Frankfort—were crucial in developing the historiography. But, as with any shift in research focus, the transformation in what is seen as important by leaders in the field could only be influenced by the increasing volume of work in the 1980s and 1990s: studies by Barbara Solomon, Joyce Antler, Rosalind Rosenberg, Margaret Rossiter, Geraldine Jonçich Clifford, Helen Horowitz, Lynn Gordon, Sally Schwager, Patricia Palmieri, Ellen Fitzpatrick, Linda Perkins, and many others. This recent scholarship has grown, as the work in women's history has had more impact on the larger body of historical scholarship on American culture and institutions. It has helped to open the door to closer examination of institutional cultures in a variety of institutions beyond the predominantly white liberal arts college and research university. The best of the scholarship cannot ignore gender, ethnicity, race, and class issues in the growth and transformation of higher education in the United States: For since the colonial period, these institutions have played key roles in forming local and national leadership and culture, in training for the professions, and in responding to state-defined needs for knowledge and technical expertise, as well as in excluding or limiting representation of nonwhites and nonmales in these activities.

If Jana Nidiffer did nothing more than to make abundantly evident the key roles that women deans assumed as advocates for marginalized women students on early coeducational campuses, that would be enough to justify this book. But she does more than that: Her analysis of Lois Kimball Mathews, Marion Talbot, Mary Bidwell Breed, and Ada Louise Comstock's efforts to gain for women not just access, but equitable treatment within coeducational universities, provides her readers with an exposition of the structural and cultural flaws in these institutions' claims to meritocracy. That these women worked against institutionalized inequities, when such colleges and universities prided themselves on being agents of credentialing and professional certification on the basis of academic competence, makes Nidiffer's story all the more compelling and necessary.

Nidiffer's book contributes measurably to our understanding of the history of higher education. We know about the major male university leaders from the 1870s to the 1940s, but far too little about women administrators; these women were absolutely critical to realizing the promise of integrating women into the university and pressuring the university to accommodate women within its definition of legitimate student. Although they were not successful in many of their efforts to attain equitable treatment for women, they were successful enough so that by the 1920s women students began to see campuses as their territory too. In addition, women students came to view deans as allies in creating institutional space and in gaining recognition from faculty, administrators, and peers.

In the end, Nidiffer's book is not merely an account of the efforts, successes, and setbacks of women deans: It is an analysis of how they developed a profession out of their dedication to making universities in the twentieth century better places for women than they were in the nineteenth century. Nidiffer's examination of the stages of the professionalization process, the strategies women deans used to solidify and institutionalize their work, and the networks and organizations they built to communicate and further their progress is an important addition to the literature. Deans of women, as she so clearly demonstrates, were the progenitors of the deans of students we know today. As much as presidents and faculty leaders influenced academic life, deans of women influenced campus life for students at coeducational universities. The time has come for their story to be told within the larger history of higher education.

Mary Ann Dzuback

PREFACE

When I entered Indiana University in the middle 1970s, a new world, hitherto unimaginable to me, opened up. The experience convinced me of the transformative potential of higher education. Yet I slowly became aware that, as a young woman, there were avenues that were closed to me and experiences that were unobtainable. My nascent feminist consciousness was only mildly angered by the exclusion. It was, to my mind, simply the way of the world. But distance, in both time and miles, sharpened my critical appraisal of my undergraduate experience and piqued my curiosity about the generations of women who braved much greater hostility and even ostracism for the opportunity to live the life of the mind. This book, with its examination of the lives of those pioneers and the professional women who eased their circumstances, is the culmination of years of interest and study and is dedicated to those women who hungered to make it better.

Jana Nidiffer
Ann Arbor, Michigan, 1999

ACKNOWLEDGMENTS

I am indebted to the creative insights, scholarly contributions, and helpful ideas of several people who enhanced my work and supported me. The initial research for the book was conducted while I was a doctoral student at the Harvard Graduate School of Education (HGSE). Therefore, my first words of thanks and profound gratitude are for the three members of my dissertation committee: Arthur Levine, Linda Eisenmann, and Judith McLaughlin. All three provided unfailing support and intellectual largess that enhanced not only this work, but my entire graduate school career. Linda was especially helpful with her understanding of feminist history and her generous mentoring into the world of academic historians. I feel personally enriched because all three are now close friends as well as colleagues.

All researchers, but perhaps especially historians, are indebted to librarians and archivists, without whom the work would be impossible. I am especially grateful to Kathleen Donovan of HGSE who, for four years, shared a laugh with me at my more ludicrous requests, but then willingly tracked down some of the most obscure information one could imagine. The core of the primary source material essential to this work was collected from several university archives and I wish to thank the archivists whose assiduous efforts are greatly appreciated: Nancy Bartlett, Bentley Historical Library, University of Michigan; Caroline Coven, University of Chicago; Thomas Malefatto, Indiana University; Steve Masar, University of Wisconsin; and Carol O'Brien, University of Minnesota.

Conversations with other historians have guided my work more often than I can name. However, many thanks especially to Carolyn Terry Bashaw for her insights and shared interest in deans of women. I also wish to acknowledge Joyce Antler, who, because of her high standards of scholarship and personal friendship during a formative period of my own intellectual life, acted as the muse, perhaps without even the knowledge that she had done so. I will also always remember my conversations with Barbara Miller Solomon, and I mourn her passing.

During the course of my research, I became especially interested in the life and career of Lois Mathews Rosenberry. I wish to thank Louise

Roberg and the members of the Winneshiek County Genealogical Society for guiding me through a history of Lois's birthplace, Cresco, Iowa. I also want to thank Nancy Rosenberry Hoit, Lois's step-granddaughter, who generously gave me time out of her impossible schedule, shared stories of her family, and allowed me to rummage through her grandmother's trunks.

I am very grateful to the Wisconsin State Historical Society for naming me the Alice E. Smith Fellow and to the Radcliffe Grants to Graduate Women Program for the Caroline Wilby Prize. In addition to the honor afforded, the two awards also provided much-needed funds for travel and research. Many thanks are also due to the editors at Teachers College Press, especially Susan Liddicoat, Lori Tate, and Faye Zucker, whose hard work and patience greatly improved my work.

My deepest thanks are extended to a core of friends who provided love and succor in a crucial time in my life that coincided with completing this book. Linda Eisenmann and Philo Hutchenson have kept me sane through almost daily email discourse. Margie Magraw, more than anyone else, made it possible for the words to flow again. I am also indebted to Theresa Brown and Debbie Paliani who kept me from floundering with innumerable words of support and countless hours of listening. With tremendous affection and gratitude I thank Jayne Thorson for bringing laughter back into my life. And words can scarcely capture my gratitude to Daphne Layton who gave unfailing acceptance and support. Her depth of friendship and her generosity with time, love, and even her home and family sustained me. I am profoundly thankful for her "large sacrifices and small kindnesses."

A final thank you goes to many of my students in the Center for the Study of Higher and Postsecondary Education at the University of Michigan and the Higher Education Program at the University of Massachusetts, Amherst, who remind me, on a regular basis, why I chose my profession and why I love it.

PIONEERING DEANS OF WOMEN

More Than Wise and Pious Matrons

Chapter 1

INTRODUCTION

At its core, George Eliot's 1872 novel *Middlemarch* is about the common life well lived. Her characters have their share of tragedies and triumphs but mostly their lives are modest. As Eliot herself states, her characters are involved in "unhistoric acts." Yet, by the end of her novel, Eliot helps the reader assess the profundity amid the common—the importance of the humanity in every human life, even if such a life is deemed insignificant by the chroniclers of society. With respect to the main character of the book, Dorothea Brooke, Eliot expresses this theme most explicitly in her last paragraph:

> Her full nature, like that river of which Cyrus broke the strength, spent itself in channels which had no great name on the earth. But the effect of her being on those around her was incalculably diffusive: for the growing good of the world is partly dependent on unhistoric acts; and that things are not so ill with you and me as they might have been, is half owing to the number who lived faithfully a hidden life, and rest in unvisited tombs. (p. 766)

It is in such a manner that I regard the first professional deans of women. By some measures their accomplishments may be deemed insignificant. Their story is certainly omitted from traditional (meaning the male-written, president-centric) histories of higher education that were typical prior to the late 1970s, but are still being published today. Yet the early deans made an enormous difference in the lives of the women students they touched and left a lasting legacy for the daughters and the granddaughters of those women as well—a legacy that was resurrected in the women's centers on campuses in the 1970s.

NOT YOUR MOTHER'S DEAN OF WOMEN

In the popular imagination deans of women are often stereotyped as either matronly, curmudgeonly chaperones dedicated to scrutinizing boyfriends and conducting bed checks or innocuous mother figures who offer advice on hem length and proper fork choice at formal dinners. In fact, on more than a few occasions, women who remember their deans have commented to me that my depiction of deans of women as *advocates* for women is a bit startling. So, if the term *dean of women* conjures up only enduring images of prudish busybodies or harmless matrons, why is a historical analysis of this position warranted?

The primary answer to this question is that neither characterization—curmudgeon or house mother— is wholly accurate. Around the turn of the 19th century, the position of dean of women was instead one "in which intelligent, well-qualified, well-educated women could exercise administrative skills and professional leadership and exert a unifying influence on behalf of women" (Treichler, 1985, p. 24). The deans of women of the Progressive Era accomplished two major goals. First, these well-qualified, well-educated deans improved the material lot and the educational experience of women students, especially at midwestern state universities. Second, and perhaps more important, the deans—at least a small cadre of leaders between the years 1892 and 1918—forged a new professional identity for themselves as the first senior women administrators on coeducational university campuses.

The deans developed a more expansive vision for the potential of the profession. Their new role, as they defined it, was one of advocacy for women students. Based on their newly developed expertise in the education of women in coeducational settings, they constructed programs and policies that helped women students cope with the inequitable and sometimes hostile environment of the university —the notorious "Chilly Climate" (Hall & Sandler, 1982; Sandler, Silverberg, & Hall, 1996) of coeducation—that was downright *cold* for women in the late 19th and early 20th centuries.

The deans began to demand that the institution provide whatever was necessary to ensure a good education for women. Nancy Fraser's (1989) discussion of the "need claims" of powerless groups is useful for understanding the way deans approached their work (see also Bashaw, 1992). Fraser identified the "thin" needs of groups, which were the basic, immediate needs such as food or shelter. Thin needs therefore required attention before what might be labeled "higher-order" needs were met. Fraser further noted that needs were "nested," meaning both types of needs were highly interconnected and the failure to meet one kind of need had consequences for the other. Fraser's ideas bear similarities to Abraham Maslow's (1954) notions of a "hierarchy of needs," but Fraser's emphasis on the effects of needs claims for powerless groups and her discussion of the interrelatedness of needs are especially pertinent to the deans' work.

Deans of women seemed to have had an intuitive understanding of Fraser's concepts. While male administrators often believed that admission to the institution was all that women needed, women deans grasped that the situation was more complex. They recognized that the immediate or thin needs of women were housing, adequate meals and rest, and good health. They further understood that such issues were necessary preconditions to addressing the remaining needs of women in college such as intellectual parity, career aspirations, leadership opportunities, and a sense of community. Most important, deans comprehended that both levels of need required consideration in order for women to have the full benefit of a university education. In modern terminology, the deans recognized that mere admission to a university of an underrepresented or marginalized group did not guarantee an equitable experience. There is a difference between *access*—simply getting in—and what I term *genuine access*—experiencing the full panoply of what the university has to offer on terms similar to those for the dominant population. Being the first administrators to fight for genuine access is the legacy of the first professional deans of women.

A NEW FIELD OF ENDEAVOR

The position of dean was significant for the functions it performed, but deans also played an important role in opening up the entire *field* of university administration on coeducational campuses to women. There was (and still is to some degree) a direct relationship between the number of women students at an institution and the presence of women on the faculty or in administration. Consequently, women as faculty or administrators were virtually unknown in all-male institutions. A few significant opportunities for professional careers as presidents or academic deans arose at women's colleges, but unfortunately these colleges were small, employed very few women, and tended to be regional—located primarily in New England and in parts of the South (Horowitz, 1984; Solomon, 1985). So, hope for new career options rested with the coeducational institutions.

Possibilities for employment in coeducational universities were scarce before 1890, but began to increase as the number of women students grew (Clifford, 1989). Women's participation in higher education exploded from 11,100 in 1870 to 56,300 in 1890 to 282,900 by 1920. What is interesting, however, is the relative distribution between single-sex and coeducational institutions during this same 50-year period. In 1870, 41.1% of all women in college were in coeducational institutions. By 1890, 70.1% of the women were in coeducational settings and that percentage grew to 81.3% by 1920 (Newcomer, 1959, p. 49). Clearly, in terms of numbers of women educated, coeducational colleges and universities played an increasingly important role.

Coeducational institutions eventually fulfilled some of the promise for women who sought professional careers in universities. This was especially true for those who lived in the Midwest or other regions of the country where single-sex education was less common. Infiltration into coeducational universities was most successful where resistance to women's presence was least—in areas defined as women's sphere or women's work (Clifford, 1989). For example, the first female faculty members were usually in normal (later, education) or domestic science departments. For administrators, deans of women positions were analogous to home economics departments for academics. As such, the dean of women's position provided opportunities, but also became a female ghetto of sorts with the inevitable glass ceiling.

The number and type of administrative careers available to women were limited. Some coeducational universities hired female physicians or health educators. Although their contributions to the lives and health of women students were substantial, such women held marginal positions, typically part-time or even done on a voluntary basis. Doctors and physical educators were unlikely to have general administrative authority and only rarely did they report to the university president, which was common practice for deans of women before 1920. Thus, as the first and often the only female administrators who either held a broad range of responsibilities or sufficient rank in the institution to initiate policy proposals, deans of women "had the most consistent effect in bringing more women into the professional community" (Clifford, 1989, p. 13). The deans, therefore, acted as the "entering wedge" (Rossiter, 1982, p. 2) of coeducational institutions. In fact, in terms of the administrative influence of deans, the first three decades of practice represented the high point in the history of the position. By mid-century, the position had suffered a considerable reduction in stature, as former deans of women, who reported directly to the president in the early decades, typically became assistants who reported to a dean or a vice-president of student affairs.

The position of dean of women also played an interesting historical role by being the first systemic administrative response in higher education to cope with a new, and essentially unwelcome, population.

There was one brief period when the College of William and Mary hired a "Master of the Indian School" to look after the few Native American students, but by 1721, the Indian School had faded away and the position was not emulated at other colonial colleges (Morpurgo, 1976; "Narrative of Bacon's Rebellion," 1896). The position of dean of women, on the other hand, was replicated widely. By 1920 it was nearly ubiquitous. After World War II and the appointment of special officers to attend to the needs of returning veterans, hiring an administrator for new or marginalized populations on campus became a very common practice in higher education. Today, especially on large campuses, it is not uncommon to find one or more special administrators for African American, Hispanic, Asian, Native American, disabled, and (occasionally) gay and lesbian students.

PROFESSIONALIZATION

The pioneering cadre of deans of women carved out a niche for themselves, and sought status and recognition by creating a profession. During the Progressive Era, the period extending roughly from the late 1880s through America's entry into the First World War, colleges and universities became integrally associated with two social impulses. The first was the national zeal for reform, and the second was the growing reliance on expertise and professionalism. Both emerging and established occupations aspired to the status of "professional," and worked to acquire the characteristics normally attributed to professions. Deans of women were no exception.

The decade from Marion Talbot's appointment at the University of Chicago in 1892 to her first suggestion that deans meet in 1901 proved to be the formative years in which the foundation of professionalization was laid. After the turn of the century, the pace of the professionalization process for deans of women quickened and the number of participants in the process grew. As events unfolded for deans of women, the years spanning 1902 to 1918 gained a special significance when the position of dean finally emerged as a full profession.

There were several women who made important contributions either to the process of professionalization or to improving the lot of college women. However, four women stand out as both true pioneers and innovators. They were unique and yet also stand as representatives of their growing cohort of colleagues. Their working and personal lives reveal a great deal about the issues, problems, successes, constraints, and frustrations faced by professional women during the Progressive Era.

Therefore, the essence of this study is told through the careers of four women whose working lives as deans span the critical era from the earliest call for organization (1902) to formal association (1918)—from relative obscurity to widespread phenomenon. This is the story of Marion Talbot (University of Chicago, 1892–1925), Mary Bidwell Breed (Indiana University, 1901–1906), Ada Louise Comstock (University of Minnesota, 1906–1912), and Lois Kimball Mathews (later Rosenberry, University of Wisconsin, 1911–1918).

The Definition of a Profession

Attempting to define formally what constitutes a "profession" is a 20th-century phenomenon, and there is a vast literature on the subject (Bledstein, 1976; Haber, 1974; Veysey, 1988). Generally Abraham Flexner's 1915 report "Is Social Work a Profession?" is considered the first formal work in the field and the catalyst for a subsequent flurry of scholarly interest and activity. Flexner was writing at the height of the Progressive Era when many of the careers now recognized as professions in the United States first became established. Prior to this time only the three "venerable" fields of law, medicine, and theology—whose historical roots, including university training, reached back into the Middle Ages—were considered professions (Haber, 1974; Hatch, 1988).

Flexner's report (1915) posited a definition of *profession* by listing essential criteria and then examining a particular field to determine whether it met the established benchmarks. He concluded that professions "involve essentially intellectual operations with large individual responsibility; they derive their raw material from science and learning; this material they work up to a practical and definite end; they possess an educationally communicable technique; they tend to self-organization; they are becoming increasingly altruistic in motivations" (p. 904). He also stated that professions needed a form of expression that was scientific rather than journalistic in character, the ability to draw a "clear line of demarcation about their respective fields" (p. 910), sufficient remuneration, and a professional spirit. Then, turning to social work, Flexner judged that because social work failed to meet all these standards, it was not a full profession.

The criteria for professions that Flexner put forth in 1915 were based on observable conditions of the venerable professions during almost 200 years of American history. More recently, historian Sammuel Haber (1974) delineated how the ideas now associated with "professionalism" came to be understood and expected. During the century from 1730 to 1830, the professionals were male doctors, lawyers, and ministers, and several important concepts about the nature of professionalism emerged. Theoretically at least, there were no class barriers to entry. Culturally, however, barriers to entry based on gender and ethnic background were considerable. Unlike their counterparts in England, young White American boys without titles or land could attend college and earn the liberal arts degree that was associated with the learned professions. In fact, professional status afforded American men what only birthright brought in 18th-century England. But despite birthright—whether humble or comfortable—professional status thrust the men into the middle, and occasionally the upper, classes of society. They became part of the political and economic power structure of their community. However, as professionals, the men then served a clientele from all strata of society. Women and members of ethnic minority groups had no choice but to seek professional services from White men. Thus the nature of the professional/client relationship frequently had gender, race, and class dimensions. Professional men were held in high esteem and well compensated for their work. In fact, Adam Smith (1776), in his book *Wealth of Nations*, stated that professional men were well paid *because* they held a public trust. Professionals had a dependent relationship with their "clients," but that too was based on a form of trust. The nature of that trust was codified when the courts upheld the confidentiality privileges of the professional/client relationship.

Haber (1974) described the next 50 years, 1830 to 1880, as the nadir of professionalism when much of society, due in part to the egalitarian impulses of Jacksonianism, became wary of "experts." The end of Reconstruction and the beginning of the 1880s brought about a renewed interest in professionalism and the drive for professionalization for all sorts of occupations reached its zenith. It was during this time that deans of women were coming of age, individually as women and collectively as deans.

During the Progressive Era, the three venerable professions reasserted their primacy in American society. Doctors and lawyers (more than ministers) secured legislation that placed control of the professions in the hands of practitioners and ensured significant financial rewards for those who practiced the profession. The notions of self-regulation and control over entry became important criteria for professions. A further significant development was the creation of medical, law, and theology graduate schools at the universities. Thus the association between professionalism and university training was firmly established (Bledstein, 1976; Rudolph, 1962).

Establishing a relationship between an occupation and higher education was a key feature of the professionalization efforts. As a consequence, new courses of study and new professional preparation programs sprang up like weeds in American universities (Rudolph, 1962).
For women, despite formal obstacles to their full participation in the
workforce, the Progressive Era was also a time of incomparable opportunity due in large part to their high participation rates in higher education. Women comprised almost 40% of all undergraduates by 1900 and
were exposed to the same rhetoric about work and professional status
as their male classmates. This rhetoric glorified the middle-class ideals
of hard work and ambition and combined these notions with a commitment to service and a faith in technology (Glazer & Slater, 1987). As historian Joyce Antler (1977) noted, the circumstances of the Progressive
Era allowed women to "seize every opening within American culture to
define new possibilities for themselves as independent individuals"
(p. 10).

Women seeking a professional career during this period followed one
of two paths, each rife with struggle and impediments (Cott, 1987). They
either entered a male-dominated profession—in an established field (e.g.,
medicine or academia) or in a feminized subspecialty (e.g., pediatrics or
home economics)—or they chose the other path and entered the women-
oriented professions. On this latter path, women either took up the older,
traditionally female fields such as teaching or nursing or they carved out
new and emerging feminized fields such as social work (Clifford, 1988,
1989; Fitzpatrick, 1990; Glazer & Slater, 1987; Harris, 1978; Rosenberg,
1982; Rossiter, 1982; Walsh, 1977).

Glazer and Slater (1987) identified four strategies that women utilized in varying combinations when entering professions at the turn of
the century: superperformance, subordination, innovation, and separatism. Superperformers sought status through extraordinary efforts and
a willingness to sacrifice traditional relationships. Another strategy was
accepting a subordinate position within a male-dominated profession.
Innovation meant establishing a new professional field. Often this allowed
women to remove themselves from direct competition with male professionals, especially if they took up work or served clients typically neglected by men. A few women were able to practice their professions in
separate, all-female environments such as women's colleges, where they
were senior administrators and faculty members, even in traditionally
male disciplines. The pioneering deans of women were superperformers
and innovators: They sought recognition through overachievement, sac-
rificed traditional relationships, carved out a new field of endeavor, and
served a "client" (women students) largely ignored by men.

The Elevation of Expertise

For both women and men, the Progressive Era provided a convergence of circumstances that made such a bustle of professionalization activity possible. The era was noted for a high degree of reformist activity in government, education, politics, and social welfare. Americans were also becoming increasingly fascinated with and convinced of the efficacy of science (Hatch, 1988). In addition, this whirl of professionalization occurred at the height of the university movement with its emphasis on modernist thinking and rationality (Veysey, 1965). Therefore, when the modernist, intellectual mode of thinking converged with the reformist's zeal, it produced an ethos that dictated that science and technology should be used to better society. For example, Woodrow Wilson as president of Princeton University called for expertise to be applied to the field of government service, ending the Jacksonian idea that government work could be performed by anyone. In 1896 he challenged Princeton's graduates to be in the "Nation's Service" and brought this same progressive ethos to the White House in 1912.

Those seeking professional status used the authority of science to elevate the prestige of their endeavor. Science even played a large role in the development of the not especially reform-oriented occupations of business and engineering. As Haber (1974) remarked, "to the extent that the technical knowledge of the profession could appear scientific in this newer sense, it appeared more authoritative" (p. 259). There was a tendency for each occupational group to establish itself as a separate entity by claiming that its knowledge base was unique and therefore required distinct training and a separate professional organization (Hatch, 1988). For example, the growing ranks of university administrators, which included bursars, registrars, deans, and so forth, did not unite as administrators but rather maintained separate professional groups. Some occupations changed their names in order to sound more scientific. Deans of women were very conscious of the fact that *dean* or even *advisor* to women had a more authoritative (and hence professional) connotation than *matron* or *preceptress* and secured official title changes for themselves and their successors.

The American confidence in science also produced a change in the way people believed that one became an expert. Expertise, once solely acquired through practice, now required significant training in theory as well. Theoretical training, regarded as the province of the universities, was another reason that higher education and the professions were brought into an even closer relationship. Burton Bledstein (1976) argued in *The Culture of Professionalism* that the symbiotic relationship between higher education and the professions was due more to the aspirations of the middle class than an absolute need for training. He asserted that the relationship between higher education and the professions was not benign, but rather elitist, self-serving, and corrupt. The gatekeeping functions of universities did indeed have profound classist, racist, and sexist implications. But whether the need for training was actual or perceived by the middle class or noble or mercenary on the part of universities, the outcome is well known. The contemporary and automatic assumption that a professional is college-trained emerged during the Progressive Era and has remained virtually unchallenged, despite a strand of the American character that is peculiarly ambivalent toward the idea of expertise in the exercise of authority.

In the decades that followed the Progressive Era, sociologists and historians continued to develop definitions for professions and examined specific occupational areas to determine if they qualified. Those occupations that did not meet the mark (and many feminized fields fell into this category) were identified as sub-, pseudo-, or semi-professions (Etzioni, 1969).

Can Women Be Professionals?

From the 1920s to the late 1960s, the professions were generally viewed in benevolent terms as "serving the needs of the public through the schooled application of their unusually esoteric and complex knowledge and skill" (Friedson, 1986, p. 28; see also Moore, 1976; Parsons, 1968; Wilensky, 1964). Some of the subsequent literature of the 1970s and 1980s illuminated the more troubling aspects of the professions, including their relationship to political and economic elites and their role in perpetuating the class and market system of society (Friedson, 1986; Geison, 1983; Schudson, 1980). Yet, despite the fact that some interpretations were benevolent and others not so, there is remarkable overlap among the scholars in the definition of a profession (Abbot, 1988; Geison, 1983; Hatch, 1988; Veysey, 1988).

Professionals have a definable body of knowledge that is based in theory and is unique to their field; they acquire this knowledge through university training and then apply it in practical ways to assist clients. They control who enters the profession, usually through a professional association, by monitoring university admissions or licensing requirements, and entry is based on merit. The professional organization is also charged with regulating its own affairs, typically via the establishment of a code of ethics. In addition, professionals have a lifelong commitment to the profession; the client relationship is based on trust; they are separate from the amateur; and they have independence, recognition, and distinction from outside the profession (Geison, 1983; Hatch, 1988; Hughes, 1965; Parsons, 1968).

The above definition of professional has an important limitation for women: It was constructed by male academics using male-dominated professions as the norm. As such, it does not consider the social milieu in which the more visible attributes of professional status manifest. Recently, feminist scholars have pointed out that the assumptions about professionalism common during the Progressive Era conflicted with the gender-role expectations of that period. For example, the presumption of an unequivocal commitment to one's work conflicted with society's expectations for women as wives and mothers. Most women struggled with this issue alone, making private decisions without social or institutional supports, and many came to the sad conclusion that it was not possible to have both a marriage and a career (Antler, 1977).

Women also had to reconcile within themselves the fact that certain notions embedded in the definition of professionalism—such as being authoritative, competitive, or objective—had also been socially constructed as "unfeminine" (Glazer & Slater, 1987, pp. 13–14). In several respects, women "understood how social reality constrained their choices," and many in women-dominated fields chose to define their work on their own terms (Antler, 1977, p. 14). As Antler (1977) noted, "they actively worked to develop a new model of professional endeavor that would give women the chance to become competent, creative human beings in spheres of action not delimited by gender" (p. 10) and they "used the rhetoric they carefully designed and promoted to propel themselves into new orbits of achievement" (p. 14). Yet by focusing their motivations on serving the client, dealing with areas often neglected by men, incorporating feminine values, and not seeking authority over issues outside the purview of the field, the feminized professions have never attained parity in stature with the older, traditional, male-dominated professions. In the "semi-professions"— the derogatory name given to many women's fields—most practitioners had limited autonomy, existed in bureaucratic structures, and earned lower wages than male professionals (Preston, 1991).

Given the list of specific definitional requirements and general connotations of "professional," it is interesting to note which specific attributes the deans of women believed were essential to their quest for professional recognition. They strove for a title that connoted administrative authority within their institution (dean versus matron); standardization in terms of title and duties; university degrees as a requirement of entry; standards of practice; sufficient remuneration so that practitioners were fully employed as deans (ending the practice of depending on volunteers or untrained women to perform the necessary duties); a knowledge base and expertise that was unique to deans and available to all practitioners; a professional literature; a method of training women aspiring to enter the field; and a professional association (Mathews, 1915, pp. 1–39).

Again, this simple list of steps is useful, but has limitations. The list delineates only the tangible and observable aspects of the professionalization process, ignoring other important factors that act as necessary precursors to the observable events. For example, instruction in a university is a commonly understood prerequisite to professional recognition. However, prior to university courses, a professional literature is needed. The literature, in turn, must be based on the standards of practice, policies, and programs that the deans developed, and informed by the theoretical underpinnings of the profession and the specific expertise of the deans. The achievements of the first professional deans—Talbot, Breed, Comstock, and Mathews—were sometimes tangible (e.g., Mathews wrote the first book on the profession in 1915), but each woman also made intermediate or incremental contributions that were necessary precursors to full professionalization.

From Position to Profession

The professionalization process for deans of women can be divided into five phases, the last three of which are the most important and come in quick succession. While not all of the phases are rigidly defined by specific benchmarks, separating the process into five phases is useful for understanding the progression from mere position to full profession. Figure 1.1 illustrates the five phases and notes the dean whose career is illustrative of the central features of each phase.

The first phase, which I refer to as the historical backdrop, lasted from Oberlin's appointment of a lady principal in 1833 until 1892 when Marion Talbot assumed her position at the University of Chicago. In the almost 60 years covered by this phase, women administrators on *college* campuses were little more than dormitory matrons. During this period, especially after the Civil War, women began attending coeducational *universities* in ever-increasing numbers. The distinction between college and university began to take on increasing importance. However, university presidents were reluctant to hire female administrators during the 1870s and 1880s. Only one or two universities experimented with deans of women and those experiments did not last and were not replicated. Without deans, female students at universities sought the advice and

I	II	III	IV	V
1833–1892	1892–1901	1901–1906	1906–1911	1911–1918
Historical Backdrop	Pre-Profession-alization	Collective Activity	Becoming an Expert	Attributes of a Profession
	Marion Talbot	Mary Bidwell Breed	Ada Louise Comstock	Lois Kimball Mathews

FIGURE 1.1. The History of the Position of Dean of Women: The Five Phases of Professionalization

counsel of volunteers—faculty wives and local club women who performed some of the duties that later became associated with the work of deans of women.

The second phase, which lasted from approximately 1892 to the first year of the 20th century, might be thought of as a pre-professionalization stage in which the groundwork was laid for subsequent accomplishments. The central feature of the second phase was the recognition by university presidents and residents of university towns that the women students had unmet needs. The presidents also recognized that such needs should be met under the direction of an officer of the institution and not by volunteers. The faculty wives and club women who had donated their talents had performed a job that had no definition, expectations, or standards; they thought only in terms of the particular tasks required for a specific time and place. Marion Talbot, however, imagined the broader applicability of a dean's activities. Therefore, the second phase began when she laid the theoretical groundwork for the new profession.

By 1901, when Mary Bidwell Breed began her career at Indiana University, it had become almost "fashionable" to have a dean of women. Therefore, there were enough practitioners to consider collective activity (Martin, 1911b). The years that Breed spent at Indiana, 1901 to 1906, approximate the duration of the third phase. For deans in this era, the tasks were to overcome resistance on the part of their "clients"— the women students—and attend to the most urgent needs of women. The first group activity on the part of deans occurs during this phase when the Conference of Deans and Advisors of Women in State Universities began biennial meetings in 1903.

The fourth phase, 1906–1911, coincided with Ada Comstock's career at the University of Minnesota. This phase was marked by a growing professional maturity among the deans. During this stage, the first statistical research project on the work of deans was conducted and distributed (Martin, 1911b). A clearer intellectual rationale for the work of the deans was developed, based on their beliefs about women's nature and their assertion that a dean's appropriate expertise should focus on the nature of women's education in a coeducational setting. This intellectual activity saved the profession from remaining at the level of matron. Comstock used this philosophical base to develop programs and policies that attended to the higher, "nested" needs of students. In addition, deans began publishing in educational journals and making connections to other professional women in education, especially the Association of Collegiate Alumnae.

During the final phase, while Lois Mathews was dean at the University of Wisconsin from 1911 to 1918, the more tangible aspects of professionalization emerged. While the Conference of Deans and Advisors of Women in State Universities continued to meet, a new professional organization, the National Association of Deans of Women, was formed in 1916 and incorporated in 1918. In addition, the first "how to be a dean of women" courses were taught at both the University of Wisconsin and Teachers College, Columbia University. And finally, the first book about the profession was published—Mathews's own *The Dean of Women* (1915).

Thus, the careers and contributions of the first professional deans are the heart of this story. However, I begin with the very first "wise and pious matrons" who lived among the college "girls" at such antebellum coeducational colleges as Oberlin and Antioch and the problems and challenges associated with women's education. This is the historical background and context that shaped the profession that Talbot, Breed, Comstock, and Mathews helped create.

Chapter 2

THE WISE AND PIOUS MATRONS

When the Oberlin Collegiate Institute of Ohio opened its doors to young women as well as young men in 1833, a "dangerous experiment" began. The founders, Reverend John J. Shipherd and Philo P. Stewart, opened the institute to train teachers and other Christian workers for the unsettled lands of the West. Believing in the "joint education of the sexes" so that women could become Christian teachers and missionaries, Philo P. Stewart stated one of the institute's primary objectives as "the elevation of the female character, bringing within the reach of the misjudged and neglected sex, all the instructive privileges which hitherto have unreasonably distinguished the leading sex from theirs" (quoted in Lasser, 1987, p. 65).

Although the first women at Oberlin took classes alongside the male students and comprised one-third of the total enrollment (15 out of 44 students), they were officially pursuing diplomas in the "Ladies Course"—a less-demanding version of the Collegiate Department in which men were enrolled. The revered classical education designed to train the logical minds of men was thought beyond women. If women must be educated, some believed, it should be in the domestic arts or in "finishing" subjects such as sewing, drawing, or French, or in disciplines of minimal rigor and importance such as science.[1] In 1837, four women, Mary Kellogg (Fairchild), Mary Caroline Rudd, Mary Hosford, and Elizabeth Prall, enrolled in the Collegiate Department, and in 1841, all but Kellogg graduated—she had left early to marry James Fairchild, a future Oberlin president. Oberlin was also one of the first institutions to enroll African American students in the 1830s, but it was not until 1862 that Mary Jane Patterson became the first African American woman in the United States to earn a college degree (Holmes, 1939; Lasser, 1987).

THE LADY PRINCIPALS

Between Oberlin's founding and the American Civil War, there were only a handful of institutions that were coeducational (Rudolph, 1962). Yet, even with the numbers so few, college officials, members of society, and especially parents were worried about the effects of coeducation. Of particular concern was the propriety of young, unmarried men and women in such close proximity. College officials quickly recognized the "problems which demanded the presence and supervision of an older woman" (Holmes, 1939, p. 109). These overseers of young women had titles such as preceptress, matron, or lady principal. Occasionally, they were employed by the college, but using the volunteer labor of the president's wife or a local club woman was not uncommon.

The first woman to serve in this position at Oberlin was Mrs. Marianne Parker Dascom, with the title "Lady Principal of the Female Department" (Kehr, 1938). The 1835 description of the Female Department in the college catalog indicated both Oberlin's desire to appease trepidation regarding coeducation and the scope of Mrs. Dascom's duties:

> Young ladies of good minds, unblemished morals, and respectable attainments are received into this department and placed under the supervision of a judicious lady, whose duty it is to correct their habits and mould the female character. They board at the public table, and perform the labor of the steward's department, together with the washing, ironing, and much of the sewing for students. They attend recitations with young gentlemen in all the departments. Their rooms are entirely separate from those of the other sex, and no calls or visits in the respective apartments are at all permitted. (Kehr, 1938, p. 6)

Mrs. Dascom's position at Oberlin illustrated two important themes in the earliest history of deans of women. First, the "Lady Principal" was hired as a direct response to prevailing concerns regarding coeducation. Second, her formal duties were limited to supervision of housing and living arrangements and the moral guardianship of the women students.

Antioch College in Yellow Springs, Ohio, was also coeducational from its opening in 1854. Antioch President Horace Mann believed that it was the responsibility of the faculty to the ensure the "complete moral protection" of women students. He also insisted on a boardinghouse for the young women. He stated, "I should deprecate exceedingly turning them out in the streets for meals" (Holmes, 1939, p. 6). The boardinghouse required a female supervisor so someone with responsibilities similar to Mrs. Dascom was hired.

In the antebellum era, a few other institutions considered admitting women. In the early 1850s, for example, a few women and their supporters began agitating for admission to the University of Michigan. After all, the 1837 charter of the university said it was "open to all persons of the state." Although the legal reasoning of the era omitted women from the category of "persons," several citizens of Michigan objected to their exclusion. In 1853, the State Teachers Association formally declared that they wanted higher education for the state's secondary school teachers, including women teachers (McGuigan, 1970). In 1858 Sara Berger petitioned the board of regents at the Commencement Meeting in June on behalf of herself and 12 other women for admission. The board of regents tabled her request.

Knowing that the petition would be considered again in September, the regents took advantage of the summer months to consult various "experts" in coeducation. Two men from whom they sought advice were Horace Mann and Charles Grandison Finney, presidents of Antioch and Oberlin, respectively. Mann acknowledged that "the advantages of joint education are very great. The dangers are terrible. . . . These dangers consist in their [students'] opportunities for association without supervision" (Holmes, 1939, p. 6). Finney replied that the results at Oberlin were "satisfactory and admirable" and offered the board the following advice for ensuring success: "You will need a wise and pious matron with such lady assistants as to keep up supervision" (Holmes, 1939, p. 7).

Both Finney and Mann limited their remarks regarding coeducation to the moral well-being of the women and the social propriety of coeducation. Both concerns could be mitigated with the help of the right "wise and pious matron." But when the Michigan Board of Regents considered Sara Berger's petition again in the autumn of 1858, they concluded that coeducation was a "dangerous experiment" and a "radical revolution" and should not be undertaken (Report on the Admission of Females, 1915). President Henry Tappan—the man hailed for building Michigan into a great university based on the idealized German model—declared his opposition on other grounds:

> After [the admission of women] no advancement is possible. . . . The standard of education must now be accommodated to the wants of girls who finish their education at 16–20, very properly, in order to get married, at the very age when young men begin their education. (quoted in McGuigan, 1970, p. 18)

With Tappan's opposition and the intervening Civil War, Michigan remained single-sex for another 12 years. The regents did not relent until 1870, when James B. Angell, a supporter of coeducation, was president. By that time, the pressure from taxpayers was too great to ignore and all efforts on behalf of creating a separate women's institution were deemed financially ruinous.

After the Civil War, coeducational liberal arts colleges became more prevalent. Following the lead of the established coeducational colleges, the newer institutions employed lady principals, matrons, or preceptresses who supervised the women's living arrangements. Swarthmore College was typical and engaged a "judicious matron" in 1872 (Holmes, 1939). By 1880, this practice was more common than not in the nation's residential liberal arts colleges (McGrath, 1936).

While the wise and pious matrons were supervising the living arrangements in liberal arts colleges, the conditions of student life for women at the newly emerging universities were quite different. Beginning in the 1850s but accelerating precipitously after 1870, several college presidents set about turning liberal arts institutions into serious research universities (Veysey, 1965). The names of these presidents are still fairly well known today and their institutions remain among the elite universities in America—a tribute to their successes of over a century ago. Among the best-known presidents are Charles Eliot of Harvard, David Starr Jordan of Stanford, Daniel Coit Gilman of Johns Hopkins, Henry Tappan and James B. Angell of the University of Michigan, Charles Van Hise of the University of Wisconsin, William Rainey Harper of the University of Chicago, and Andrew White of Cornell (Rudolph, 1962; Veysey, 1965).

Based on an American interpretation of the German research universities that were so admired, these presidential visionaries followed similar paths to building a university. They hired the best established faculty members they could induce and lured bright young intellectual stars. They also began requiring that all new faculty hold the Ph.D. The presidents added graduate and professional schools, put research at the center of the enterprise and scrambled for the resources to support it, dramatically altered the curriculum, and paid as little heed as possible to the out-of-classroom lives of students. Students were thought to be adults capable of fending for themselves. In the younger state universities, this point of view was also financially expedient. Most state universities were quite resource-poor in the 1870s and 1880s (Rudolph, 1962; Veysey, 1965). As a general rule, universities could not afford to build dormitories so both men and women students were expected to find lodging in nearby rooms and boardinghouses. University officials believed that because they provided no residential housing for women, no matron was needed.

Despite the official attitude that students should be on their own, the young women attending universities in the 1870s and 1880s often did require assistance. On campuses, a popular teacher or occasionally the president's wife had the responsibility of supervising or guiding the female students (Merrill & Bragdon, 1926). Campuses also formed Women's League chapters, many based on the exemplary model started at the University of Michigan. The goal of the Indiana University Women's League was typical: "to promote a more general acquaintance among the women students; to foster a spirit of helpfulness and womanly kindness; to meet and welcome the new girls." League members gave "receptions, musicals, and entertainments" for students. Members also met each incoming train with a new female student passenger and helped her find a lodging room (Indiana University, 1897, p. 19).

If assistance on campus was not available, help came from the wider community. All across the Midwest, YWCA members and club women took the local university students under their wings (Holmes, 1939). The primary disadvantage of such voluntary service was that the women did not have the imprimatur of the university and held no administrative authority. Without such an administrator, the women students had to rely on volunteers.

Of course there were the occasional exceptions. At the University of Wisconsin, President Paul Chadbourne (whom history has labeled "great"), unlike many of his contemporaries, was very much concerned about the living arrangements of students. He was also an outspoken and virulent critic of coeducation. Wisconsin opened in 1858 with two residence halls, one for men and one for women, but Chadbourne gave the on-campus residence hall built for women to the men. To distance the women from the campus even further, Chadbourne built the Female College off-campus and required women to reside in it or at home with family members. In 1871, he hired a "judicious matron" to supervise the college (Teicher & Jenkins, 1987, pp. 5–6). Later, when the women were given a new dormitory, it was named Chadbourne Hall with deliberate irony (Shay, 1966; Teicher & Jenkins, 1987).

Occasionally, administrators at an institution without dormitories believed that women students needed supervision. Indiana University (IU) experimented briefly with the position of Social Advisor to women when Sarah Parke Morrison was employed in 1869. Morrison was the first woman to earn a full baccalaureate degree (commensurate with that conferred on men) from a state university when she graduated from Indiana in 1869. She was hired in 1873, but stayed on campus for only 2 years. The university let her position remain unfilled for over 25 years until Mary Bidwell Breed became Indiana's first professional dean of women in 1901 (Rothenberger, 1942).

At a few universities, women students, their parents, or community members agitated for the universities to offer some living arrangements for the women students. When there was no supervised housing, upper-middle-class parents and families who lived long distances from the campuses expressed reluctance to send daughters to college (Gordon, 1990). Yet, if boardinghouses, residence halls, or sorority houses were created, an administrator was needed. Such was the case at Cornell when a private donation was received in 1871 to build Sage College as the residence for women. In 1884, the president of Cornell hired a Lady Principal of Sage College whose only qualification for the position was that she possessed "social poise and good judgment" (Holmes, 1939, p. 37).

What lay at the heart of the parental uneasiness that manifested at Cornell and elsewhere was the significant controversy surrounding the issue of coeducation. The great social debate regarding the question of higher education for women had a profound impact on the first professional deans of women. First, the majority of the deans were students themselves in the 1870s and 1880s and experienced firsthand the slights and hostility directed toward women on campuses. Second, the acceleration of anticoeducation sentiment during the 1890s was a direct catalyst for creation of the first professional deans. Third, fighting the ill effects of such sentiment on the women students in their charge became the deans' *raison d'être*.

CONTROVERSY AND CONTENTIOUSNESS

In the very first novel written by a woman graduate of a coeducational university describing her experience, Olive San Louie Anderson (1878, publishing under an anagram of her name, SOLA) barely concealed her frustration and dismay. Even her title, *An American Girl and Her Four Years in a Boy's College*, was revealing. Locating her story at the fictitious University of Ortonville, but in reality writing about the University of Michigan, Anderson spoke of her isolation and lack of integration into full university life. Although Michigan was regarded as one of the better universities in terms of providing opportunities for women, Anderson's story unmasks any pretense that women's admission to a university implied equal opportunity. "The girls are not expected to have much class spirit yet, but are supposed to sit meekly by and say 'Thank you' for the crumbs that fall from the boys table" (pp. 49–50) she wrote. Yet at the same time Anderson felt her "bosom swell with pride" (p. 50) to be included in such a great institution and knew she was given an opportunity that very few women before her had ever had.

Such was the dilemma of coeducation. The climate was hostile and the social cost was enormous, but the opportunities were unparalleled. From the time women entered Oberlin in the 1830s through to almost the

1930s, the myriad arguments against women's higher education in general, and coeducation in particular, were articulated and refuted. The religious, intellectual, biological, and social reasons cited against women's higher education reveal a great deal about the attitudes and beliefs of America's dominant class, as well as the growing importance of higher education in the social and economic welfare of the nation.

The World as It Should Be

The cornerstone of resistance to women's higher education was the very Judeo-Christian heritage on which the country was founded. Both laws and social practice were informed by the pan-Protestantism integral to early America. Included among this belief system was a conviction that women were to be subservient, first to a father, then to a husband, and, at all times, to God. People believed in a divinely ordained world order. God meant things to be exactly as they are. It followed therefore that women were confined to one sphere of life, the domestic, and only men were part of the political, economic, and social spheres of the communities (Rosenberg, 1982). Women were expected to conform to the "cult of true womanhood," which demanded piety, obedience, purity, and domesticity (Welter, 1976).

By the mid-19th century, the growth in common schooling combined with increased economic opportunities in business for men created a demand for teachers that could be filled by women. The revivalist spirit also spurred a need for missionaries. Beginning in the 1830s, a smattering of colleges such as Troy Seminary and Mount Holyoke, Oberlin, and Antioch Colleges seized the chance to educate women to these two new roles. A social contract was struck. Women could continue their education and find intellectual and professional fulfillment in work that was genuinely needed. Yet these two roles only minimally pushed the edges of the female sphere—although technically in the workforce, the college graduate remained an obedient Christian woman and a nurturer of children.

The passage of the Morrill Act in 1862 brought several changes to American higher education, but no single change was more important than the development of a significant sector of public higher education. Prior to 1860, the majority of institutions were private—at least in the contemporary understanding of that term. By and large, coeducation was a phenomenon of the public sector, either at the smaller normal schools or at the state universities. As more and more public institutions admitted women, the debate regarding coeducation grew (Schwager, 1978, 1987; Woody, 1929). The debate was acrimonious and long-lasting and has been compared to the debate surrounding abolition in terms of the intensity of emotions on both sides of the issue and the numbers of middle-class men and women involved (Palmeri, 1987).

The Biological Bogey

By the middle of the 19th century, science—specifically biology—was used to justify the differences between the genders. Much of this type of thinking was inspired by Herbert Spencer. Spencer believed that the body was a closed biological system—the expenditure of energy in one part necessarily deprived another part. Spencer also had a particular take on one of the newest ideas in the scientific community at the time. He believed that evolution had caused civilization to develop as it had relying increasingly on the specialization of function. This included specialization between men and women, who had prescribed roles (Rosenberg, 1982). So the separate spheres were not only as God ordained, they were as Darwin predicted.

Rosalind Rosenberg (1982) noted that the "growing emphasis on the power of biology revealed anxiety over the increasing instability of sex roles" (p. 6). It was therefore fitting that one of the first widely read attacks on coeducation emerged from the medical community. In 1873 a former member of the Harvard Medical School faculty, Dr. Edward H. Clarke, published his views on women's education in a small book entitled *Sex in Education: Or, a Fair Chance for the Girls*. Clarke's views were based on a position that biology was destiny (see also Zschoche, 1989). He argued that women's brains were less developed and could not tolerate the same level of mental stimulation (meaning higher education) as men so they should not be taught in the same manner as men. More important, however, Clarke linked intense brain activity with the potential for malfunction of the reproductive "apparatus," especially if women were overtaxed during the "catamenial function" (menstruation) (p. 48). Therefore a separate system of women's higher education was needed rather than coeducation, which was a "crime before God and humanity" (p. 127).

Clarke's (1873) book had a tremendous impact and was extensively used by opponents of women's education. It was also extremely popular. On one hand, *Sex in Education* addressed two issues that fascinated the educated public—the "experiment" of women's higher education and the application of evolutionary biology to social issues. The book discussed these issues with "readable prose and decidedly non-Victorian candor about female physiology" (Zschoche, 1989, p. 547). It was almost titillating.

Response on campuses—and in college towns, women's clubs, medical schools, reading circles, and anywhere that people were debating women's education—was overwhelming. Although the University of Michigan had been coeducational for 3 years by 1873, "everyone" was reading the book and on one occasion 200 copies were sold in one day! At the University of Wisconsin, where antagonism toward coeducation was intense in the 1870s, President Chadbourne and the regents of the university used Clarke's findings to justify withdrawing support for women's education. "It is better that the future matrons of the state should be without university training than that it should be produced at the fearful expense of ruined health," commented a regent (Rosenberg, 1982, p. 12).

Proponents of women's education were shocked and angered by Clarke's theories, but aware of their persuasiveness. M. Carey Thomas, future president of Bryn Mawr College, recalled, "We did not know when we began whether women's health could stand the strain of education. We were haunted in those days by the clanging chains of the gloomy specter, Dr. Edward Clarke's *Sex in Education*" (quoted in Rosenberg, 1982, p. 12). Feminists denounced Clarke, including suffragist Julia Ward Howe (1874), who edited a collection of essays in response to the book. Other critics responded as well, arguing that Clarke's conclusions were faulty, and pointed out that his theory was based on only seven case studies, one of whom was not even a college student! Of those subjects who were students, not even one woman attended a coeducational institution (Duffey, 1874). Proponents wrote several articles in the leading women's publication, *Women's Journal*, illustrating the good health and stamina of college women. In 1885 members of the Association of Collegiate Alumnae (ACA) conducted and published a survey using empirical evidence to refute Clarke, stating that 78% of college women were in good health (Howes, 1885; Rosenberg, 1982).

Socially Undesirable

While many opponents latched onto the "ruined health" thesis of Dr. Clarke, others opposed women's education because it was "socially undesirable" (Eschbach, 1993; Gordon, 1979). Throughout the 1870s and 1880s, the anxiousness surrounding the changing gender roles was often expressed as a fear of "masculating" or "unsexing" women, making them unfit for marriage. Annie Nathan Meyer, founder of Barnard College, recalled with sadness what her father said when she announced her intention to seek higher education. "You will never be married," he said. "Men hate intelligent wives" (quoted in Eschbach, 1993, p. 87).

Although critics were numerous, coeducation also had influential friends. Early women's rights advocates believed that coeducation was the only way to achieve equity for women so that they might emerge from their "separate sphere" (Rosenberg, 1988). Although suffrage remained a goal, most political energy on behalf of women from the late 1860s to the turn of the century was focused on winning the chance to go to college (Kraditor, 1981). Activists such as Susan B. Anthony, Lucy Stone, and Julia Ward Howe argued that coeducation was "the only means of reaching the ideal of equal education" (Eschbach, 1993, p. 99). Others such as Elizabeth Cady Stanton believed coeducation would improve relationships between the sexes. "If the sexes were educated together," she said, "we should have the healthy, moral, and intellectual stimulus of sex everquickening and refining all the faculties without the undue excitement of senses that results from novelty in the present system of isolation" (quoted in Eschbach, 1993, p. 100). Most middle-class feminists believed in the need for education to improve social and domestic conditions for women.

After the Civil War, there were also strong pockets of local-level support and women's clubs of the era were active campaigners for coeducation. These clubs were comprised of older women who, denied the opportunity of a college education, worked on behalf of their daughters and younger sisters. They lobbied university administrations and state legislatures, and convinced husbands and brothers to support legislation that would open public colleges to women (Gordon, 1990).

Colleges and universities, however, were not "overwhelmed by egalitarian considerations" (Gordon, 1990, p. 21) and on the whole did not admit women enthusiastically. Only a few institutions were persuaded to adopt coeducation as a result of women's campaigns. Cornell, located not too far from Seneca Falls (the site of the first Women's Rights convention in 1848), admitted women in 1872 after a long campaign by both male and female women's rights advocates (Rosenberg, 1988).

Pragmatism Wins Out

Pragmatic need, state interest, and economic insecurity were the real catalysts for the initiation of coeducation in public universities. The shortage of college-ready students (and their resulting tuition dollars) caused acute problems. The statistics from the U.S. Commissioner of Education revealed the scarcity of students: in 1876–1877, the University of California had 177 students, the University of Illinois had only 41, the University of Minnesota had 107, and the University of Wisconsin with its large preparatory department claimed only 225 students (Eddy, 1956). The paucity of students prompted institutions to enact a variety of strategies including lowering admission standards, instituting preparatory departments, and going coeducational. As President Charles Van Hise of the University of Wisconsin noted in 1907, "The reasons which led to coeducation were then purely economic. The western states in these early days were too poor to support two high grade educational institutions [male and female]" (pp. 509–511).

A war-induced dearth of potential male workers combined with a growing number of students in public elementary schools prompted states to seek a cheap supply of teachers—women, who were typically paid only half of what men earned. State teachers' associations were active lobbyists on behalf of coeducation in a number of states. They knew the universities needed tuition revenue, the state needed teachers, and separate public women's colleges were too expensive (Gordon, 1990; Rosenberg, 1988).

When introducing coeducation, many institutions did so reluctantly and only gradually. At first, women were permitted to enroll just in certain departments such as domestic science or the normal program. More time had to pass before women were permitted in all courses of study available at the university. Yet, no matter the reason they were let in or limitations placed on them, young women took advantage of the opportunity presented in the midwestern universities. The women who went to college between 1870 and 1890 are often referred to as the "first generation."[2] These pioneers were serious, purposeful, and single-minded. They were stereotyped as mannish and often joyless, yet they were very much aware that they were the first of their gender to have such opportunities—and such expectations placed on them.

The first woman to attend Indiana University, Sarah Parke Morrison, reflecting in 1919 on her experiences back in 1867, said, "When the decision was announced [that she would attend the university] no one in the family encouraged it. This was more than they bargained for" (p. 532). But she did attend and was so aware of the many stares she received that she wore a large hat her first few months on campus to avoid men's eyes. She was also aware that she was scrutinized and felt considerable pressure to perform well. "A woman must come up to the mark, must be careful to establish no precedent injurious to her interests. . . . To fail would be worse than not to try" she said (p. 531). To cope, she often overcompensated: "I think that perhaps I had had about of enough Latin, I had chosen to make a point of it, but I rather read more than really required 'to not lower the standard'" (p. 533).

First-generation women represented only 2.2% of their age cohort (18- to 21-year-old women), but they represented 35% of all college students. Slightly over 70% of all first-generation students were in coeducational institutions (Gordon, 1979; Newcomer, 1959). By example, they illustrated that women could withstand the intellectual rigors of college and remain healthy. They performed well academically and several went on to careers in medicine, science, teaching, social work, and higher education—a few as professors. Others were the first professional women administrators—deans of women, physicians, or health and physical education supervisors (Gordon, 1990).

Race Suicide

In the beginning of coeducation, critics charged that educating women was an abomination before God. Within a few years the argument was more personal—the strain of education hurt the individual woman. At first there was fear of her masculinization and then of her "ruined health" as predicted by Dr. Clarke. As the 19th century came to a close, coeducation was deemed to be causing grievous harm to the larger society. The academic success and low birth rates of college women caused the arguments against coeducation to shift to the slightly different, yet integrally related, notion of "race suicide."

Anxiety regarding acceptable sex roles had combined with increasing xenophobia and anti-immigration sentiments. This wave of attacks on women's education focused on the fact that college-educated women married later, if at all, and had fewer children then their less-educated contemporaries. Critics held that a college education was responsible for the falling marriage and birth rates and increasing divorce rates among White, native-born Americans (Palmeri, 1987).

The critics were numerous and prominent. Charles Eliot of Harvard, psychologist G. Stanley Hall (1906), and President Theodore Roosevelt warned against the trend and told Americans that the "best classes" were not reproducing themselves (Palmeri, 1987). Throughout the Progressive Era, scholars and commentators published articles on the issue. In 1907, German-born Dr. Möebius wrote, "If we wish a woman to fulfill her task of motherhood fully, she cannot possess a masculine brain. If the feminine abilities were developed to the same degree as those of the male, woman's maternal organs would suffer and we should have a repulsive and useless hybrid" (1991, p. 195).

Another example, even more racist in tone, was a 1915 *Journal of Heredity* article simply entitled, "Education and Race Suicide," in which the author argued that every college-educated woman should have at least three children "in order to prevent the race from actually declining in numbers" (Sprague, 1915, p. 159). The topic was even the subject of concern in college courses. Albert Waite was a student in Harvard's Principles of Sociology. In 1904 he recorded in his class notebook, "Higher education has somewhat the same effect [on population] as celibacy. Those securing higher training multiply less rapidly than others. Whether this is due to education or not is undecided, but it seems to be. Now it seems certain that if the educated people multiply slower than non-educated, intellectual deterioration is sure" (n.p.).

The critics did have the advantage of statistics. Approximately one-half of the first-generation women married, in contrast to marriage rates of 90% for non–college educated women (Gordon, 1990). Women who went to college after 1890 had higher marriage and birth rates than the first generation, although they were still lower than the rest of the population. However, the percentage of women in college was still so small that even if one-half or one-third of them did not marry, the vehemence of the attacks was out of proportion to any real population danger.

Feminization

In addition to race suicide, a new criticism emerged during the Progressive Era accusing coeducation of feminizing both male students and the institutions themselves. Women students were the catalyst for changes in the curriculum, including the introduction of normal departments and "domestic" studies. One of the earliest home economics departments was at the University of Iowa in 1871, but several other state universities followed within a decade or two. Teacher preparation and home economics absorbed the majority of female enrollments in the 19th century. By 1900 there were 61,000 women in coeducational institutions; 43,000 were enrolled in education departments and 2,000 were studying home economics (Newcomer, 1959). After 1900, women students and educators pushed for other types of courses related to women's interests and the growing numbers of women involved in the reformist movements of the Progressive Era. Such topics included child psychology, marriage and family studies, social work, settlement work, poverty, and charity.

Feminization was also cited as the cause of changes in the course-taking patterns of women and men. Men were deserting the humanities and languages. They gravitated instead toward the sciences, now deemed rigorous and important, and newer disciplines such as economics and political economy. Women did the opposite; they chose the humanities and languages (the very disciplines they were thought incapable of understanding a few decades earlier!) and the new discipline of sociology. Faculty members in the humanities complained vociferously that women were feminizing (and therefore devaluing) their disciplines by driving the men away. Historian Barbara Miller Solomon (1985) described the no-win situation that women found themselves in:

> Women, charged with sex repulsion and sex attraction, both of which interfered with the holy process of educating the future leaders (males) of the country, simply could not win. They either drove men out of the classroom, or they attracted them into it and then distracted them too much. The best solution was to have women attend their own schools. (p. 61)

Deans Marion Talbot and Mary Bidwell Breed spoke out on the issue, stating that men and women were choosing different courses based on vocational interests and employment possibilities, rather than inherent differences in aptitude or ability (Breed, 1907; Gordon, 1979). Women entering teaching or social work still benefited from the humanities, languages, or sociology. Men, the majority of whom planned to enter business or the professions, found less use for humanities courses.

Despite this explanation for the phenomenon, it was argued that reversing the effects of feminization required more male students, separate courses of study for each gender, and the addition of programs and graduate schools that attracted men. Several universities contemplated restricting female enrollment, segregating men and women in all subjects, or eliminating coeducation altogether. Stanford's benefactor and mother of the institution's namesake decreed that female enrollment could never exceed 500. Boston University initiated a "More Men Movement" and Wesleyan abandoned coeducation altogether. Even at the University of Chicago, where coeducation had been part of the university from the beginning, President William Rainey Harper had deep reservations about educating men and women together.

The professional schools of law, medicine, business, and divinity were dominated by male students and a strong ethos that women did not belong. Only the newly forming social work graduate programs had significant female enrollments. Therefore, it was reasoned that establishing more professional schools would increase the number of male students on a campus, and the new universities established such schools at an accelerated rate. An economist at the University of Chicago summed up the thinking of the era in 1902:

> The congestion of numbers [of women students] is now largely due to the fact that the undergraduate courses are practically used by women as an advanced normal school to prepare for teaching. Just so soon as proper support and endowments are given to work which offers training for ca-

reers in engineering, railways, banking, trade and industry, law and medicine, etc. the disproportion of men will doubtless remedy itself. (Rosenberg, 1982, pp. 48–49)

The fear of feminization also received considerable attention in the popular press, where American men were encouraged to be more manly, athletic, and aggressive. A commonly held belief was that increasing industrialization and urbanization were rendering men too soft. But many critics thought higher education was the real culprit. They charged that coeducation was responsible for the loss of manly verve. The fact that such criticism implied that women wielded enormous power and depicted men in quite unfavorable terms seemed lost on the critics. Such criticism was, in fact, a response to the growing prevalence of coeducation and, especially, the academic success of women students (Rosenberg, 1982). As Mary Cheyney, the secretary of the Western Association of Collegiate Alumnae commented adroitly in 1905, "The very success of the movement, which amounts to a great revolution affecting one-half of the human race, has roused men to resist its progress" (Cheyney, 1905, quoted in Palmeri, 1987, p. 57).

Despite It All!

The "success" of coeducation was measured in two ways. The first was simply the sheer number of women in colleges and universities. The second benchmark was the intellectual success of women. At the University of Chicago between 1892 and 1902, women earned 46% of the baccalaureate degrees but 56.3% of the Phi Beta Kappa keys. Similar levels of accomplishment occurred elsewhere and this prompted some universities to impose a limit on the number of honors women were eligible to earn. At Berkeley, for example, Lillian Moller (later, Gilbreth) earned Phi Beta Kappa recognition in 1900 but also learned that no women were awarded the key. The university reasoned that men were in greater need of the honor when looking for a job (Gordon, 1979).

Another manifestation of the antagonism was the inequitable distribution of resources that universities bestowed on women, an inequity that deans of women fought for years to reverse. In general, the midwestern universities did not provide women with housing, medical care, or physical education facilities, despite the fact that the latter services were available for men by the 1870s.

Access to a gymnasium was quite important because of the concerns regarding the health and fitness of women students. Typically, universities barred women from the gyms at first and then gradually relented to pressure by granting limited access. When access was granted, it was usually at times deemed less desirable by men, during the dinner hour, for example. President William Rainey Harper of the University of Chicago argued that women and men could not use the gymnasium at the same time for reasons of propriety. To Harper's declaration, Dean Marion Talbot (1936) wryly noted that "they [men and women] could swim together in the ocean and dance together on the ballroom floor even though, in the former case, the costumes of women were much scantier than those allowed in the gymnasium" (p. 177).

Of equal concern was the paucity of scholarship money available to women. Universities gave little, if any, of their available funds to female students. From the class of 1903 at the University of Chicago, 88 men (12.6% of the total male undergraduates) and 85 women (14.2% of the female total) were admitted to Chicago's graduate school. Ten of the men received fellowships while only three of the women received financial assistance (Talbot, 1936). In response, local club women and YWCAs developed the practice of raising scholarship money for students.

In an interesting fashion, the criticism leveled at coeducation also spoke volumes about the changing nature of the relationship between higher education and the economy. Higher education assumed the role of gatekeeper to the professions and, consequently, the middle class. As entry to high-status jobs depended less on family name, men resented the places taken and honors won by women at the premier state universities.

Male students made it difficult for women to enter their preserve. Photographs of lecture halls of the era revealed a pattern of strict segregation. Women were explicitly ridiculed under the guise of humor as misogynistic cartoons and stories filled campus newspapers, literary magazines, and yearbooks. "Coeds," as they came to be called, were excluded from clubs, eating halls, music groups, honorary societies, and most activities associated with campus prestige (Gordon, 1979). Men also did not allow women's participation in activities deemed useful to future careers.

Faculty members sometimes ignored women in the classroom, refused to answer questions, or prohibited discussion. Professors often addressed mixed classes as "gentlemen" and called women "Mr. _____," ignoring their gender. On some occasions, official university policy ignored or excluded women. In response, college women established a separate student culture in much the same manner as adult women in the larger society (Rosenberg, 1988). They had women's literary and debating clubs and women's magazines and newspapers or special "women's pages" inside the dominant campus publications, and they formed sororities. As depicted in the diaries and letters of women students as well as in the fiction written by and about them, these special, all-female worlds were cozy and a valuable asset in coping with the daily indignities of life (Marchalonis, 1995). Despite their obvious drawbacks, these female worlds were fondly remembered by the alumnae.

The presence of women on a campus was a tangible sign of an institution's lack of wealth and prestige. The rather condescending attitudes of eastern educators, especially Charles Eliot, also fueled resentment. Speaking in 1894, Eliot stated that men and women 15 to 20 years of age were not "best educated in intimate association" but he also noted that coeducation may "nevertheless be justifiable in a community which cannot afford anything better. . . . Coeducation has the advantage of economy . . . because the churches or the people could not afford two colleges in a single commonwealth" (quoted in Woody, 1929, vol. 2, p. 257).

As a consequence, seeing women on campus reminded the men at Wisconsin or Michigan that they were not at Harvard or Yale and they took umbrage. In response, a few institutions—Wisconsin, Stanford, Chicago, and Wesleyan, for example—on much stronger fiscal ground after 1900 than before, attempted to limit or eliminate coeducation. These attempts, however, were socially, politically, or financially costly and were not sustained.[3] In the generally expansive and pro-democracy mood of the Progressive Era, a retreat from access was unacceptable.

Yet the resistance that had fueled attempts to prevent women's entry in the first place did not magically disappear once the doors were officially opened. Virginia Woolf described the underlying subtext against which women struggled as habits of mind that were "tough as roots, but intangible as sea-mist" (quoted in McGuigan, 1970, p. 106). The antagonism hit a fevered pitch in the 1890s and shaped the struggles and the agendas of the new cohort of professional deans of women.

THE WOMAN PROBLEM

The resurgence of anti-coeducation sentiment coincided with another development on university campuses that precipitated the hiring of deans of women. As the 1890s progressed, faculty members around the country grew increasingly concerned about the extracurricular activities and the anti-intellectual posturing of students. Even the image of women students, once thought so serious as to be dour, was changing slightly. The so-called second generation of women students was perceived as less serious and more in need of supervision. As Dean Lois Mathews (1915) noted:

> The problem was the same in both the coeducational institution and the women's college—a changing and enlarging student body with less interest in intellectual things, a more complex and elaborate social life within the college, less intimate relations between faculty and students, and more problems of so-called discipline. The women's college met the situation in part by self-government associations; the coeducational institutions met it so far as their women students were concerned in quite another way. Then it was that the "dean (or adviser) of women" came into being. (pp. 6–7)

At the same time, faculty reluctance to handle such matters became obvious. The growing demand for research productivity placed new pressures on faculty and created an unwillingness on their part to spend vast amounts of time on administrative details or student discipline. Nor would a president interested in research results want a faculty so engaged. The role of the president was changing. The early 19th-century image of a college president—Mark Hopkins on one end of a log with an eager male student on the other—was no longer applicable by 1890s at the research universities (Rudolph, 1956).[4] Presidents were unlikely to spend much of their time in the classroom (or on a log); they were, instead, managing and providing the vision for increasingly large and diverse enterprises.

Most faculty members and presidents did not believe that a matron in the residence halls could adequately monitor the socializing that went on among men and women outside the classroom. Other issues, such as the health of women students, also required attention, but this was not a chore for which the faculty wanted direct responsibility either. Making sure that women were not crowding men out of humanities courses, that their health and virtue were intact, and that they had a place to reside on campus with proper supervision came to be known among college presidents as the "Woman Problem." Hiring a dean of women freed the president from dealing with it any more than he had to. For the president, the dean could be both a tangible asset—actually solving some of the campus concerns regarding the housing, health, and social habits of the women students—and a public relations ploy. As a former faculty member of the University of Wisconsin noted:

> The time came when the faculty had to remind the enthusiast that the university is a place where some studying ought to be done and lay a curbing hand on extra-curricular pursuits. About the middle of President

Adams' administration the need for improved means of establishing standards of social expedience and propriety became apparent, and the office
of "dean of women" was created. Miss Annie C. Emery, a woman of distinguished qualities, was appointed to this post in 1897. (Pyre, 1920, p. 323)

Thus a new cohort of deans of women appeared who had university-wide authority (at least with respect to women) and were not limited to matron-esque duties. The University of Chicago was first when
President Harper hired a dean of women, Alice Freeman Palmer, and her
associate Marion Talbot, in 1892. Northwestern hired a lady principal in
1892, but changed her title to dean in 1898 when the president told that
board that it would be "a mistake to relegate her to a subordinate position" (Holmes, 1939, p. 35). The University of Michigan was the first state
university to hire a woman with the title "dean," in 1896, and was followed
by the University of Wisconsin in 1897. Michigan was unusual in that
President Angell hired a female doctor, Eliza Mosher, who handled the
duties of dean and took care of the health needs of women. The University of Oregon appointed a dean in 1899, although no housing was provided for women until 1918. That institution tapped the services of a
female professor, Luella Carson. In her first 2 years, Professor Carson
devoted only 3 hours per week to her dean's duties and the rest to teaching, but the balance eventually tipped in the other direction (Holmes,
1939).

Only one university appointed an administrator during the 1890s to
help curb the excesses of the young men. In 1891, President Eliot of Harvard
University appointed a 35-year-old professor of English, LeBaron Russell
Briggs, Dean of Harvard College with responsibilities to oversee the undergraduates. Dean Briggs, as his biographer noted, "became the first officer
in the history of American higher education charged with responsibility
for student relations as separate and distinct from instruction" (Fley, 1979,
p. 24). As the early history of deans of women suggests, this boast was
not wholly accurate. However, bestowing the title "dean" on the officer
looking after undergraduate students at an institution of Harvard's prestige was new. In general, institutions were much slower in appointing administrators whose sole responsibility was looking after men. It was almost
another two decades before the title "dean" was conferred on such a man.
However, President Harper of the University of Chicago must have felt
encouraged by Harvard's example when he gave his newly hired female
administrators the title only one year after Dean Briggs was appointed.

The previous work experience of the newly hired deans of women
clearly revealed that there was no single career trajectory. Some had no

prior work experience, but most had previous teaching or administrative experience, typically in a women's college. A few others had experience outside of academe running women's clubs or civic organizations (Holmes, 1939).

Whatever their previous work experience—faculty member, dormitory matron, women's college administrator, or officer of a women's organization—the deans of women hired by universities in the 1890s shared similar ideas about the nature of the tasks before them. They looked to the work of their predecessors in liberal arts colleges, but they also had another source of information—the quasi-official work done for the university by the YWCA and Women's League members, none of whom held an official appointment.

In the 1890s, no two deans had identical duties or work conditions because the situation on each university campus was different. The presidents who hired the deans had three responsibilities uppermost in their minds—housing, health, and social supervision. Although this list of formal obligations looked similar to the tasks of early deans in liberal arts colleges, there was an important difference. The work of university deans involved campuswide—sometimes even community-wide—management.

Two historical studies confirmed that the growth in the early years of the 20th century was dramatic. One study of eight state institutions revealed that none of them had a dean in 1890; yet three had a dean by 1900, half had a dean by 1910, and all eight institutions employed a dean of women by 1930 (McGrath, 1936). In a 1911 study of her peers, Gertrude Martin (1911b), Advisor of Women at Cornell, surveyed 68 coeducational institutions and received 55 usable responses. She found that the majority of institutions had a dean of women at the time of her survey and that the average length of service was 9 years. Her study confirmed that the practice of hiring a dean of women became prevalent around the turn of the century.

In the first few years of the new century, a fresh set of personal and professional characteristics for deans became typical. Martin's study (1911b) revealed that the title of "dean" rather than "advisor" or "matron" had become the norm. The majority of this new cohort of deans possessed an advanced academic degree and, despite the challenges inherent therein, had faculty responsibilities as well as administrative duties. Another study revealed that the most common academic disciplines of deans who taught were literature and modern languages. This was followed in prevalence by the social sciences, which included the relatively new field of domestic economy (McGrath, 1936). These findings were not surprising given that literature, language, and home economics were (and remain) "women's fields." However, a few other fields were also represented. Mary Bidwell Breed of Indiana University, for example, held a Ph.D. in chemistry from Bryn Mawr (Rothenberger, 1942).

As mentioned above, the presidents who hired deans of women to deal with the woman problem envisioned a prescribed role emphasizing housing, health, and social supervision. However, they hired women with serious academic credentials while at the same time emphasizing the aspect of the job that least needed such qualifications. This disparity was not lost on the deans in Martin's sample (1911b), who were driven to make the job more suitable to their qualifications.

With minimal job descriptions provided by the presidents, deans were generally left to fashion their own way. This presented the opportunity for a few leaders among the deans to forge ahead in making their work into a new profession. The catalyst and central actor in this process was Marion Talbot. Her vision for the potential of dean of women, her skill at organizing professional meetings, and her contributions to the field of women's education made her integral to the professionalization process. In fact, Gertrude Martin (1911b) even credited the rapid growth in deans' positions to the presence of Talbot at the University of Chicago: "I myself remember when it began to be 'good form' among the colleges to appoint a dean of women. I am sure that it was the University of Chicago that really made it fashionable" (p. 66).

Marion Talbot, circa 1892. Assistant Professor of Sanitary Science, Dean of Undergraduate Women, 1892–1899 and Dean of Women for the University, 1899–1924, University of Chicago. (Courtesy Department of Special Collections, University of Chicago Library)

Chapter 3

THE CATALYST AND THE HUB

Marion Talbot's contributions to women's education were extraordinary. She fought for intellectual equity for women. In 1881 she co-founded the Association of Collegiate Alumnae (ACA), the most important organization for university-trained women of the Progressive Era. She was one of the first female educators to write authoritatively on issues in women's education (Talbot, 1897). She wielded considerable influence, especially over women, at the young but vital University of Chicago. Her tenure at Chicago lasted from 1892 until her retirement in 1925, much longer than most other deans, for whom the average tenure was under 10 years (Martin, 1911b; McGrath, 1936). Indefatigable, she remained active in her post-Chicago years, continuing to publish in the field of women's education, including a history of the American Association of University Women (AAUW) (which originated as the ACA) that she co-wrote with colleague Dean Lois Mathews Rosenberry (Talbot & Rosenberry, 1931). She also extended her administrative career beyond retirement and twice served as the acting president of a women's college in Turkey.

Talbot also had a profound impact on the profession of dean of women. Her own career encompassed all the phases of professional development—from pre-professionalization activity to attainment of full professional status. She offered an intellectual rationale for the profession in the second phase, initiated professional meetings during the third phase, and published material on women's education and helped the struggling profession gain prestige during the last two phases.

Considering all her attainments, however, perhaps the greatest was that of catalyst for the professional meetings. Talbot brought other deans of women into her professional circle and around to her way of thinking. They joined her in the push for professionalization, extended her influence, and became key figures themselves in the process (Fitzpatrick, 1989; Rosenberg, 1982; Storr, 1971; Talbot, 1936).

AN INDOMITABLE YANKEE SPIRIT

Marion Talbot was born in 1858 and lived for just over 90 years. Born in Europe while her parents were "sojourning," she was raised in Boston amid economic comfort and "social amenity," coming from a long line of New England families (Storr, 1971). She traveled in influential circles, and interesting women such as Julia Ward Howe and Louisa May Alcott were in her social milieu. Her father, Israel Tisdale Talbot, was passionate about health reform and a specialist in homeopathic medicine. He became the first dean of Boston University's medical school in 1873. Marion's mother, Emily Talbot, was also a committed health reformer, but the cause she held most dear was expanding women's educational opportunities.

Emily Talbot had an enormous influence on her daughter. Frustrated by the paucity of her own schooling, Mrs. Talbot wanted to secure a better education for her daughters, Marion and Edith. She embarked on her quest after witnessing the difficulties Marion encountered trying to obtain a classical, college preparatory education on a par with young Boston men (Fitzpatrick, 1989; Rosenberg, 1982; Storr, 1971). Marion attended the reluctantly coeducational Chauncy Hill School where the instructors taught the girls at a slower pace than the boys. To strengthen Marion's education, Emily Talbot provided private tutoring in the classical languages and moved the family to Europe for 15 months so Marion could learn German and French. Mrs. Talbot finally secured a place for her daughter in Boston University in 1876, but Marion had considerable academic difficulty compared with the young men prepared in academies (Fitzpatrick, 1989). In 1877, after Marion began college, Mrs. Talbot succeeded in convincing city officials to open the Latin School for Girls in Boston so that other women's daughters would not suffer in college as Marion had. For Emily Talbot, this was a compromise because she wanted one, coeducational Boston Latin School. She was further bothered when the city refused to allow "Boston" in the school's name, but it was a start.

In post–Civil War New England there were several fine preparatory academies for boys, but education for young girls was limited to learning the skills deemed necessary for domesticity. Emily Talbot and other New England reformers began discussing the ill effects of commercialization and the growing problems of urbanization. They were a bit ahead of their time; during the Progressive Era, trepidation over these issues became a nationwide concern. However, Emily Talbot's thinking bridged her concern with social issues and her quest for women's education. She thought educated women should become more than teachers. She was convinced that "higher education provided the key to both female fulfillment and social reform" (Rosenberg, 1982, p. 4) so along with other

Boston women she agitated for more education for girls and college opportunities for young women.

Marion Talbot graduated from Boston University with a bachelor of arts degree in 1880, after which she "fell victim to a kind of aimlessness and uncertainty" (Fitzpatrick, 1989, p. 88) not uncommon to the small number of women earning college degrees in this era. Her college training had cut her "off from her girlhood friends. No 'Junior League' or 'Sewing Circle' or 'Vincent Club' of those days wanted as a member a young woman whose aims were so different from their own" (Talbot & Rosenberry, 1931, pp. 4–5). Marion herself commented: "The satisfactions obtained in the pursuit of truth make other searches seem trivial in the comparison, and the use of one's mind becomes not only fascinating, but a compelling task" (p. 6). Sadly, she had no immediate peer group.

Emily Talbot understood and sympathized with Marion's malaise. She astutely realized that Marion's feelings were probably shared by the ever-growing number of women receiving college degrees across New England. Mrs. Talbot had a vision of "college women from all over the country joining together to advance their own and other noble causes" (Fitzpatrick, 1989, p. 89). She told her dream to Marion, who asked Ellen Richards, a professor at MIT, to help her organize a meeting in the autumn of 1881 of women who had recently graduated from college. The Association of Collegiate Alumnae grew out of this first assembly (Talbot & Rosenberry, 1931, pp. 8–9).

The ACA was an important organization for Marion. It supplied her with a much-needed circle of friends who shared an interest in intellectual fulfillment and professional accomplishment. Further, the ACA became an organizational base for her own maturing interests in women's education, and she served as its secretary for the first 14 years (Fitzpatrick, 1989). It also provided a model of collective action to which she would return when she started organizing deans of women in 1902.

The ACA had the twofold purpose of "offering encouragement to young women wanting to go to college and expanding the opportunities for women graduates" (Rosenberg, 1982, p. 19). Its members accepted as their first challenge a refutation of the arguments of Dr. Clarke's (1873) book *Sex in Education*. Marion had read Dr. Clarke when she was only 15 and was upset by his claims that women were physically damaged by intellectual work, but she had remained determined to go to college. She and other ACA members promptly conducted a survey of the health of college women to illustrate that the fears of illness were unfounded. The ACA made several important contributions to women's higher education over the years, including the establishment of fellowships for graduate study that helped several women earn doctorates. During her years as dean of women at Chicago, Marion served as ACA president (1895–1897) and remained connected to the organization until her death. Urged by Marion in 1912, the ACA changed its criteria for accrediting institutions and demanded, among other things, that the college or university have a dean of women. In 1921, the ACA became the American Association of University Women, and later in 1931, Talbot became its historian along with Lois Mathews Rosenberry.

In the earliest days of the ACA, however, Marion was endeavoring to find a calling that justified her education to her own mind and fulfilled her sense of social obligation. Her passion to find socially useful work led her to resume academic study. After earning a master's degree from Boston University, she enrolled at MIT in 1884, studied with Ellen Richards, and graduated in 1888 with a bachelor of science degree in sanitary (later domestic) science (Rosenberg, 1982). Her choice of domestic science "reflected an attempt to elevate the domestic interest widely accepted as woman's 'proper' domain to a respectable position as a professional, scientific field" (Fitzpatrick, 1989, p. 89). For Talbot, this was key. She believed, like many of her contemporaries, that women were uniquely qualified to bring about the reform of social ills. Domestic science taught women how to make the home free of disease and filth, and Talbot believed that women should take that knowledge into the public arena and eradicate many problems associated with urbanization. It was a field where women could find work that was "socially useful, intellectually challenging, and available to her sex" (p. 89).

Talbot was appointed an instructor of domestic science at Wellesley in 1890 at the behest of its president, Alice Freeman (later, Palmer). In many ways, Palmer was Talbot's mentor. Palmer was a member of the ACA and had been impressed by Talbot's leadership ability. Wellesley, however, remained committed to a traditional liberal arts curriculum, and Talbot grew fatigued of New England's "conservative" attitudes toward women's education (Fitzpatrick, 1989).

AT THE UNIVERSITY OF CHICAGO

Her opportunity to leave Wellesley was made possible by the same woman who brought her to campus, Alice Freeman Palmer. In 1892, William Rainey Harper began building the University of Chicago. He dreamt of making it a western Yale, and the generosity of John D. Rockefeller gave him the resources to lure prestigious eastern academics to the shores of Lake Michigan. Harper was determined to fashion a great university quickly and did so by hiring proven administrators and established scholars (Goodspeed, 1916; Gordon, 1990; Storr, 1966). Harper was not an enthusiast for coeducation, but the charter of the university demanded it. In keeping with his desire to hire the most talented faculty that he could find and the social expectation that college women needed supervision, Harper offered Alice Freeman Palmer the position of professor of history and dean of women for the university. Palmer was reluctant to turn down an opportunity to become a female professor in a coeducational institution, for there were precious few such offers in 1892. Although she had served as a president of a women's college, Palmer was interested in and committed to coeducation, probably due to her relatively positive undergraduate experience at the University of Michigan and her long-standing friendship with James B. Angell. She agreed, however, on two conditions. Because her Harvard professor husband, George Herbert Palmer, was unwilling to leave Cambridge, Alice Palmer said she would work in Chicago only 12 weeks a year. She also demanded that Marion Talbot be appointed her deputy. Talbot's title was Dean of Undergraduate Women and Assistant Professor of Sanitary Science (Fitzpatrick, 1989).

With some trepidation, Talbot prepared to move to Chicago. Her Boston friends were rather horrified that she, being quite small in stature and weighing only 93 pounds, would move to such a "wild and woolly place" (Talbot, 1936, p. 6). However, they wished her well and gave her a modest trousseau as if she were getting married. One friend even gave her a piece of Plymouth Rock to remind her of her New England roots. Actually, the move west appealed to Talbot's pioneering spirit and the new opportunities at Chicago "promised an escape from the restrictive conception of feminine capacity and purpose that had plagued her youth" (quoted in Rosenberg, 1982, p. 2).

Harper's standards for his faculty and students were high. He hired talented scholars and tolerated little nonserious behavior in his students. He made no intellectual exception when hiring a dean of women. In this regard, Harper was the first president to break the mold of the "wise and pious matron," expecting his dean to be a serious scholar and much more than a monitor or mere guardian.

The new University of Chicago was a singular place for women. It was a private institution with aspirations to "Ivy League" eminence, but it was born in the age of the university with few of the traditions associated with the old eastern colleges, including the custom of educating only men. Located in the Midwest, surrounded by coeducational state universities, Chicago was coeducational from the beginning. From very early on, it had a critical mass of women that few other universities achieved until much later in the 20th century. In 1892, just under 200 women attended, but they were one-quarter of all undergraduates. By 1897 there were over 1,000 college women; in the 1901–1902 academic year, women were 52% of all undergraduates. The absence of old college traditions such as "rushes," the large presence of women on campus, and Harper's intolerance for adolescent behavior made Chicago a less hostile environment for women than many other coeducational universities, although hardly a panacea (Gordon, 1990).

Women were central in the graduate school as well. In 1892 the largest collection of students entering from any one institution was from Wellesley. The percentage of women academics was much less impressive, but Chicago had more women faculty than other coeducational universities. Eleven women held academic posts in 1897 (Fitzpatrick, 1989).

Toward the turn of the century, Chicago was also the home of an important women's community off-campus. Women were active in several fields, but the most notable was the large women-dominated reformist community in Chicago. Imbued with the spirit of Progressivism and dedicated to ameliorating various social problems, especially those associated with poverty and immigration, women in large cities were becoming reform-oriented activists. One common form of activism was the Settlement Houses founded in New York, Boston, Chicago, and Philadelphia. Built in the middle of the poorest neighborhoods, settlements housed privileged and educated women who chose to live among the poor in order to improve social conditions within those neighborhoods. The most famous settlement was led by Jane Addams and her associates at Hull House, founded in Chicago in 1899. Addams was so frequent a speaker on campus (and Hull House so often the host to many of the university's prominent sociologists) that she was virtually an adjunct faculty member. Palmer and Talbot used all the resources available to create the sense of community they had known at Wellesley and combined "community" with the intellectual opportunities available at a university as energetic and vibrant as Chicago (Fitzpatrick, 1989; Gordon, 1990).

From the beginning, although Talbot was officially charged with looking after the undergraduate women, she actually considered all the women of the university community her constituency. When Alice Freeman Palmer officially left Chicago in 1899, Talbot was promoted to dean of women for the university, but in fact she had done the preponderance of the work from the start. She was an uncompromising advocate for women and a formidable foe to anyone she perceived as the opposition. She regularly surveyed "the women of the university" from her vantage point as dean and presented her findings in her annual reports to the president. She emphasized the accomplishments of female professors, undergraduates, and graduate students to illustrate that "the presence of women did not mean the lowering of any standards" (Fitzpatrick, 1989, p. 92).

She also wrote of difficulties and losses for women at Chicago. She rarely missed the opportunity to remind Harper that the women needed additional university funds and support (Talbot 1897, 1903, 1908). In her 1905–1906 report to the president, she rather caustically pointed out that "the work in Physical Culture continues to gain in effectiveness in spite of the fact that the increase in the number of students is not accompanied by the corresponding increase in instructional force or equipment" (quoted in Fitzpatrick, 1989, p. 105). Her use of graphs, charts, and statistics sometimes allowed "the status of Chicago's women [to] speak for themselves" (Fitzpatrick, 1989, p. 92). On one occasion, she illustrated that the number of women faculty members was actually declining as time passed rather than increasing despite gains in the number of women earning Ph.Ds. She noted that there were 52 women of academic rank in 1902–1903 but only 45 in 1903–1904, a loss of 14% (Fish, 1985). As historian Ellen Fitzpatrick (1989) noted, "Whatever her technique, Talbot's insistent refrain ensured that nothing would silence the voice of what William Rainey Harper called 'the woman side of the university'" (p. 92).

Her most pitched battle in her role as women's advocate began in 1900 when the university administration proposed the segregation of instruction for men and women into a newly proposed Junior College (Brint & Karabel, 1989; Harper, 1900). Harper was a proponent of separating the first 2 from the last years of undergraduate study. He expected the less serious students (a category into which he hoped all women would fall) would leave after 2 years with a certificate or associates degree and let the university train only the serious advanced undergraduates and graduate students. Advocates for women knew that behind Harper's proposal was his strong desire to limit the university to training only advanced undergraduates and graduate students coupled with his lukewarm acceptance of coeducation. It was feared that the inevitable result of this plan would be fewer women as university students. Although the plan was largely Harper's, well over one-half of the male faculty supported the idea (Gordon, 1990).

Harper's idea received national attention and opposition came from many quarters. The issue was described by Thomas W. Goodspeed (1916), the university's earliest historian, as "the first and only civil war during the first quarter century" (p. 407) of the university's history. University alumnae and representatives from national women's organizations protested to the president. On campus, assertive faculty members challenged Harper in "A Memorial to President Harper and the Trustees," a petition signed by all female faculty members and by 50 men, including John Dewey. Dewey, in fact, became one of the strongest male voices in opposition to Harper's plan:

> The argument implies that the proper basis of the relation of the sexes is the life of amusement and recreation, instead of that of serious pursuit of truth in mutual competition and co-operation. The proposed measure thus takes away the chief safeguard of co-education and leaves all its weak points exposed and multiplied. Quadrangles contiguous to each other for social purpose and absolutely remote for intellectual purposes are a standing invitation to silliness. (quoted in Harper, n.d.; also quoted in Gordon, 1990, p. 115)

But it was Marion Talbot who led the opposition. Separate classrooms "threatened her lifelong crusade to establish the intellectual equality of the sexes, and the expense of dual classrooms meant women might receive less qualified teachers. Furthermore, whatever the university said, the public would view segregation as a response to some failure by women students" (Harper, 1902; also quoted in Gordon, 1990, p. 115). She wrote letters and spoke at gatherings and officially protested to Harper:

> The atmosphere of intellectual freedom enjoyed by our students, through which they have exercised their mental powers as human beings without reference to the fact that they are either men or women has been appreciated by them and admired by the world. Separate instruction would introduce an element which would affect this condition unfavorably. If the trustees could know how eager girls and women are to study as thinking beings and not as females, they would hesitate in justice to women to adopt this measure. (Harper, January 16, 1902, also quoted in Gordon, 1990, p. 115)

Such opposition did not sway the faculty, which voted to approve Harper's plan in the summer of 1902; it took effect in the winter of 1903. Yet the plan never became fully operational. The administration voted to offer segregated sections of required courses with expectations of doing the same for electives as it became economically feasible. By 1906–1907, however, only 50% of the students in the Junior College had even one segregated course in their plan of study. After 1907, there was no mention in university records or the *President's Reports* of segregated instruction (Gordon, 1990). Apparently, the idea simply atrophied. By 1907, it was evident that the plan was far too costly and its instigator, President Harper, was dead.

Advocates of coeducation had won only a relative "triumph," because the gains for women at the university actually peaked in 1902. The proportions of women earning academic honors, receiving fellowships, and gaining faculty appointments or promotions fell between 1902 and Talbot's retirement in 1925. The relative strength of the women's community off-campus grew until the 1920s, however, providing Chicago's undergraduates with "richer campus experiences than their counterparts at other coeducational schools" (Gordon, 1990, p. 119).

One of Talbot's successes in fostering a community for women on campus was the creation of the Women's Union building in 1901. She was strongly opposed to sororities and secret societies. She was concerned that national sororities exacerbated social class distinctions, and this interfered with her vision of community. So although the men had fraternities, Talbot banned sororities for women. The students circumvented her wishes and formed a few secret societies, but the clubs often languished without the imprimatur of the university. She founded and ran the Women's Union. As she reported to President Harper in her annual reports, the Women's Union is "for making more attractive, interesting, and profitable the life of women students in the University" (Fitzpatrick, 1989, p. 111). The work of the union fell into four categories, performing services not unlike modern women's centers on campuses: "1) the provision of material contributions to the physical comfort of students, ... 2) Opportunities for social enjoyment, ... 3) The service of attention and help to all women students needing sympathy or assistance, ... 4) In addition, . . . the Women's Union is the link between the students of the University and organizations for social and civic improvement in the city of Chicago" (Fitzpatrick, 1989, pp. 111–112).

The union was open to all the university women who paid the dues of $1 per year. It was an especially effective mechanism for involving nonresident women in the life of the campus. The union was replaced in 1915 with another of Talbot's projects—Ida Noyes Hall, which had a larger clubhouse and a gymnasium, lunchroom, and swimming pool. Throughout her entire career as dean, Talbot always "sponsored some sort of organization open to every woman on campus" (Gordon, 1990, p. 99).

Her efforts were appreciated by undergraduates. Lucy Lucille Tasker, who was an undergraduate from 1921 to 1926, wrote of Marion Talbot:

> Yes, all of us shall remember Miss Talbot for there is no forgetting her thoughtfulness as she met each of us Freshmen. Some of us were here to stay a year, some four or more but her vigor and vitality sustained us. . . .
>
> Then there were Sunday afternoons with music in the parlor and after the social hour one might be invited into Miss Talbot's apartment as a special privilege. Here the beautiful mementos of her travels, the bright

cheerfulness of the fire and eager vitality of the spirit that filled the room made any future possible. Adventure and gayety made her ours for the moment and we forgot her importance in the immense world of scholarship and loved her for her own great gift of understanding. . . . Yes, we shall remember. (Haddock, 1952, pp. 345–346)

Talbot also sponsored meetings of Women Fellows (graduate students with fellowships) and other types of formal and informal gatherings of students and faculty. She had other duties as well, many of them traditionally associated with deans of women. It was this aspect of her job in which her modern notions of women's capabilities and her 19th-century social sensibilities were fused. As dean, she was responsible for the provision and superintendence of adequate housing and the social supervision of students. In the residence halls where students of all ages mixed, she advocated a "house plan," which meant that the students were largely self-governed although each dorm had a woman with an academic appointment as the head resident. The freedom from supervision that this afforded was a tribute to Talbot's liberal attitudes toward and confidence in women students. A former student and faculty colleague of Talbot recalled that she had a "warmheartedness, a quick understanding and sympathy, and a sincere and uncompromising evaluation of the rights and wrongs of a case. Her desire was always that women should go forth from the University with ability to think for themselves, to develop their powers to the utmost and to lead useful and gracious lives" (Haddock, 1952, pp. 346–347).

However, in matters of social propriety, she was often strict. As Fitzpatrick (1989) noted, "decorum was maintained in accordance with social values that Talbot considered fundamental. The drinking of wine and attendance at off-campus parties fell victim to Marion's proper rule at an early date" (p. 93). In general, Talbot believed in the power of persuasion and tried to avoid petty rules. As she stated in her 1936 autobiography, *More Than Lore: Reminiscences of Marion Talbot*, she was

> wholly unwilling to have a new rule passed whenever an objectionable situation occurred. A much better way seemed to be to advise with the student concerned. This was, of course, a long-drawn-out process; but I doubt if it consumed more time or effort than would have been necessary to enforce a body of minute rules and, moreover, it resulted in the development of a kind of morale which was very effective. "It isn't done" proved more of a deterrent than "It's against the rules." (p. 162)

An example of her style was evident in an encounter she had with President Harper's daughter, whom she chastised for walking on campus in an outlandish costume for a club initiation. Miss Harper responded that she had seen the men do the same thing and then rather mockingly questioned the dean, saying didn't the "women have the same rights as men in the university?" Dean Talbot drew an important distinction for her: "women ha[ve] the same rights to do anything credible, but no right at all to do anything dis-credible, even if the majority of the men set the example" (Talbot, 1936, pp. 161–162). Talbot felt satisfied in how she handled the incident and reported that such occurrences were not repeated.

TRUE WOMANHOOD/NEW WOMANHOOD

Talbot's turn-of-the-century view of women was fundamental to her work as both a dean and a scholar. She combined three strains of 19th-century thought. She believed in modernist ideas about the inherent rationality of all human beings, which implied that women were as capable of intellectual thought as men. Yet she never completely let go of all the vestiges of Victorian notions of propriety and separate spheres, other than intellectual. She also accepted Darwinian ideas of biological differences between the genders—that differences between men and women were designed by God to ensure reproduction. Her convictions were shared with many other women's educators, feminists, reformers, and suffragists, of which she was one.

Her view was three-pronged: Women were simultaneously equal with, different from, and in one sense morally superior to men (Ferguson, 1988). Talbot believed that women were intellectually equal to men and therefore entitled to equivalent educational opportunities. This belief was at the heart of her opposition to Harper's plan of segregated education. As she stated unequivocally in her 1910 book *The Education of Women*, "Women have proved their ability to enter every realm of knowledge. They must have the right to do it. No province of the mind should be peculiarly the man's. Unhampered by traditions of sex, women will naturally and without comment seek the intellectual goal which they think good and fit" (p. 22).

The second component of her belief was that women were different from men and required an environment that was special or distinct. Her beliefs in the benefits of a separate women's community placed Talbot firmly within the tradition of late-19th-century feminists. Feminists of the day adopted what Estelle Freedman (1979) described as "separatism as strategy" where "they preferred to retain membership in a separate female sphere, one which they did not believe to be inferior to men's sphere and one in which women could be free to create their own forms of personal, social, and political relationships" (p. 514).

On coeducational campuses, the special environments were created in women's housing or in a women's building such as Talbot's Women's Union. Antagonists of coeducation sometimes used this very argument against women. Opponents countered that female needs for a special environment implied single-sex classrooms. Talbot held firm, however, stating that mixed classrooms were the only way to ensure equivalent educational opportunities and that a "special" environment could be created for the out-of-classroom lives of women. In this view, she was an intellectual bridge from the older view that feminine uniqueness implied intellectual limitations. Or, put succinctly, she was a bridge between what Freedman (1979) and other feminist historians have labeled "true womanhood" and the "new womanhood." By asserting that women were academically capable in any field and relegating the need for unique circumstances to realm of the social, she secured for women a safe place in the university, maintained propriety, and yet kept all avenues of mental exploration open.

The third aspect of her philosophy, which was similar to views expounded by her mother, was that women were in one sense morally superior to men. This superiority compelled women to enter professions such as the one she loved—sanitary science—and other fields such as teaching, social work, or, as the suffragists argued, politics so that society might be improved. Although Talbot did not believe that reform work was the exclusive task of women—indeed, she believed it suffered from a neglect by both genders—she did believe that educated women should be so engaged (Rosenberg, 1982). Talbot expressed her view in an 1898 article:

> In my opinion, this period of four years' training is not intended to fit a young person to earn her living and to do something which will have a direct and definite market value. That function belongs rather to the trade, graduate, or professional school. But it is of great importance, under existing social conditions, to train the women who are going to our colleges to *spend* wisely, and to use their privileges and meet their responsibilities as members of the leisure class. For, after all, what is involved in this aim of securing the proper discipline of all the higher powers, except that they be used as the tools in social service? The college, then, should give ample opportunity for the direction and expression of these powers as they develop. (p. 26)

She never veered from this position. "One of the greatest gains needed in education," she wrote 12 years later, "is a revival, through adequate training, of their peculiar influences in unorganized social activities and then out and beyond into the organized social activities in which they are destined to play a part" (Talbot, 1910, p. 204).

Talbot's view of women drove her scholarly ambition as well. Talbot had a faculty career of some note but it was her dual role of administrator/teacher that provided the core of her experience at Chicago. The two were quite fused in her mind. Yet despite some academic success, it was primarily her position as dean of women that "made her a highly visible figure within the university community and brought to her a kind of recognition that her work as a professor never quite afforded" (Fitzpatrick, 1989, p. 91). In this respect, Talbot was typical. Many women faculty members, relegated to doing "women's work," which included being a dean of women, found that their scholarly contributions were ignored as feminine or trivial or eclipsed by the administrative aspects of their jobs (Rossiter, 1982).

When Talbot initially was approached by President Harper in 1892, she requested a position of associate professor, but he offered the rank of assistant instead. She moved to Chicago anyway, which seemed to her full of boundless possibilities, with the dream of establishing her own department of sanitary science, believing that such a department was key to the progress of women in the university and larger society. Harper steadfastly refused her request for a new department, arguing that it was an unreasonable use of university resources in the early years. Harper's resistance was her first sign (and one of her hardest lessons) that her genuine affection for him coexisted "with a frustrating recognition that the Chicago president sometimes stood in the path of women's progress" (Fitzpatrick, 1989, pp. 93–94). Talbot's disappointment with the president who had hired her was not unique. Dean of Women at Berkeley, Lucy Sprague (later, Mitchell) felt unease at times with the generally supportive President Benjamin Wheeler (Antler, 1987), and Lois Mathews was sometimes frustrated with President Charles Van Hise at the University of Wisconsin. Male support often had bounds.

Talbot became instead a member of the sociology department, where she experienced some success. For example, when Albion Small began the *American Journal of Sociology* in 1895, Talbot was invited to be a member of the editorial board. Of most significance, however, was that she was a "pivotal figure in this community of activists and scholars, a kind of chief of employment for Chicago's women students and academic dean for Chicago reformers" (Rosenberg, 1982, p. 34). She was promoted to associate professor of sociology in 1895.

A growing acceptance and enthusiasm for domestic science finally convinced Harper in 1904 to create the new department of Household Administration, of which Talbot, now a full professor, was head. She used her position as department head to secure the appointments of talented protégées, including Sophonisba Breckinridge, a lifelong friend for whom she battled for years for higher pay and recognition (Gordon, 1990). She also instigated graduate fellowships for students. Her new department stressed the intellectual aspects of the field and was deeply rooted in the liberal arts tradition.

Talbot, in fact, was actively involved in the professionalization of home economics as well as the professionalization of deaning. She took part in the Lake Placid Conferences, under the leadership of Ellen Richards, that led to the development of the American Home Economics Association in 1908. Her major publication as department head was the 1912 book *The Modern Household*, in which she argued that educated women should act as modern administrators and exert the influence of the home in the larger society. The woman should consider herself "as placed at the real heart of things, responsible for the conduct of that institution [the home] which is the unit of social organization" (Talbot & Breckinridge, 1912, p. 8).

Her department was attractive to women students. Although domestic science did perpetuate women's interests in "proper sphere" issues such as food, clothing, nutrition, and children, it also provided women with jobs in something other than teaching. By creating a department that catered to women, Talbot "furthered a trend that saw women moving away from advanced study of traditional and predominantly male social sciences toward training in more 'feminine' fields" (Fitzpatrick, 1989, p. 94). While the women in her department may have benefited from the enclave she created, it was ironic that by creating a "women's" department, "she fell victim to the very process of academic sexual segregation that she was trying to fight" (Rosenberg, 1982, p. 49).

When Talbot retired from the university in 1925, President Charles "Max" Mason did not appoint a successor, and the record is not clear as to why that decision was made. Instead, he divided her duties among several committees (Gordon, 1990). The testimonials from former students that poured in at her retirement were surely gratifying to Talbot, who commented near the end of her life: "For thirty-three years I gave all I had to the university, and reaped a rich harvest of happiness and content" (Fitzpatrick, 1989, p. 95). Perhaps the highest compliment a dean of women was ever paid by male officials at a university was bestowed on Talbot in the early years of her career in 1902. A decennial publication compared her to the legendary football coach of the university, Amos Alonzo Stagg. The article said, "As Mr. Stagg is 'first in the hearts of Chicago men,' so she might well be proclaimed first in the affection of the gentler sex" to which Ellen Fitzpatrick aptly noted, "That an academic institution could celebrate the talents of a woman who made a career of critiquing the university's treatment of her sex is perhaps Marion Talbot's most impressive and telling legacy" (p. 96).

THE BEGINNINGS OF PROFESSIONALIZATION

It was Marion Talbot's influence beyond the University of Chicago, however, that made her pivotal to the professionalization of deans of women. Talbot was a pioneer in many respects and often, but not always, the University of Chicago led the field in innovative ideas for women. Of course she was not the only dean who wrote on the subject of women's education or the nature of deaning. Rather, her significance came from the role she played in gathering other deans together at a propitious place and time, articulating a philosophical basis for their work, and providing leadership throughout her career.

Talbot's critical contribution during the phase of pre-professionalization (1892 to 1901) was her eloquence in discussing an educational philosophy for women with other deans. She was neither the first nor the only educator to hold such beliefs, but through the ACA *Journal* and meetings and other sources, Talbot effectively communicated her ideas. Lulu Holmes, author of *A History of the Position of Dean of Women* (1939), later remembered how Talbot defined "the objective of higher education for women and then move[d] toward it actually from all fronts" (Haddock, 1952, p. 349).

Her unequivocal faith that women were the intellectual equals of men, even if they sometimes needed special protections or environments, provided a theoretical underpinning for the new profession. The new professional deans were still obligated to fulfill the duties of the "wise and pious matron" by looking after the behavior of young women. However, deans were also members of the growing ranks of college-educated women in the United States seeking new professional opportunities and an expanded role on campus. It was the three-pronged nature of the turn-of-the-century view of women's education (as articulated most forcefully by Talbot) that provided the rationale for the expanded role of deans.

Subscribing to a belief that women were intellectually equal provided the deans with a justification for their involvement in curricular and other academic matters aimed at ensuring equal educational opportunities. The belief that women needed a community on a coeducational campus to counteract the antagonism against them thrust deans into a new advocacy role. In this capacity, deans defended competing for university resources for women's housing, women's buildings, and other projects designed to benefit women. During the Progressive Era, American women felt a tremendous pressure to justify the investments that families and society were making in their higher education. The movement of women into socially useful professions (and especially benevolence work) was in response to this pressure. Deans eventually included career counseling among their repertoire and sponsored vocational conferences that frequently highlighted social work, but provided young women with information on all types of careers, including those defined as exclusively male.

Lois Mathews (later Rosenberry), author of *The Dean of Women* (1915) and co-author with Talbot of *The History of the American Association of University Women* (1931), reflected on Talbot's contribution at the time of her death in 1948:

> My friendship with Miss Talbot covers a span of nearly forty years. As I think of her it is her integrity, personal and intellectual which stand out most prominently. But her idealism for women, her belief in their capacity, her visions for their future—these rare traits also characterized her. She was a splendid person and the world of women is richer for her long service to them. (quoted in Haddock, 1952, p. 349)

When Talbot organized the first meeting of midwestern deans in 1902, she initiated the third phase of professionalization, and this was probably her most tangible contribution. The idea of gathering women together for mutual support and the furtherance of their goals was, of course, not new to her because she had done so 20 years earlier with the ACA. Professional associations were very important to women. They were necessary for professionalization, but they were equally important as part of the "separatism as strategy" movement of late 19th-century feminists (Antler, 1977; Freedman, 1979). Talbot brought the first group of deans together in Chicago, where they met on Northwestern's campus. The purpose of the meeting, which became a regular conference, was to share information, discuss policy and practice, and assist each other in coping with the stress of the job. As Ada Comstock, who became a dean of women at the University of Minnesota in 1906, recalled many years later:

> In the early part of this century, the office of the dean of women was established in many of our coeducational institutions. Those of us appointed to these posts had to define their scope as well as to meet the daily responsibilities. By way of help we formed a small group of deans of women in state universities which met annually to discuss problems and formulate policies. Our usual meeting place was Chicago and although the University of

Chicago was not a state university, we always insisted that Miss Talbot should attend our meetings. The rapid spread of higher education for women was due in an appreciable degree to Marion Talbot's insistence on standards of achievement and proper arrangements in coeducational institutions for the life and work of women students. (quoted in Haddock, 1952, p. 347)

Comstock's reminiscences are confirmed by the minutes of these early deans' meetings. After the conferences were firmly established, Talbot was one of the few women to attend who did not represent a public university.

In many respects, the third aspect of Talbot's central role in the professionalization process was the result of a fortuitous historical accident. She worked in a prestigious private university located in a region of the country where the dominant form of university education was public. In the heart of the Midwest, she found the deans of women of coeducational state universities in close geographical proximity. These were highly trained women with excellent academic credentials, capable and talented, and committed to advancing women's education and their own professional careers. Although Talbot was in the private sector, she reached out to these women in the public sector of higher education, and it was there that the position of women deans expanded into a recognized profession.

Because of her central role in founding the conferences, Talbot was regarded as the "expert" to whom new deans turned and someone with whom experienced deans shared professional advice. Among the young deans who attended the first meeting was Mary Bidwell Breed, the newly appointed dean of women at Indiana University, who became the secretary of the new organization and a central actor in the professionalization process.

Mary Bidwell Breed, circa 1905. Assistant Professor of Chemistry,
Dean of Women, 1901–1906, Indiana University.
(Courtesy Indiana University Archives)

Chapter 4

GETTING ORGANIZED

Where Marion Talbot's career was exceptional, Mary Bidwell Breed's was more typical; while the history of the position of dean of women at the University of Chicago was remarkable, at Indiana it was paradigmatic. Breed's career at Indiana (1901–1906) was representative of the third phase of professionalization for several reasons. Like Talbot, Breed held the title "dean," rather than matron or preceptress, and was a member of the regular teaching faculty (Rothenberger, 1942). Her tenure was characterized by initial resistance from students and faculty members who resented her presence. She had to cope with an administration that committed too few resources to her proposals and her work was dominated by the issue of housing women. When Breed accepted her position, deans of women had none of the trappings of a profession, but by the time she left a few important steps had been taken, including the regular Conference of Deans. Under Breed's leadership of the conference, the locus of control of the profession was assumed by deans from large midwestern public universities. There the deans developed standards of practice that became the foundation of both a professional literature and the subsequent phases of professionalization.

DEANS OF WOMEN IN STATE UNIVERSITIES

The evolution of the office of dean of women at Indiana University (IU) was illustrative of the general history of the profession in state universities. In 1867, Indiana opened its doors to women and 2 years later conferred a full bachelor's degree on Sarah Parke Morrison. Responding to criticisms and fears surrounding coeducation, President Cyrus Nutt hired Morrison as an "advisor to women" in 1873. She was regarded as a too-stern disciplinarian; she had no clear mandate, and little support for her job. She left the university in 1875. For the next quarter of a century the university failed to replace Morrison, whose duties went undone or were absorbed by women of the community, the Women's League, and the president's wife (Rothenberger, 1942).

Near the turn of the century, Indiana again typified what was in vogue. As early as 1898, following Chicago's "fashionable" (Martin, 1911b, p. 65) lead and responding to a new wave of concern regarding coeducation, housing, and student health, President Joseph Swain decided he wanted a female administrator on his staff. At the strong urging of his wife, a year later he began searching for a female medical doctor who was also a "woman of superior training and refinement," or as Thomas Clark (1970–1973), university historian, wryly noted, an "angel with an M.D. degree" (v. 1, p. 318).

Swain's desire to hire a woman physician as dean grew after consultation with a friend, President James B. Angell of the University of Michigan. Angell had finally persuaded Dr. Eliza Mosher to leave a successful practice and move to Ann Arbor as Dean of Women and Professor of Hygiene in 1896 (McGuigan, 1970). That made her Michigan's first woman professor.

In the 1870s and 1880s Michigan had a reputation as a campus more hospitable than most to women. It certainly was the largest public coeducational institution in the country and the most prestigious. It also had more than its share of remarkable women graduates, but the struggle for acceptance was as arduous there as elsewhere. Lucy Salmon, an 1874 graduate of Michigan and a future Vassar professor, tired of hearing criticism about women violating their proper sphere in the Sunday sermons at her church. Once, she felt so angry that she wrote her pastor quite a vituperative note (Clifford, 1989, p. 5). Even Alice Freeman Palmer, perhaps Michigan's most notable woman graduate, summed up her undergraduate experience by saying that "coeducation was not for the timid" (Antler, 1987, p. 96).

In 1870 Michigan became one of the first universities to open its medical school to women. Eliza Mosher's Quaker upbringing had instilled in her a sense that women were equal to men. She thought her mother believed so too and was a bit shocked when her announcement about entering medical school brought the following response: "I would sooner pay to have thee shut up in a lunatic asylum . . . than to have thee study medicine" (McGuigan, 1970, p. 63). Eventually, Mosher's mother relented and Mosher became one of Michigan's earliest woman graduates of the medical school in 1875. The taunts and teases of her male "colleagues" disturbed but strengthened her. In an alumnae survey completed sometime after the turn of the century, she stated, "opposition increased my power of resistance, deepened my determination to prove that I had both the ability and the right to become a physician and practice medicine beside the best men in the profession" (Mosher, n.d., n.p.). She was discouraged or ignored by most of her professors and even though she considered President Angell a friend, she was aware that he sometimes referred to women doctors as "hen medics."

Mosher lasted as dean of women for 6 years, but did not like her role. Her first professional loyalty was to medicine. As such, she used her position to usher in health reforms and encouraged women to get more exercise, abandon their corsets, and wear sensible shoes. Although doctors/administrators such as Mosher provided an invaluable service to women, and some were on the forefront of women's health issues, the few who served in this position were less likely to aspire to the status of professional dean or even afforded that opportunity. At Berkeley, for example, the first female administrator was a physician, but Dr. Mary Ritter's position was only half-time and her dean status was unofficial (Antler, 1987). In hindsight, it was probably fortunate for the young women at Indiana that President Swain, even after 2 years of searching, could not find his "angel with an M.D." and hired Mary Breed instead.

President Swain worked hard finding a dean. In his presidential report of November 1899, he devoted a special section to "Women in the University" (p. 33). He noted that the number of women students had almost doubled in less than 8 years, growing from 160 students in 1892 to 318 for the academic year 1898–1899, 30% of the student body. He advised the board of trustees that the chronically impecunious university needed the tuition generated by women students, but propriety demanded that attention be paid to women's needs. It was clear in Swain's mind that the position of dean of women and the solution to the housing problem were integrally related. He related:

> For some time I have wished to visit representative institutions to investigate more thoroughly the advantages of a dean of women. I feel that we can increase here the value of an education to women, and also increase our attendance of women by better facilities for them. I think we can improve these conditions in two ways: 1. By the establishment of a Dean of Women, provided that the right woman can be found. 2. By the establishment of a small dormitory for women in [the?] charge of a woman appointed by the University. The latter will of necessity need to be supplied by private capital. I have no recommendation to make at this time. If it is thought wise by the Trustees, I will investigate these matters and report at a future time. (p. 33)

While searching for "just the right woman," he wrote the presidents of the Universities of Illinois, Michigan, and Wisconsin seeking their advice on hiring a dean. On the advice of the other presidents, he and Mrs. Swain visited the campuses of Michigan, Vassar, Western Reserve, Chicago, Smith, Mount Holyoke, Barnard, Pennsylvania, and Bryn Mawr.

Swain summed up the collective wisdom of several presidents he had consulted for the trustees: "All the men agree that the Dean of Women should be a teacher of high standing in the faculty; that her powers should be advisory, not mandatory; that all methods possible should be devised that her influence should be natural, flowing out of her work; and that unless the right woman is secured, better have none" (Swain, 1900, p. 3).

During his first visit to Bryn Mawr in 1899, he briefly met Breed, who was working on her Ph.D., but he did not consider her at that time. Instead he pursued several other candidates. He consulted other university presidents and Marion Talbot for recommendations. He offered the job to four other women who, for various reasons, did not accept the post. Swain told the board, "I am convinced still more strongly that women who are fitted for our position and whom we can secure are scarce" (Swain, 1901b, pp. 16–19).

There is no record of why President Swain next chose to pursue Breed or who recommended her to him, but in June of 1901 Swain wrote to Breed inviting her to apply for the job. He said that the "duties of this position would be a matter somewhat of development. Our present idea is that she should teach perhaps seven or eight hours and give the rest of her time to helpful assistance of the college young women in educational, social and personal ways" (Swain, 1901a, June 21). Breed responded, indicating interest if the position had faculty rank[1] and Swain promised that it did (Swain, 1901a, July 1). After meeting him, Breed accepted Swain's offer to become the dean and assistant professor of chemistry teaching elementary chemistry and a 5-hour course in mathematics—all for a salary of $1,300 with the promise of $100 raise a year for the next 2 years if her work was satisfactory (Swain, 1901a, July 21). Swain reported to the board that he finally had found a dean of women and that she had a "pleasing personality, good common sense, and [an] intelligent and sympathetic interest in young women" (Swain, 1901c, p. 6).

Swain thought Breed eastern in her "sense of decorum" and yet "strict enough to enforce her code of gentle-womanly behavior" (Clark, 1970–1973, v. 1, p. 320). It was typical of Swain to want a woman who combined scholarly accomplishment with gentlewomanly grace. Thus were the two spheres deans of women were expected to straddle.

Breed accepted the post of dean of women in 1901 and stayed at Indiana only 5 years. The overwhelming task of housing left little time for meeting the other needs of women students. Following Talbot's lead, Breed was among a growing cohort who sought to expand the traditional role and advocated broadly for the women of the university. She made strides in several directions, enhancing university life for women in the process. She was dedicated to women's education, so despite the discouraging conditions, she remained committed to the importance of her work. With a handful of other deans, and at the instigation of Marion Talbot, she actively participated in the initial steps toward turning her job into an acknowledged profession by organizing the first series of Conferences for Deans of Women in Midwestern Universities.

A WOMAN OF SCIENCE, BUT WITH GOOD BREEDING

Breed was born in Pittsburgh, Pennsylvania, on September 15, 1870, the daughter of Henry Atwood and Cornelia Bidwell Breed, prominent citizens of the town. Her family tree included eight participants in the American Revolution, so not surprisingly, she was a member of the Daughters of the American Revolution (DAR). Her pedigree, which impressed President Swain, also listed notable educators including Jonathan Edwards, the theologian and philosopher who served as the third president of the College of New Jersey, later Princeton University (Breed, 1949; Fley, 1980; Leonard, 1914; Rothenberger, 1942).

Growing up, while in college, and all through her adult life, she was active in the Episcopal Church and religion seems to have played an important role in her life. Not much is known about her personal affairs, but Rothenberger (1942) recorded the impressions of Indiana faculty who remembered her. The list of adjectives is long and, for the most part, complimentary. Only 31 when she became dean, she apparently successfully struck the characteristic balance required of deans of women—a stern and serious enough countenance to please parents and presidents, yet a personality kindly and humorous enough to reach students. Breed appeared a bit severe, with pulled-back hair and pince-nez glasses, but was remembered as pleasant and positive in outlook. She was determined and poised, but with a sense of humor, and "a sympathetic interest in young women" (Rothenberger, 1942, p. 38).

Breed attended Bryn Mawr College as an undergraduate and earned an A.B. degree in Chemistry in 1894. Like the majority of women who assumed dean's positions within higher education, participation in formal organizations played an enormously important role in both her personal and her professional life. As an undergraduate, Breed was a member of the Self-governing Board of Students, and a member of Bryn Mawr Advisory Board while a graduate student. Between her studies at Bryn Mawr and her appointment as dean at Indiana, Breed also served as the president of the Pittsburgh chapter of the Association of Collegiate Alumnae

(ACA), an organization she promoted throughout her career (Rothenberger, 1942).

Breed's graduate training reflected the options available to American women in the late 19th century. Most women in science found prestigious research universities reluctant to accept them as full-time nonspecial students with access to research facilities and laboratories. Even if accepted, women were often denied degrees after completion of their studies (Rossiter, 1982). Women's colleges and women's organizations—most notably Bryn Mawr and the Association of Collegiate Alumnae—stepped in to fill the breach. M. Carey Thomas, president of Bryn Mawr, succeeded in having her college offer fellowships for European study and grant doctoral degrees at home. The ACA worked to open German graduate schools to American women and provided fellowships to make graduate study financially feasible. Although some women gained entrance and even degrees, the struggles of American women in the German universities were legion. Ida Hyde (1938), one of the first women to earn a Ph.D. in Germany, later humorously recounted her experiences in an article entitled "Before Women Were Human Beings." The ACA largely abandoned the European strategy after 1900. American graduate schools began offering more opportunities to women and the prestige of the German university waned in American academic circles. Ironically, the strategies of the ACA and Bryn Mawr proved more beneficial to German women than to Americans (Rossiter, 1982).

Breed, however, benefited. She was awarded the Bryn Mawr European Fellowship for the 1894–1895 academic year. While in Europe, she studied in the chemistry laboratory of Victor Meyer of the University of Heidelberg, apparently the first woman to have done so. Her work in Germany earned her a master's degree from Bryn Mawr in 1895.

On her return from Europe, Breed accepted a post as instructor of science at the Pennsylvania College for Women in Pittsburgh for 2 years. In 1899, she re-enrolled in Bryn Mawr and earned her Ph.D. in chemistry in 1901, one of the earliest doctoral degrees awarded by the college in chemistry (Fley, 1980). By 1901, she had published three scholarly articles in her field, including one in the *American Chemical Journal*. Her dissertation was published as the first in the series Bryn Mawr College Monographs, published between 1901 and 1926. The monographs were an important source of scholarly output for women and were notable for publishing examples of important pioneering work (Rossiter, 1982). Inclusion in the monographs was an indication of her scholarly promise.

Despite the promise of her early years, Breed's scholarly career after she entered administration was also, unfortunately, typical. Women with

doctorates in science often found it difficult to obtain full-time employment as scientists. Women employed in coeducational universities often
settled for working in some kind of "women's work" in science. Usually
this implied working in a "feminine" field such as home economics or
hygiene. Others, like Breed, accepted what historian Margaret Rossiter
(1982) called "academic-hybrid" positions such as dean of women, but
the exigencies of these positions made scholarly progress unlikely. Breed
remained on the faculty while at Indiana, but taught only during the first
3 years of her appointment. She noted in her last dean's report some
disappointment over the lack of teaching, but felt that the paucity of such
classroom opportunities was not detrimental to her dean's work. She
strongly asserted the principle of teaching deans, however, in her dean's
report of 1906: "I feel that the recognition of the Dean of Women as a
member of the Faculty is an essential condition for her highest success
among the students" (1906d). She never published again in her field of
chemistry. Instead, her subsequent publications were germane to her new
profession.

ISOLATION AND RESENTMENT IN BLOOMINGTON

At the turn of the century Indiana University, having been founded as a
seminary in 1820, was old relative to other midwestern state institutions.
It was not a land-grant college and regularly competed for funds from
the notoriously tight-fisted legislature with the state's Morrill Act institution, Purdue University. Located in Bloomington in the rural, southern
part of the state, it was 60 miles from Indianapolis and 220 miles from
Chicago. Its isolation from large cities coupled with poor train service
and abysmal roads caused constant problems. One of the most severe
problems caused by rural isolation and an unfortunate spate of droughts
was an inadequate water supply. On occasion, the university was forced
to shut down due to a lack of potable drinking water and poor sanitary
conditions. From the 1880s until well into the early 1900s, there were
outbreaks of typhoid, malarial fever, la grippe, dysentery, and smallpox.
Students were warned to boil all water, but several became ill, and a few
died. Angry students occasionally threatened collective action against
the university. To the legislature, President Swain blamed the falling enrollments of 1899 on the water problem (Clark, 1970–1973).

The academic side of the university was faring better than the physical plant, but had its share of difficulties as well. In 1885 David Starr Jordan became president with a vision of moving Indiana fully into the university movement. He succeeded in breaking some of the last vestiges

of a sectarian hold on the curriculum, hired an able faculty, and began the process of administrative change. Unfortunately for the university, parsimonious salaries and chronic underfunding by the state made the probability of holding on to talented scholars unlikely. In 1891, Governor and Mrs. Leland Stanford succeeded in luring Jordan to California and raised his $4,000 per year salary to $10,000. Impressed with the talent he saw in Bloomington, Stanford promised Jordan a bonus for every IU professor that followed him. In all, 12 of the university's 29 faculty members left. Joseph Swain was part of the exodus and became a vice-president of Stanford, but he returned as president of Indiana in 1893 to help rebuild the university, an unenviable task given the current conditions (Clark, 1970–1973).

Bloomington was not an especially cosmopolitan environment in 1900. There was some heterogeneity, including a few African American students and a small but growing number of international students from Japan, China, and Eastern Europe. In May 1899, student Edith B. Wright wrote in a letter home to a friend. She said that the campus had a small but representative selection of people from around the world, a microcosm of sorts. "Most of the students are from this State; but there are some from others, and occasionally there is one from beyond the seas. So you see, there is not a '*multum in parvo*' here, but a '*mundus in parvo*.'" Most students, however, were of "provincial Hoosier origins" (quoted in Clark, 1970–1973, v. 2, p. 41).

There was little social life for students in town and transportation to nearby cities was difficult. Student clubs were popular, but many were organized off-campus because there was no student union or building. The position of editor of the *Daily Student*, which began in 1867, was a prestigious one, and the newspaper was generally highly regarded as student publications go. The state of Indiana had a strong tradition of "newspapering" and the university opened a school of journalism in 1895. Athletics was another activity that held students loyal to their alma mater, but these activities were reserved for men (Clark, 1970–1973) so women had fewer choices. "Class" affiliation was important and for years male students made a great ado about class rituals and customs. Women, on the other hand, were undifferentiated by class and simply known as "coeds."

With few other opportunities for social interaction, the majority of students joined fraternities or sororities. While Greek-letter organizations were important to students on numerous campuses, they held a particularly elevated status at places as isolated as Bloomington. Until the presidency of Joseph Swain, the university administration paid little official attention to such activities. That changed, however, when Swain learned that three members of the Glee Club got drunk while on a university outing. Outraged, he began checking into the social habits of students (Clark, 1970–1973). His investigation led him to believe that some form of supervision was necessary.

When Breed took up residence in Bloomington in the fall of 1901, she met with resentment from both students and faculty. Swain and some faculty members thought deans of women were necessary, even desirable. Other faculty, however, resisted any form of administration that might coddle students, whom they felt were already too immature. They argued that treating students as adults was preferable to developing systems, including deans of women, designed to monitor students' every behavior. A handful of men expressed resistance to the very idea of a dean of women, but not because of her potential effect on students. Instead, they objected to having a woman with any administrative authority at any level on campus (Rothenberger, 1942). By the time of Breed's appointment only three other women had *ever* been employed by the university. Instead, the female contributors to the university were professors' wives and town women. As Thomas Clark (1970–1973) noted, "women appeared in generous numbers at all university and public affairs, but they appeared as almost faceless individuals so far as the university was officially concerned" (v. 1, p. 316).

Students also resented the new dean. Despite the fears of the anti-coeducationists, during the 1870s and 1880s men and women on campuses did not fraternize much. Lack of interaction was partially due to mutual antagonism, largely due to Victorian sensibilities and mores, but not due to explicit rules. Yet, by the turn of the century, the rigid Victorian social codes were easing slightly. Bold students experimented with new ways of conducting social relations, and there was little in the way of university policy to stop them (Rosenberg, 1988). Many students, especially the men who had just discovered that college women were worth dating, feared that a dean of women would limit their newly found freedom.

Women students saw the presence of a dean as an affront to their integrity. Gertrude Martin (1911b), who later became a dean herself, recalled her undergraduate days at the University of Michigan when they learned of Marion Talbot at nearby University of Chicago: "We resented that Chicago dean of women as an unwarrantable criticism of the conduct of college women in general. In our self-sufficiency we could conceive of only one possible function for a dean of women—disciplinary function; and we were very certain we needed no disciplining" (p. 66).

Martin was not alone in her sentiments. In her 1915 history of the profession, Lois Mathews commented that acrimony at first was common. New deans of women were "received resentfully and even antagonistically, for it was felt by many that when students came to college they were no longer boys and girls, but young men and young women, quite capable of looking after themselves" (pp. 9–10). Mathews further noted that under such conditions, the dean had "her own way to make and her position to form in the midst of difficulties of all sorts" (p. 10). Yet, in the end most deans were highly regarded by their professional peers and students alike.

Breed, like many of her contemporaries, moved from being resented to being appreciated. Her administration "disarmed the campus of its resentment toward a dean of women and undoubtedly smoothed the way for those who came later," wrote Katharine Rothenberger (1942), a historian of Indiana's deans, "her rare intelligence, good humor, and self-confidence won for her the cooperation and respect of the whole . . . campus" (pp. 49–50).

The strategy used by Breed and her colleagues elsewhere to win over opponents was rather straightforward. She expanded her role beyond discipline, involved students in creating policies and programs, and advocated for women in ways that made tangible differences in their lives. Deans used intelligence and a sympathetic predisposition toward women students as well as the necessary dose of charm and warmth to effect change. Evidence left by students including letters, diaries, published tributes, and occasionally oral recollections collected by institutional historians suggested that the deans on many campuses were remarkably successful in reversing resentment and converting it into respect that sometimes verged on reverence. Breed, for example, received a gift from students—a photograph of the statue of Hermes by the Greek sculptor Praxiteles (Words of thanks, 1905). The artifacts of former students indicate that deans often became important in their lives. Even allowing for the purplishness of late-19th-century prose, the high level of regard is telling (Antler, 1987; Eisenmann, 1991; Fitzpatrick, 1989; Haddock, 1952; Talbot, 1936; see also H. R. Stephens, personal communication, July 20, 1992).

Although no student correspondence mentioning Breed has survived, a tangible tribute to her remains. Representing a significant departure from custom, the senior class of 1905 dedicated the *Arbutus* (yearbook) to her. Prior to that time, the yearbook had been dedicated to sitting or former presidents or occasionally anonymous groups of university supporters such as the alumni or "the people of the state." Only twice before had the yearbook been dedicated to a faculty member and never had the male-run *Arbutus* paid tribute to a woman (Fley, 1980).

Such high regard should not obscure the fact that deans and female students were not always of one mind. There were components of a generation gap and elements of a disciplinarian/disciplined relationship. For example, students and deans shared many political objectives, especially in reform-oriented areas, but students increasingly agitated for more freedom in male-female socialization, causing a split between the two generations of women (Gordon, 1990). Deans often thought many students were too frivolous, overly interested in social activities and dating (Mathews, 1915). In response, students sometimes thought deans were old-fashioned. Some went so far as to think the generally unmarried deans might be sexually unfulfilled or perhaps even "deviant" (Gordon, 1990, p. 39). But overall, female students had very few adult female role models on coeducational campuses between 1900 and 1920 and even fewer advocates. When Breed resigned, the *Daily Student* said she would be leaving behind a "wide circle of friends" (Dean Breed resigns, 1906).

THE MOST URGENT NEED OF ALL

Of the many tangible contributions made by deans to the daily life of women students, none was more important than improving where and how they lived. All early deans dealt with the issue of housing; indeed it was the reason most were appointed (Holmes, 1939). Invoking Nancy Fraser's (1989) framework of "thin" and "nested" needs, housing was perhaps the "thinnest" need of all. Women attending public universities, and not living with their families, had three housing options at the turn of the century: boardinghouses, sororities, and, where available, dormitories. Deans of women were responsible for women students in all three circumstances.

In 1900, there were almost no residence halls in state universities (Cowley, 1934a, 1934b; Shay, 1966). Most American colleges began as residential, based on the collegiate model of Oxford and Cambridge. Faculty saw their role as educating all aspects of the young men in their charge—intellectual, physical, and moral. College students were boys to be molded and required constant vigilance on the part of the adult males.

After the Civil War, the view taken by faculty members gradually changed. Following the lead of Henry Tappan, president of the University of Michigan at mid-century, American educators came to believe that college students were men and the purpose of the university was exclusively teaching and research. German institutions, after all, extended no effort to regulate the out-of-classroom lives of students, and it was those

German universities that late-19th-century American university leaders were emulating. So why not leave American students to fend for themselves as well? Those students who did not live with relatives took room and board with local families. In several "gown towns" of the 1870s and 1880s, it was not uncommon to find families who had moved to the vicinity so that their children could attend college. These families made extra income by taking in boarders. Occasionally, young instructors found that renting a small number of rooms augmented their often paltry income (Mathews, 1915). These environments were thought to be wholesome and conducive to university life. Unfortunately, the number of rooms available with "proper" families never kept pace with the quickly expanding enrollments of state universities.

In the 1880s, campus fraternities (sororities came a bit later) filled some of the gap. Fraternities were started as social organizations but later more of them built houses to accommodate members (Cowley, 1934a, 1934b; Shay, 1966). Fraternity housing had a divisive effect on most public campuses and made social-class distinctions more obvious. For other students, a new kind of boardinghouse came into being. These were frequently run by widows, and their purpose was to board students rather than to provide a family-like atmosphere; profit was the sole motive.

By the mid-1890s, the predisposition against dormitories was waning. William Rainey Harper assumed the presidency of the University of Chicago with an enthusiasm for the possibilities of residential living. In this, Harper and Marion Talbot were in complete agreement. She wrote, "It was agreed that it was a fitting undertaking to supplement the intellectual and educational advantages of the institution with a corresponding care for the physical requirements of students" (quoted in Haddock, 1952, p. 37). Chicago had four halls in 1893 and seven by 1900. Other private universities eventually followed Harper's lead. Woodrow Wilson introduced a preceptorial plan at Princeton in 1905 and President Lowell of Harvard ushered in the house plan in 1909 (Cowley, 1934b).

The situation at public universities was more complicated, even with presidents persuaded to Harper's point of view. Efforts by presidents and deans were often thwarted by the constant shortage of money. Students longed for dormitories, hoping that on-campus living would increase their opportunities for socializing and participating in "college life" (Cowley, 1934b). Dorms were also needed simply because the fraternities and boardinghouses could not keep up with the growing numbers of students. The 16 largest state universities grew by 150% between 1895 and 1910. By way of contrast, growth at comparable private institutions was only 75% (Claxton, 1912, p. 59). Therein lay the tension—large numbers of students were necessary for the tuition they generated, but they never created enough revenue to pay for the buildings needed to house them.

What finally convinced most state universities to start acting on the housing issue, however, was the constant urging of the deans of women that housing women must be addressed (Cowley, 1934b). Young men were thought able to look after themselves with few social ramifications. Unsupervised young women were far more vulnerable to harm, either physical or reputational. If parents discovered their daughters in unsupervised situations, deans argued, they threatened to withdraw them (and their tuition money) from college (Gordon, 1990; Horowitz, 1987).

Beyond the propriety concerns, deans argued for university-owned housing on the basis of its educational value as well as its potential social benefit. Marion Talbot was an outspoken proponent of residence halls for women. She wanted to touch the inner lives of students, help them learn cooperation and group living, foster personal growth, teach them social graces, and instill the skills needed in future professional lives. "It is from the natural relationships and problems of simple every-day life that may be secured the fine democracy and social power demanded of the educated woman of today" (p. 46) she wrote in 1909. Lois Mathews (1915) argued that university-run dorms helped set a cost-of-living standard in the community and prevented price-gouging by landlords. More important, however, dorms afforded deans a mechanism for reaching large groups of women students and thus a means of social control based on persuasion and self-government.

Philosophically President Swain supported the idea of residential living. As early as 1896, he and Mrs. Swain told the board that dorms were needed. They set about raising private capital because the university did not have the necessary resources. Mrs. Swain harnessed the energies of the Women's League, which took up raising money for a women's building as its first major project on behalf of the university, but Indiana's struggle with student housing continued.

When Breed arrived on campus, one of her first acts was to poll several other universities about the housing situation on each campus (Breed, 1901). In almost every dean's report she brought up the subject. A change in presidents in 1902 did not alter the situation for her because President William Lowe Bryan (1903a) was as concerned as his predecessor. He wrote in his first president's report:

> I believe the university must assume a somewhat closer guardianship over the women students, at least over those whose parents desire this. I believe, therefore, with the Dean of Women that we should endeavor to ar-

range as soon as possible for the establishment of dormitories for women which should be subject to University supervision. (n.p)

Despite the desires of both Breed and Bryan, a dormitory for women was not built for several years. The women's building project begun by Mrs. Swain was under way, but with considerable alterations to her original plan. Needing money, the university secured a $50,000 matching grant from John D. Rockefeller but on the condition that what was built was a student center (rather than a dorm) open to both genders. After years of delays and problems, the student building finally opened in 1906, but it did not house students, and the rooms women used were relegated to one wing (Clark, 1970–1973; Rothenberger, 1942).

In the absence of dormitories, Breed's most pressing problem became improving the boardinghouses. Her first task was overcoming long-held prejudices against boarding women students. A description of landlady ignorance and intolerance from Olive San Louie Anderson's 1878 novel about college life at the University of Michigan was very revealing. The protagonist, Wilhelmine, met with several rejections before she found a home. Making the rounds of Ann Arbor, the daughter of one potential landlady rejected her by saying, "Mamma don't want girls" (p. 36). Another landlady was equally off-putting: "I could not think of taking a lady student, it's so odd, you know; we can't tell what they might be like" (pp. 36–37). It was not until landladies discovered that women boarders were quieter, neater, and rarely drunk that their disposition improved. To help ease the shortage of rooms in the years before Breed arrived, the local YWCA and Women's League worked to change landladies' minds and set up referral services for new students. However, there was no oversight in terms of quality, and, in Breed's opinion, many of the boardinghouses in town were unacceptable.

To ascertain the exact nature of conditions, Breed frequently visited every boardinghouse in Bloomington, trudging up and down the unpaved, muddy streets. From Breed's perspective, having men and women reside under the same roof was the most objectionable aspect of a boardinghouse. She worked toward the goal, supported by the president, of requiring all students to live in single-sex housing (Swain, 1902). At first she tried to educate the landladies to the wisdom of her plan. Next, just as Talbot was doing in Chicago, Breed secured the cooperation of the YWCA and other Christian organizations, which, after 1904, refused to list mixed-gender houses on their "approved list." She made some headway, cutting the number of mixed-gender houses in half by 1905 (Breed, 1905b).

She disapproved of houses with no parlors for entertaining gentlemen callers, poorly prepared food, and the absence of proper manners at mealtime. Young women paid as much as $3 per week (equivalent to almost $550 per month in 1999 dollars) for a thin-walled room with little privacy and much noise. In a 1909 article, Breed illustrated the compounding role of boardinghouse owners in preventing universities from building dormitories. As a constituency of taxpayers, landladies successfully convinced state legislatures that apportions for residence halls were equivalent to robbing them of their livelihood.

The third facet of Breed's responsibilities in the area of housing was the supervision of sorority houses. Breed generally thought that they had a positive influence on the campus because, being organized, they were easier to control. Also, she felt the sorority women often came from cultured homes and exerted a positive influence on the campus. She was aware of the social divisions they sometimes caused, but did not feel as strongly about this as Marion Talbot, who forbade them at Chicago. To handle the sororities, Breed first engaged the assistance of local women, including many faculty wives. She encouraged them to become house heads for sororities, to offer supervision as well as advice and counsel. Her next step was to meet regularly with sorority women and gain their confidence and support and work collectively to change regulations (Breed, 1903a, 1905b; Bryan, 1903b; Those regulations, 1903). Students did turn to her. When a group of fraternities (The Big Five) threatened to boycott any sorority whose members dated men from their opposing faction, a group of sororities (The Little Three) went to Breed. She met with them in long sessions, proposed a strategy, and swore them to secrecy. There is no record of what Breed told the women, but her proposed solution worked and the campus crisis, which was deemed serious enough at the time to be discussed in the Indianapolis papers, was averted. The fraternities resumed normal relations with the sororities (*Daily Student*, 1903a).

Sorority members agreed to end social activities at reasonable hours, to have chaperones at gatherings with men, and to have all activities approved by the dean beforehand. In all houses, senior women were part of the governing committee, along with house matrons and the dean. In her 1905 "Dean's Report," Breed (1905b) commented on the willingness of students to be regulated:

Whereas the students formerly tried to justify their exceptional late hours, they now excuse and apologize for them; and the number of requests for special indulgences itself indicates a recognition of the new order. The four sororities have given further evidence of this spirit by incorporating in a formal agreement concerning the "rushing" of new members next Fall Term, a provision that all "rushing" parties end at half past ten. I regard this agreement as a great step in advance especially as it was done without any direct suggestion from me on the subject. (n.p.)

Overall, early deans of women were successful in bringing about changes in living conditions for many students. The ground swell of pressures for dormitories caused most public universities to build at least one dorm for women before World War I, although it was never enough to house all the women who needed it. Housing for men soon followed (Claxton, 1912; Cowley, 1934b). The style of administration with respect to housing illustrates a key distinction between professional deans and pious matrons. The modern dean was not a house mother. Instead, she was a manager, responsible for a whole system of residence life that involved the coordination of various members of the community and the supervision of a professional staff reporting to her (Holmes, 1939; Mathews, 1915).

Beyond Housing

Although Breed's work was dominated by the issue of housing, there were other student needs that demanded attention. During one outbreak of smallpox in 1902, angry students argued that the administration had an obligation "to see that students did not injure their health by overexertion or foolish habits" (Clark, 1970–1973, v. 1, p. 313). Breed appealed to the fraternities and sororities, which agreed to end social functions at 10:30 P.M. on weeknights and midnight on weekends. Even the faculty agreed to halt their social functions at 11:00 P.M. After several robberies, assaults on women, and a much-publicized incident of the whipping of a prostitute, Breed also enforced a rule that did not allow women to drive or walk for pleasure alone after dark (Breed, 1903a; Clark, 1970–1973).

Breed was also responsible for curbing what was described as "excess in social conditions," meaning simply that students spent more time on social activities than academics. She was concerned by a general decline in social standards throughout society. On the campus, she wanted to rely on the influence of cultured people as models for young women and the civilizing effect of liberal studies. She did not believe in elaborate "machinery" to regulate people (Breed, 1908a). She wanted to use self-government, much like the system used at Bryn Mawr when she was a student (Breed, 1901). She asked students for their cooperation with her policies and responded in kind by fighting for little amenities and larger benefits. For example, once a student building was finally completed in the last months of her deanship, she argued for cooking facilities for the women's wing and coffee service in the women's parlor (Breed, 1906c).

The Association of Collegiate Alumnae

The larger benefits came in the form of social opportunities and permanent recognition for Indiana women by the ACA. Breed knew that students required more from college than a place to live, however important that might be, and Bloomington had little to offer. Breed found time to offer embellishments in the form of social gatherings and intellectual stimulation. As the university's historian put it, Dean Breed was "taxed to the limit of imagination and energy to break the drab monotony of college girls' lives" (Clark, 1970–1973, v. 2, p. 26).

She occasionally offered lecture series on various subjects. She spoke on etiquette and the challenges of entering a professional field not already identified as acceptable for women (science, for example). She gave several talks about her trip through France the previous summer of 1904 (*Daily Student*, 1903b, 1904, 1906). Such travelogue lectures were an extremely popular form of entertainment at the turn of the century.

She hosted meetings for the Women's League, gave candy and chafing-dish parties, provided opportunities for students and faculty to mix, and attended numerous receptions. On one occasion, she directed a play. She also attended the annual Panthygatric—a banquet sponsored by women students that offered cold beans, ham, and pumpkin pie—despite the obvious gastronomical risks. The number of opportunities for socializing that Breed offered was small, but her efforts represented some of the only such events on campus. Breed, however, set her sights on providing Indiana's students and alumnae with a more tangible benefit—membership in the ACA.

The ACA provided opportunities for leadership and support. Official recognition, an early form of accreditation, brought material benefits. For example, women from recognized institutions were eligible for certain scholarships and more competitive in graduate school admission. Breed, a former president of the Pittsburgh Chapter, was convinced of the long-term benefits to women students and set out to make Indiana a member institution. It was often Breed's lot to fall prey to the slowly grinding wheels of change. In terms of housing, she clearly set things in motion, but failed to see her vision come to fruition during her tenure. This was also true of her efforts to secure membership in the ACA for IU's women.

In 1892, Indiana was denied admission to the ACA because the association believed the standard of Indiana's high schools, and therefore the
corresponding admissions standards of the university, were poor (Platter, 1892). Breed took up the cause early in her career, urging Indiana to
push for membership. In 1903, she wrote an article for the student newspaper outlining the work of the ACA and stated her appeal:

> For a college not to have its alumnae eligible to the A.C.A. is regarded in
> many educational circles as a mark of inferiority. For example, one of the
> great eastern colleges refuses to accept credits from any institution not
> recognized by the A.C.A., and has refused Indiana credits within the past
> year. This ought not so to be. It is extremely desirable that enough inter-
> est be taken in the University to push the campaign for its admission to
> the A.C.A. (1903b, p. 1)

She continued her work with the ACA, attempting to have the university meet every requirement for admission, and reported her progress
to the president in her dean's reports (Breed, 1903a, 1904b, 1906a). She
hosted meetings and receptions and corresponded with the leaders of
the ACA and attended their national conventions. Just weeks before she
left Indiana, she sent a long letter to alumnae about the ACA, appealing to
their loyalty for Alma Mater. Several alumnae promised to join if the ACA
recognized Indiana, but that was slow in coming (Breed, 1906b). Near the
end of her career at Indiana, she told President Bryan, "I have done all
that an untrained politician could do in a very difficult situation, and I
still have hopes that Indiana will be admitted next year" (Breed, 1906a).
It took a while, but eventually what she had hoped for came to pass and
Indiana became a member of ACA in 1912.

CONFERENCE OF DEANS AND ADVISORS OF WOMEN
IN STATE UNIVERSITIES

An important first step toward professionalization for deans of women
was gathering with colleagues from other universities. In 1902 Marion
Talbot thought such meeting would prove useful (Potter, 1927). Gathering together women with like-minded interests was a strategy familiar to
her; that was how she founded the ACA. So Talbot asked her friend Martha
Foote Crow—a former assistant to Alice Freeman Palmer at Wellesley, a
former English professor at the University of Chicago, and, by 1902, dean
of women at Northwestern University—to meet with her. The dean of
women from nearby University of Michigan, Myra Jordan, was also invited, as was Dean Evans from Carleton College, and possibly a fifth per-

son. Breed was not present at this little conclave, but those who met decided to invite several other women from nearby colleges and universities for a two-day conference on November 3 and 4, 1903, to be co-hosted by the University of Chicago and Northwestern University. Breed eagerly accepted the invitation.

Eighteen women arrived in Chicago in the autumn of 1903 as the guests of both Talbot and Crow. All the deans represented institutions in the Midwest (except the dean at Barnard College), so it was not surprising that the meeting's official title was the Conference of Deans of Women of the Middle West. Ten of the women were from private institutions while eight represented state universities. Twelve of the women held faculty appointments in addition to their work as dean. Dean Evans of Carleton was selected as the president of the meeting and Breed was chosen as secretary (Conference of Deans of Women of the Middle West [hereafter, CDWMW], 1903; Potter, 1927).

The first action taken by the group was to exclude newspaper reporters and guests, although the reasons they thought this necessary were not recorded in the minutes. They next appointed a committee to pursue the idea of forming a permanent organization. They also formed a committee for the purpose of data-gathering about all the roles and responsibilities of deans in an attempt to have "scientific" data at their disposal.

Not surprisingly, the first substantive topic addressed was the issue of dormitories and women's housing. Only the handful of deans from liberal arts colleges worked on campuses where dorms existed. Nevertheless, all discussed the benefits of dormitory living. Breed added that dormitories provided more healthful food, which was needed by women doing brain work. They went on to talk about the problems of boarding-houses, the helpfulness of the Women's League, the concern of breaking down the distinctions between sorority and nonsorority women, and the benefits of sororities to freshmen. Time and again, the subject of housing arose.

"Ways of Influencing Young Women" was the next subject on the agenda. They discussed the effectiveness of official occasions, social occasions, and "at-homes" with the dean. Breed reported that it had become too difficult to talk with all students where they lived so she now entertained them at her home. Talbot recommended that clear distinctions be drawn between social and official business, which should only be conducted at the dean's office. They noted that YWCAs were quite useful.

They debated self-government versus direct government. One woman spoke in favor of the dean's having a great deal of "machinery," meaning rules and policies, but the majority opinion was "less is better." Self-government contributed to the positive development of college women and "tended to a more self-respecting feeling on both sides" (CDWMW, 1903, p. 9).

They spoke of parties, dances, and social life in general and decided all functions should end at midnight on the weekend. They worried that some students spread themselves too thinly and concentrated on social life to excess. They expressed fears of women riding alone at night. They agreed, however, that the overall health of women students was good. They condemned intercollegiate athletics for women, and they debated whether to exclude men from the women's gymnasium because of the "tendency of women in coeducational colleges to recite and behave in general with constant consciousness of the presence of men" (CDWMW, 1903, p. 18).

The deans voted to meet 2 years hence and passed a series of resolutions summing up the collective opinion of the group on housing, self-government, social life, and intercollegiate athletics. Some time in the intervening 2 years, a decision was made to limit the membership of the group to deans of women in state universities with the exception of Talbot. No record exists of who made the decision or why, but when the deans met in Chicago in December 1905, the gathering was convened as the first meeting of "The Conference of Deans and Advisors of Women in State Universities." With the exception of Lucy Sprague from the University of California, all participants were from midwestern institutions. Breed was chair of the conference.

The topics of consideration at the 1905 conference were similar to those of the first meeting (Conference of Deans and Advisors of Women in State Universities [hereafter CDAWSU], 1905; Potter, 1927). Housing, athletics, and social life were all discussed. The deans resolved that private boardinghouses should be supervised and that dormitories were necessary, and reiterated that social functions should end at midnight.

At Breed's urging, there was a joint session with delegates from the national Panhellenic Conference. The group resolved that large numbers of sorority chapters on campus dissipated social inequities, that excessive "rushing" was harmful, and that extravagant expenditures were condemned. Breed spoke frequently on the need to involve sorority women in setting the standard for behavior on campus. She said, "We must make them do the right thing. . . . I have thrown responsibility upon them constantly and have always endeavored to make them do their own disciplining, and make their own regulations so far as possible, and work out their own salvation, and in that way have an influence over the rest of the students that I think on the whole is a good influence. . . . I think sorority women should stand for the highest scholarship" (CDAWSU, 1905, p. 18).

A critical development, however, was that the deans were able to go beyond deliberations of the thin needs of students. They expressed their concern for the need to create a "community" for women on campus. The first resolution passed at this meeting stated that some "unification of women" was "absolutely necessary" (Potter, 1927, p. 217). The deans also discussed levels of scholarship and the place of domestic science in the curriculum, and held almost unanimous agreement that the classroom should not be segregated by gender. This resolution followed closely on the heels of Marion Talbot's struggle with President Harper at Chicago.

The minutes also revealed that deans were against "spooning" and worried about a lax moral code in society with respect to sexuality. Night driving and unsupervised outings were problems. The deans also chatted about campus regulations regarding married students. At some institutions, if the marriage was public, the woman was "dropped"; if it was a secret and then discovered, the woman was expelled. Apparently the deans did not disagree with these policies; at least they made no resolutions to amend them. Interestingly they were silent on the fate of the young student husbands once a marriage was revealed.

The meetings served three important purposes. Many a dean felt that she was inventing her job as she went along and perhaps floundering in the process. The first purpose of the meeting was to provide information and support. As one dean said in 1926 when recalling the early years, "It was a more effective and less burdensome and happier means of exchanging ideas" (Potter, 1927). In providing and sharing information, a second purpose was fulfilled. The deans were able to establish standards of practice that defined the nature and scope of the job. It was clear that Breed's work was influenced by the discussions and resolutions of the two meetings she attended while at Indiana. In her 1903 dean's report (1903a), she reprinted the resolutions adopted at the meeting for President Bryan. In her January 1906 dean's report (1906d) she stated, "I feel that I have gotten many useful ideas" (n.p.). It was also clear in many of the policies she put into effect that her approach to her responsibilities was consistent with the views and ideas expressed at the two conferences.

The third purpose of the meeting was to establish a collective identity and form a professional organization. The efforts of deans of women to organize, develop administrative structures, and attempt to standardize practice placed them firmly within a larger movement within higher education during this era. Attempts at routinizing practices within institutions began as early as the 1890s. Harvard introduced assembly-line registration in 1891. At several universities, courses were rationalized

and described in numbers of "credits" and the catalog began to resemble "the inventory of a well-stocked and neatly labeled general
store" (Veysey, 1965, p. 312).

One interpretation of the bureaucratic impulse was that of pragmatic necessity—it was simply a rational response to growth and com-
plexity aimed at rendering the institution more manageable (Rudolph,
1962). Also, a Weberian-constructed bureaucracy held the promise of
meritocracy—an appealing concept to Americans. Yet the zeal with
which bureaucratization was embraced suggested another, deeper,
explanation.

By 1900, the American university had become something that contemporaries of the era could not easily define. Compared with its predecessor, it seemed too diverse and heterogeneous to manage—rootless
and without focus. Even in the popular imagination, it seemed unwieldy.
For example, the University of Chicago and its myriad activities earned
the nickname "Harper's Bazaar" (Veysey, 1965, p. 311).

Without a core of shared values among all the participants in higher
education, bureaucratic administration was the structural device chosen to facilitate institution-building. As historian Laurence Veysey (1965)
explained, "Thus while unity of purpose disintegrated, a uniformity of
standardized practice was coming into being" (p. 311). Heterogeneity
forced individuals to adopt a coping mechanism appropriate to the circumstances. When presidents or deans wanted the community to operate in a specific fashion, they created rules, guidelines, and procedures—more predictable than moral persuasion and more palatable
than coercion. In these times, the collegial ethos of the university came
to fruition.

ON TO MISSOURI

Mary Bidwell Breed spent 5 years at Indiana, where she was ultimately
highly regarded by both president and students. President Bryan (1904)
described her as a woman of "rock bottom integrity" and reported to the
board in 1904 that her work had become increasingly useful (p. 33). Despite her successes, Breed was constantly frustrated by the university's
failure to construct a residence hall for women or to implement her other
suggestions. The lack of physical resources at her disposal prompted
her to tell Bryan that she felt "handicapped by conditions" (Clark, 1970–
1973, v. 2, p. 26).

In early 1906, President Jesse of the University of Missouri came to
see President Bryan about hiring Breed. Bryan reportedly told Jesse, "You

can't have Miss Breed. It is harder to find a Dean of Women than to get a university president" (p. 48). To this Jesse replied in a southern drawl, "Doctah Bryan, Ah could get a cah load of University presidents befoah Ah could find one Dean of Women!" (Rothenberger, 1942, p. 48). Whether such statements were truth or hyperbole, it was a compliment to Breed, who had been unanimously approved for the job by the board of the University of Missouri (Dean Breed resigns, 1906). As an extra inducement, the University of Missouri even placed a horse and carriage at the disposal of the dean.

In her resignation letter, Breed indicated that she would receive both a higher salary and the opportunity to head Read Hall, a residence hall for women. She also referred to her work as her profession:

> I wish to present my resignation of the position of Dean of Women in Indiana University, to take effect at the end of the current academic year. I have been elected to the corresponding position at the University of Missouri, and after long and careful consideration I have decided to accept their offer. The reasons for my decision it is unnecessary to give in detail, but I may say that the University of Missouri offers me in salary, living, &c., the equivalent of about $2200; and, what is more important, it owns a model hall of residence for women students, of which I shall be head. The hall is conducted by the University in an enlightened way, and is an invaluable tool in my profession. (Breed, 1906c)

Before she left, Breed gave one last list of needs to Bryan on behalf of IU's women. She said that the campus needed, in addition to the long-sought-after dormitory, a female physician, more organizations for women, and more university-controlled entertainments.

Breed became the Advisor to Women and Head of Read Hall at Missouri in 1906 and stayed in that position until 1912. She continued her struggle against problem boardinghouses and used Read Hall as a "laboratory and gathering center for all women students" (Fley, 1980, p. 34). She was able to work on issues beyond housing and initiated such projects as a loan fund and a self-perpetuating senior honor society. There is no indication that she ever taught chemistry again or held a faculty appointment at Missouri. Instead, she concentrated her efforts on becoming an expert in her new profession. She spoke at ACA conferences and published three articles on aspects of student life and women's education, including the educational value of residence halls and the problem of gender polarization in the liberal arts curriculum (Breed, 1907, 1908a, 1909).

Ada Louise Comstock, circa 1910. Assistant Professor of Rhetoric, Dean of Women, 1906–1912, University of Minnesota. (Courtesy University of Minnesota Archives)

Chapter 5

OPENING MINDS
AND OPENING DOORS

Ada Comstock assumed her responsibilities as dean of women under conditions that Mary Bidwell Breed would have found enviable. At the University of Minnesota in 1907, the women students did not resent the presence of a dean; in fact they had agitated for her appointment. In addition, the housing situation at Minnesota was moderately better than that at Indiana. Although there was not a dormitory for women in the college of arts and sciences until 1909, there was a small amount of housing already available for women in the school of agriculture, and the city of Minneapolis offered more opportunities for boarding than did the small town of Bloomington. Comstock had another advantage. When she undertook management of the boardinghouses, she could rely on the experience of the deans who had come before her. Comstock attended her first Conference of Deans and Advisors of Women in State Universities (CDAWSU) in the fall of 1907, and there she found established guidelines regarding the regulation of off-campus housing.

Like Breed, Comstock addressed problems of student discipline and worked to secure a dormitory for women, but overall, the conditions at Minnesota allowed her to concentrate on higher-order nested needs. Perhaps what Breed would have envied most was that Ada Comstock had a women's building on her campus. Alice Shevlin Hall opened in 1906 and became central to Comstock's work.

Historian Carolyn Bashaw (1992) commented that deans who responded to the higher, more complex needs of students "believed that if women students were to enjoy the full range of college life, they must claim not only the classroom but also the campus—its social, extracurricular, and athletic spaces—as their proper domain" (p. 7). Comstock therefore focused her considerable energies on providing possibilities. As with other deans working in the penultimate phase of professionalization, creating opportunity and community became the heart and soul of the job. How to initiate and manage the programs and policies that brought their vision to fruition was the subject of much of the professional literature.

Comstock's career exemplified another important trend in the young profession. She thought it was important for a dean to bring to her position an expertise in women's education, an expertise that informed her views on all aspects of her job. As Lois Mathews (1915) noted in *The Dean of Women*:

> The inception of the office of dean of women in state universities may be assumed to have lain in a practical need and vague fumbling about how to meet it. Out of that earlier situation emerged a large necessity with more precise definitions, and the position of dean of women should have grown and developed in corresponding degree. This large necessity is concerned first and foremost with the intellectual life of the women students. . . . Just here is to the writers mind where the position of dean of women has greatest possibilities—in making her . . . an expert on women's education in a coeducational institution. (pp. 13–16)

This represented a significant departure from pre-20th-century beliefs that all a dean of women needed was a "sympathetic understanding" of the problems of young women. During the fourth phase of the professionalization process (generally from 1906 to 1911) Comstock and her contemporaries addressed significant questions regarding the nature and purpose of higher education for women in coeducational settings.

GROWING UP IN MINNESOTA

Like many "first-generation" college women, Ada Comstock had an educated and supportive father. Solomon Gilman Comstock (who preferred to be called S. G.) moved from Maine to the prairies of Minnesota in the early 1870s along with the railroads. He was a lawyer and an early settler of Moorhead, Minnesota, a small dot on the map in the Red River Valley of the North. Living conditions were at first primitive, but the White settlers went about building a town among the Chippewa and Sioux tribes already residing there. In 1874, S. G. Comstock married Sarah Ball and in December 1876, they had Ada Louise, named after S. G.'s mother and sister. Comstock grew up being told that she was the first White baby born in the region (Blanshard, 1974; Downs, 1934; Smith, 1977; Solomon, 1980, 1985, 1987, 1993).

The Comstocks were prominent and prosperous members of their community with an estimated worth of $200,000 by 1888. S. G. was a lawyer, a businessman, and on occasion, a politician. He served one term in the U.S. Congress, from 1889 to 1891, but subsequent political campaigns resulted in defeat. Sarah Comstock was a "joiner," as were many American women in Victorian America. She was briefly the leader of the Ladies General Benevolent Society, and a charter member of the Reading Room and the Clay County Auxiliary of the Women's Colombian Exposition. She was a leading figure in Moorhead's efforts to secure a Carnegie grant to fund a public library. She was also a founding member and president of the Moorhead Women's Club and a member of the Moorhead Literary Society, which put on dramatic plays, an interest she passed along to her daughter. She was committed to providing local housewives with mental stimulation as a "change from the routine of household duties" (Solomon, 1993, pp. 12–14).

S. G.'s activities benefited education in Minnesota and, at times, had an influence on Ada's educational career. S. G. persuaded the legislature to place the state's fourth normal school in Moorhead and served briefly as its director. He also devoted energy to assisting the state university, and from 1905 to 1908 (during which time Ada was appointed dean of women), he served on the board of regents of the University of Minnesota (Solomon, 1993).

Ada Comstock was a tomboyish, athletic young girl with a confidence inspired especially by a loving father. As she commented much later in her life, "My father thought I was perfect from the day I was born. My mother had no such illusions" (Blanshard, 1974, pp. 4–5). She often had a distant and turbulent relationship with her mother, but as an adult she exhibited many of her mother's qualities, particularly her commitment to community and duty, skills in organization, and practical turn of mind. Historian Barbara Miller Solomon (1987), her principal biographer, described Ada as "a thoughtful pragmatist" ("Postscript" to the "Introduction," n.p.). When indoors, young Ada was a voracious reader and her devotion to books and learning was fostered by both parents, who worked to create avenues of formal education in the town and make their home "a center for informal education" (Solomon, 1993, p. 19).

Ada was a precocious pupil and quickly outgrew the small private elementary school of the town. She then attended the local high school, from which she graduated at the age of 15. She was encouraged by her father to attend college, but he felt she was too young to travel back East to a women's college, so she enrolled in the University of Minnesota (some 450 miles away) in 1892. Moving between the coeducational world of the state university and the single-sex environment of women's colleges characterized both her undergraduate years and her professional career.

Comstock's early intellectual and professional life was intimately associated with the University of Minnesota. Founded in 1851, the young college barely managed to stay open during its first decade. University

historian James Gray (1951) described the sparse campus as a "grandi-
ose fragment" (vol. 1, p. 22). During the 1860s, 1870s, and 1880s, Minnesota, like most other state institutions, suffered from a lack of funds and
a lack of students. Only 74 students graduated before 1880. To compen-
sate, the university opened a preparatory department with enrollments
that far exceeded the number of students in the college of liberal arts
until well into the 1880s. By the time that Ada enrolled in 1892, however,
the preparatory program had closed, and the institution had moved toward achieving university status by offering graduate work (Johnson,
1910). The University of Minnesota was coeducational from the beginning, although no women actually graduated from the university, even
from the preparatory department, before 1875. There were occasional
protests over the official policy, but overall, there was relatively little
public acrimony regarding women students attending classes (Gray,
1951). By 1890, 160 of the 781 students on campus were women. Rather
than being the objects of explicit protests or objections, women on campus were simply ignored and relegated to the periphery of the community in all matters of importance.

Governor John Pillsbury, whose philanthropy had kept the institution afloat, persuaded Cyrus Northrup to leave his home in New Haven,
Connecticut, and accept the post as the second president of the university in 1884. Northrup held both undergraduate and law degrees from
Yale, where he also taught rhetoric and English literature. Northrup was
an amiable man with an avuncular style who ran the university in a rather
informal fashion, but he was credited with overseeing tremendous growth
and advancement during his tenure (Johnson, 1910).

Northrup was liked by students and showed an interest in their welfare. As was common in those days, Northrup was affectionately referred
to as "Prexy" in student publications. He was also an outspoken supporter
of coeducation in public institutions. In one interview Northrup said:

> For a state university, coeducation is in every way desirable. The state
> should furnish higher education for its women as well as for its men. In
> the private college I believe it is better that there should be either men
> alone or women alone. I do not see that the girl is coarsened by her uni-
> versity life, and I am sure it is beneficial for the men. Men become more
> gentlemanly. The women do not become less womanly.
>
> It is natural and right that the sons and the daughters of the state who
> have grown up together—gone to high school together and been associ-
> ated together in their homes, should continue to live their lives in com-
> mon in the university. (Is co-education a success?, 1906, p. 14)

Perhaps Northrup's sympathetic and supportive position toward
women students stemmed from the very close relationship he had with

his own daughter, Elizabeth. Both his wife and his son suffered from serious physical problems that prevented Northrup from sharing with them the type of relationship he enjoyed with his daughter. His friendship with Elizabeth was vigorous and eventually quite intellectual as well (Gray, 1951). On several occasions he took a young woman under his wing at the request of a worried parent. One story that circulated on campus told how he once came upon a crying student who was both discouraged and hungry. He took the young woman home, provided her with a meal, and then made sure she found permanent employment (Johnson, 1910).

From the beginning, Northrup took an interest in young Ada and her career. During registration for her freshman year she was introduced to him. Later, when her plan of study was questioned, she did not hesitate to call on the president. She wrote to her father saying, "The Registrar objected to my taking both French and German but I went to President Northrup and had it fixed" (Solomon, 1993, p. 21). S. G.'s social prominence and connections provided Ada with many opportunities, and she lived in privileged circumstances while an undergraduate. Ada stayed in the home of William Pattee, dean of the Law School and friend of her father, with two other women boarders. On occasion, Northrup called on Ada, inviting her to tea. Ada also became a friend of Elizabeth Northrup.

The Minneapolis campus was bleak, with only a few buildings and no library. Women were scarce and scattered about the campus. There were no community-building programs or central meeting place. Many women felt at sea, unconnected to the campus or each other. Yet Ada felt quite conspicuous on campus because of the long dresses women wore, "dragging on the ground; high collars, long hair, hats perched atop and skewered with long hatpins and the sandburrs which gathered in the hems of their long dresses" (Solomon, 1993, p. 22). This combination of being both invisible and extravisible (Clifford, 1989) left her with a very uncomfortable feeling.

Ada was not dissatisfied with her education at the University of Minnesota, where she had good professors, many social opportunities among a close circle of women friends, and family connections. Yet her father wanted her to reap the benefits of an eastern education. After 2 years, he decided to send Ada to Smith College to finish her undergraduate degree. She studied at Smith for 3 years, living in the "cottage system" on the Northampton campus. The cottages were small houses built to hold a few women each. They provided a homelike atmosphere and the opportunity for students to develop close friendships. For Ada, "the great richness of female companionship" was the highlight of her years at Smith (Solomon, 1993, p. 26). Free from the pressures of dating, she believed that the single-sex environment allowed women to explore their capabilities more fully (Smith, 1977, p. 210).

After graduating with Phi Beta Kappa honors from Smith in 1897, Ada wanted to reconnect with her family and prepare to earn her own living. Although her father was well off financially, he encouraged all three of his children to make their own way. She enrolled in the Moorhead Normal School for the second year of a 2-year program. After her year at Moorhead, Ada was encouraged to continue her studies in education at Columbia, where she studied under the young Nicholas Murray Butler. Columbia did not technically admit women so Ada was enrolled in Barnard College, but Butler was supportive of providing graduate work for women. In New York, she continued her studies in modern languages, rhetoric, and the philosophy of education, working with professors from the growing Teachers College. She graduated with an M.A. in 1899. When she returned home, she found that her father's connections had once again provided an opportunity for her. She was offered a "modest post" as an assistant in the Department of English and Rhetoric at the University of Minnesota (Solomon, 1993).

THE HALCYON YEARS

In November 1940, while giving a speech at the dedication of the University of Minnesota's new women's dormitory named in her honor, Comstock (1940) reflected on her career at the university from 1899 to 1912: "Those years . . . seem to me now, as I look back on them, to have been the halcyon years. (We did not think so at the time)" (p. 191). While dean, she confronted many personal and professional challenges, but from her vantage point as the long-term president of Radcliffe College in 1940, the years at Minnesota were calm by comparison. The world before 1912 seemed peaceful compared with the social upheaval that followed—World War I, Prohibition, and the Great Depression. Professionally, the battles she fought in Minnesota paled against the fight she waged with presidents over the acceptance of Radcliffe women as full members of the Harvard community. But it was during her years at Minnesota that she became a skilled university administrator, dedicated to improving educational opportunities for women.

When Ada Comstock started teaching at the university in 1899, she noticed there were more women students than when she was an undergraduate. The campus finally had a new library building, but no progress, in terms of material facilities for women, had been made. She was teaching in a department headed by Maria Sanford, with whom she sometimes had a difficult relationship. Sanford was a controversial figure whose feminist ideas and eccentric methods, both personal and professional, placed her at odds with the administration (Gray, 1951). Rhetoric was a required course for freshman so Comstock had a full teaching schedule and taught students of widely varying backgrounds. Comstock was adept at public speaking, with experience in theatricals, and enjoyed a reputation as a good, albeit demanding teacher. On one occasion, a student publication humorously pointed out that the library was a source of "inestimable value should any of you ever take Rhetoric from Miss Comstock" (Solomon, 1993, p. 36).

She had a reputation of being formidable, occasionally intimidating, to a few, but she was also known as someone who listened to students and understood their needs. During one year when the English department did not offer a course in modern drama, she met with a group of students privately to read and enjoy contemporary plays. As an assistant in the department, Ada earned only $225 dollars a year, which left her financially dependent on her father. This rather paltry salary was granted by the university regents, who were well aware that S. G. Comstock had the resources to look after his daughter (Solomon, 1993).

She was promoted to instructor in her second year and this brought with it a small raise in salary, to $400. Apparently she contemplated leaving the university, but decided to stay after receiving a "kind and encouraging" note from President Northrup (Northrup, 1901). Her relationship with Northrup was quite affectionate. She had easy access to him and he was supportive of her positions on women (B. M. Solomon, personal communication, June 25, 1991). In 1903 she wrote and told him that she loved and respected him with all her heart (Northrup, 1903). She had also given her heart to a young man, Maria Sanford's nephew Edward. They were engaged, but her father did not approve so he arranged for Ada to study at the Sorbonne and travel abroad during the 1903–1904 academic year (Solomon, 1993). The relationship with Edward ended, leaving her quite sad, but she remained focused on her career. Believing that her additional training while in Europe improved her background as teacher, she wrote Northrup asking for a promotion. "I am hoping that the opening of the next college year may find me an assistant professor on a munificent salary. Is that too much to ask?" she inquired (Northrup, 1904). Her request was granted and she returned in the fall of 1904 as an assistant professor earning $1,200.

During her teaching years, Comstock was increasingly drawn into the work of the Women's League, the organization in which townswomen and faculty wives worked to help meet the needs of women students. Throughout her career, she worked closely with this group and with other women who sought to improve the situation of the "university girls," a term Comstock used in lieu of the hated "coed" (Comstock, 1906b, p. 18). Comstock knew that the women "were still essentially outside the life of the school, and their efforts were not taken seriously" (Smith, 1977,

p. 212). In fact, one reason Comstock joined the fray was annoyance at the attitude of many who considered the education of women a humorous subject, the butt of a joke. She once visited the editor-in-chief of one of the Minneapolis papers and asked him not to refer to women students as coeds or write about them in a facetious vein. The editor laughed at her and never took her request seriously (Comstock, 1940).

Comstock argued that intellectual achievement and physical well-being were inseparable and that the university was responsible for both. Students spent long hours on campus with almost nowhere to rest, seek recreation, or socialize with classmates. For women, there was only the mouse-infested "Ladies Parlor" in Old Main (the largest building on campus). When Old Main burned down in 1904, students were left in even more desperate circumstances (Solomon, 1993).

Comstock ardently believed that women needed opportunities for social growth and leadership. She joined those who were fighting for a women's center to be built on campus. Funding such an "air-castle" was another matter (Comstock, 1906b). Obviously, a project of this magnitude required the approval of the administration and the regents, all of whom had other priorities. She felt a bit uncomfortable asking "rich men for donations" and at times "hung back a little" (Solomon, 1993, p. 38). A donation from Thomas Shevlin was eventually secured, officially by President Northrup, but Ada had played the role of women's advocate by speaking with Shevlin and his wife on the plight of women students. To her utter dismay, her beloved President Northrup designated the gift for a new chemistry building. As Marion Talbot found at Chicago and Lucy Sprague experienced at Berkeley, a university president again turned his back on the dean and the women students she represented. For Comstock, however, her friendship with Northrup's daughter proved fortuitous. When she was caught weeping by Elizabeth Northrup, Comstock's feelings must have moved the president. Somehow Thomas Shevlin was persuaded to make a second gift and the women's building was completed in 1906 and named in honor of his wife, Alice Shevlin (Blanshard, 1974).

In the autumn of the same year that Alice Shevlin Hall opened, a public plea by students requesting a dean of women was printed in the student newspaper. It was the first time that the students had made such a request. They sought someone who was a member of the faculty who could offer advice and counsel:

> With the many boasted additions to and improvements in the faculty, one important omission was made. A dean of women has not yet been provided.
>
> Last year there were more than 900 girls registered. This year there are over 1000. There are few girls' colleges in the United States which have

an attendance equal to this, and none which do not provide amply for their care and supervision. Many other state universities such as Wisconsin and Northwestern also have deans of women.

Of our 1000 girls more than half live out of town, usually in small towns, and are having their first experience away from home. These girls do not need critical, meddling supervision, but they would be much happier if they could get advice and help on all matters from the choice of a course of study or a boarding place, to questions of dress, etiquette, health, social duties, etc.

A dean of women would be a member of the faculty, whose chief duty would be to consult with girls at all times, look out for their wellfore [sic] and enjoyments, know each individual and bring the women of the university closer together.

The Woman's building will do a great deal toward unifying them, the more united the body of girls becomes, the more their activities grow centralized, the more they need a women to lead them. The faculty women, the secretary of the Y.W.C.A. and the matron of the Woman's building can none of them fulfill this need, because they have so many other duties to perform. (Dean of women, 1906a, p. 2)

The sentiments of the students were echoed in the *Minnesota Alumni Weekly* (*MAW*), a publication for faculty and alumni. The *MAW* article used even more forceful language: "We do not hesitate to say that such an officer is the greatest need of the University at the present time. No other institution, of similar rank, pretends to do without a dean of women. . . . The university must have a dean of women. Cannot something else wait until this need which is so very pressing is provided for?" (Dean of women, 1906b, p. 1).

Fortunately for the advocates of the dean's position, President Northrup and the board of regents shared their point of view. At its December meeting, the board voted to secure a dean (Comstock, 1906b, p. 1; University of Minnesota, 1906). A list of candidates was generated with the expectation that the board would make a final selection at their May 1907 meeting. At least six candidates were considered, with Ada Comstock among them (Office of women's dean sought, 1907, p. 1).

Although no record of either the deliberations of the board or Northrup's reasoning survived, the choice of Comstock as the first dean of women for the University of Minnesota was not surprising. Comstock's work on behalf of women prior to her official appointment did not go unnoticed by either the students or the administration. She was appointed in May and assumed her duties in July 1907 at a salary of $2,000. Finally, her emolument made her feel sufficiently financially compensated and independent from her father (Blanshard, 1974). The new dean was officially welcomed at a reception sponsored by the Women's League in October. The occasion was described as one "calculated to show Dean

Comstock how warm a place she holds in the heart of the university community, and must have inspired her with new hopes and ambitions for the future of the work which is before her" (Honor Dean Comstock, 1907, p. 5).

OPENING MINDS

Comstock, like many other early deans, was the only female administrator on campus during her tenure. Once again she felt conspicuous as a woman on Minnesota's campus, but her stately manner, poise, and good humor served her well, as did her demonstrated facility for administration. Although she was promoted to full professor in 1909 and held that appointment until her resignation in 1912, the amount of time she spent teaching declined over the years. Her new administrative tasks were varied and interesting to her, providing sufficient challenge for a few years. Comstock once referred to her tasks as the most "delightful work in the university" (Comstock, 1908a, pp. 4–5).

What Comstock chose to focus on during her years as dean was dictated only in part by necessity. Like all administrators, she had fires to extinguish, but the preponderance of her work was not prescribed by exigency. Rather, her work was guided by her view of what was required for the successful education of women on a coeducational campus. Like her colleagues, she believed that deans should bring a specific area of expertise with them to the job, separate from any disciplinary expertise they held as faculty members. A dean of women should be an expert in the various aspects of women's education. This shift in attitude was marked by an increase in the number of publications by deans on pertinent topics and a noticeable change in the subjects discussed by the deans at the biennial meetings. Even women who had been deans in the earliest years published more during this era. For example, Marion Talbot published her seminal work *The Education of Women* in 1910. Mary Bidwell Breed published her three most notable articles between 1907 and 1909. In the 1907 article, "Women and the Academic Curriculum," chemist Breed addressed the problem of women abandoning the sciences and the resulting loss of status associated with fields that became feminized.

Comstock used her expertise as the basis for the programs and policies she initiated. She was an eloquent speaker on the subject of women's education. Through her leadership at the Conference of Deans and Advisors of Women in State Universities she shared her ideas with others. Lucy Sprague, dean of women at Berkeley and a frequent roommate of Comstock at the deans' meetings, felt that Comstock was among women with whom she could discuss the "substantive concerns about the higher education of women, not merely questions about dormitory rules, financial aid, student dances, and the like" (quoted in Antler, 1977, p. 112; also J. Antler, personal communication, May 14, 1991). Comstock was a pragmatist so she did not ignore the more mundane issues, but she "approached particular problems and then related them to the larger issues of women's higher education" (Solomon, 1987, in "Postscript" to the "Introduction," n.p.). By the time she resigned from her position, she was a nationally recognized leader in women's education, and Mount Holyoke College had bestowed upon her the first of her 14 honorary degrees (Solomon, 1980).

Comstock's view of women's education, first and foremost, was that it had to be taken seriously. This explained her deep annoyance with the manner in which newspapers reported the activities of women on campus, emphasizing the frivolous and ignoring the substantial (Comstock, 1940). Her primary academic concern was creating an intellectual environment in which women were allowed to work up to their full potential, fostering the complete development of their minds. "Giving the mind greater encouragement to develop its precious endowment is my purpose" (Comstock, 1929, p. 411), she once remarked. Greater encouragement meant creating surroundings that were as conducive to reflection as they were stimulating (Comstock, 1925b). "Our ideal college girl," she wrote in 1907, "is thoughtful as well as energetic, reposeful as well as efficient. . . . Herself she values, too. She regulates her life that public duties shall not rob her of her right to a peaceful development of mind and heart" (Comstock, 1907c, p. 276).

In general, however, Comstock did not focus the majority of her time on issues of curriculum or the classroom experience per se, almost as if she took that aspect of education for granted or believed that was one battle she need not fight. She did not, for example, publish on the issues of special courses of study for women, the inclusion of home economics, or the gender-segregated liberal arts curriculum, although other deans did pay attention to such matters. She sat on academic committees including the Committee for Student Work, which gave permission for students to take an extra load and dealt with academically deficient students. Comstock thought her role on this committee quite valuable. Occasionally she lamented that while the university was not adept at dealing with exceptionally talented students, methods for disciplining unsatisfactory students were commonly understood (Comstock, 1925b).

She commented frequently on the need to develop the whole individual. It was through the creation of a "good" environment, the opportunity for leadership experiences, and meaningful work that young women developed into productive, intelligent adults. For Comstock (1925b), being "concerned first and foremost with the intellectual life of the women students" (p. 426) meant paying attention to the environment in which women did academic work.

For Comstock, a "good" environment was one that provided for all facets of personal development. Ample provision for sufficient physical comfort for study and opportunities for physical exercise and recreation were needed. Central to her thinking, however, was an environment dedicated to high taste and conduct. She believed women should be in surroundings where individuals acted morally and with great civility, demonstrating trustworthiness and responsibility (Comstock, 1940). In the last paragraph of her final "Report of the Dean of Women," she clearly communicated her views on the role of the dean:

> The Dean of Women shall be aided in all her efforts to raise the standards of taste and conduct among women students. Minnesota women as a class are conscientious, earnest, and exceedingly amenable to good influences. They can not, however, by themselves escape the outbreak of vulgarity and lawlessness of which complaint is made all over this country, and which has either as its source or its expression in much of our contemporary music, drama, and literature. To fight against these debasing tendencies and to help college women to realize their responsibility in maintaining high standards is one of the tasks of a dean of women; and in her endeavors she needs constantly the sympathy and support of the administration of the university. (Comstock, 1913, p. 162)

OPENING DOORS

Comstock began her work as dean by learning all she could about the young women in her charge. It was her aim "to become personally acquainted with each girl in the college, by meeting her in the early part of the fall and keeping in touch with her for the year" (Co-ed dean has plans, 1907, p. 7). She wrote personal notes to students and attempted to learn what conditions affected students' lives outside the classroom as well as each woman's interests and aspirations. To do so, Comstock vowed to be accessible to any woman student who needed assistance and established an office in Alice Shevlin Hall, where she was available for 2 hours every morning.

The device Comstock used to learn about each student was quite simple, but it reflected a more administrative (even bureaucratic) approach to the job than that taken by Mary Bidwell Breed. Comstock asked each young woman to fill out a registration card and file it at the dean's office. Each card listed the organizations and clubs to which the student belonged, and Comstock used the back to mark academic progress. From these cards, Comstock created guest lists for the frequent teas she gave for students (Comstock, 1908a, pp. 4–5). The use of registration cards for various purposes became *de rigueur* for deans and was recommended by Lois Mathews (1915) in her primer, *The Dean of Women*. Mathews went so far as to provide a diagram of such a card and describe how it might be used to help the dean find suitable housing for women (p. 89).

Comstock concerned herself with almost all activities on campus that pertained to women. She sat on the governing body of the Cap and Gown Society, the Women's League, the Pan-Hellenic Association, and the Student Government Association. She also helped place interested women students in Unity House, a settlement house in Minneapolis (Students are doing noble work at settlements, 1910, p. 1).

She became involved in the women's publications on campus. The editorial control of most university publications on coeducational campuses rested with men. Occasionally, women held positions of leadership, but frequently they were not represented at all. One common response to exclusion was the creation of a special "women's number" of a campus publication, a volume dedicated to and produced by women. During Comstock's tenure this practice began at Minnesota. The *Minnesota Magazine*, the *Minnesota Alumni Weekly*, and the *Minne-Ha-Ha!* (the campus humor magazine) all issued women's editions, and Comstock was called on to offer editorial assistance, advice, or critique (Dean Comstock praises first number, 1908, p. 1). She also occasionally contributed articles.

In 1907, Comstock wrote "A Spring Reckoning" for the women's edition of the *Minnesota Magazine*, which was a pep talk of sorts to the students. She spoke of the material gains for women at the university and called these signs "that the college life of the Minnesota girl is growing more rich and full. No one who has been here a number of years can fail to note the new spirit which is steadily increasing among our women students. It is a generous spirit, a spirit of fellowship, and of enthusiasm for the University" (1907c, p. 276). In 1908, Comstock used the women's edition of the *Minnesota Magazine* to plead her case for a new women's dormitory (Women's mag to feature need for dormitories, 1908, p. 1).

The first women's version of the humor magazine was published in 1909, and Comstock, who was known for her wit, was sent the final version for proof and approval. There was a prevailing sense on the campus that women were acceptable as the objects of humor, but not as the source of humor. "For the first time at Minnesota, the college public will learn what co-ed humor is like when the Women's number of the *Minne-Ha-Ha!* appears on May 5th. The insinuation has been going the rounds for countless years that woman has no sense of humor" (Ha-Ha! Minne comes again, 1909, p. 1). Comstock wanted to provide the women with opportunities to make the campus laugh, without being laughed at. In her praise of the second edition, Comstock said, "Woman has again demonstrated that her sense of humor is of superior quality. Every page of the Woman's *Minne-Ha-Ha* is funny and the number contains nothing offensive" (Dean Comstock praises, 1910, p. 1).

A Place to Live

Like all deans, before and after her, who are responsible for students, Comstock had to deal with the housing problem (1913, p. 162). The boardinghouses of St. Paul and Minneapolis, although relatively plentiful, had other problems. Comstock (1907b) complained that the food was bad and the houses lacked privacy or any other refining influences. "There have been tragic happenings, and I know of one terrible case of blackmail" (p. 10), she remarked before a committee of state legislators . Learning from Mary Breed, she subsequently developed a list of "approved" houses (Dean Comstock desires approved boarding houses, 1908).

The lack of a women's dormitory on campus was a constant headache and Comstock was an unwavering crusader for her cause. She spoke before state legislative committees and wrote several articles in local publications. She was a proponent of dormitories for several reasons. Like Breed, she hoped that university-run housing would establish a community standard for a fair price for room and board. She also believed that a dormitory might boost female enrollment. Primarily, however, Comstock felt that a dormitory provided for students, 24 hours a day and 7 days a week, the advantages that Shevlin Hall offered during the work week.

She told the state legislature, "A college may train minds to be as keen as sword blades; but if it does not also teach its students to be genuine in their judgments, humane in their sympathies, and democratic in their whole scheme of thought, it has failed, I think, in its duty to the state" (Comstock, 1908b, p. 263). Her entreaty failed to secure a state appropriation immediately, but eventually the regents agreed with Comstock and listed a dormitory for women as a high priority. In 1909, Stanford Hall was built with a $100,000 state appropriation. It housed 90 women (Comstock, 1911). The college of arts and sciences did not build another dormitory for women for 32 years, until Comstock Hall opened in 1941.

An Opportunity to Work

Accruing leadership experience was critical to producing good character, she believed, so it followed naturally that Comstock initiated activities that provided women with such opportunities. But for Comstock, the key to women's full development was in the preparation for meaningful work, whether that work was paid, voluntary, or within the home. Comstock found purpose in her work and believed that the seeds of satisfaction were the same in most people. She said, "It is in some sort of purposeful activity, some sort of work that human lives seem to find their fulfillment" (1925a, pp. 448–449). However, finding fulfilling work presented special challenges to women, of which Comstock was thoroughly aware:

> Especially do the circumstances of life make the finding and accomplishment of satisfying work a difficult thing for a woman. More than men is she encumbered by tradition and convention. Less than men is she expected to make her mark upon the world, to justify her existence by some activity. The delusion that her function is largely decorative has not vanished from the world; nor the sanction upon her spending her days in silly and useless activity just as the shops are filled with useless and ugly things for her to buy. (p. 450)

Comstock believed that college should prepare *all* women for work. She argued that while young and in college, most women do not know whether they will marry and should therefore prepare for a career. She argued that marriage did not preclude opportunities for useful work— while childless or after the children have grown (1925a, p. 451). For Comstock and other college-educated feminists, the nascent vocational guidance movement offered intriguing possibilities (Strom, 1992). Deans began to believe that they could, through guidance, role-modeling, and exposure to new ideas and possibilities, change the career aspirations of young women away from the traditionally female, typically underpaid vocations.

In May 1907, shortly after being selected by the board of regents, Comstock gave a short speech at a faculty banquet outlining her intent to devote considerable attention to the vocational and career-oriented needs of Minnesota's women. Like many women of the Progressive Era, she was interested in reforming society and upholding and improving civilization (Smith, 1977; Solomon, 1993). She also felt that women had a unique role to play in this process. It was commonly held that work in progressive causes was especially well suited to women's abilities and provided a profound justification for their higher education. It was clear from Comstock's remarks at the faculty banquet that her approach at Minnesota would be an integrated one in which leadership, preparation to be useful in life, and high ideals were the aim of every program under the new dean's purview:

> College training should do more than inform the mind. It should add to the student's usefulness in society. To be a useful member of society one must be aware of one's duty to the world, and must be able to work with other people to good ends. The quality which enables a man to be thus

useful we call good citizenship. To the same quality in a woman we may give the name social efficiency.

Social efficiency cannot be taught in the class room. College life, however, offers opportunity for the development of this quality. Every student organization offers training in good citizenship and in social efficiency. Fraternities, sororities, the Christian associations, the boards of control, the Women's League, the Student Government association—in all of these students are learning how to live in society. Such lessons are not forgotten. They mould the student's after life. It is of supreme importance, therefore, that all the activities of college life should be governed by high ideals. ("Co-ed dean has plans," 1907, p. 11)

Three years later, when writing for an alumni publication, it was clear that her views were essentially unchanged. "Work among the women students of the University is likely to develop it seems to me in two ways: in the fitting of women for a greater variety of gainful occupations, while retaining for them the broad training which we associate with the bachelor's degree; and in the creation for them of influences tending toward the refinement and cultivations which we love to call womanly" (in Johnson, 1910, pp. 194–195).

Comstock's goal was helping students to finance their education and, in the process, develop long-range career aspirations—beyond, it was hoped, the typical choice of teaching. Pragmatism dictated that she first attend to the issue of paying for college, so Comstock worked on finding suitable part-time jobs for women. In 1909, it was estimated that average students needed between $350 and $450 to attend the university if they did not have free board with their families in the Minneapolis area (Johnson, 1910). Comstock conducted research and found that 15% of women students were at least partially self-supporting (compared with 64% of the men). On average, the women earned $191 while their male classmates earned $306 per year on the job. The women worked in female-oriented occupations including housekeeping, child care, office clerking, tutoring, and secretarial work. Comstock believed that low salaries obligated women to work longer hours and she observed that the women often suffered from overwork and exhaustion. She also discovered that despite the hardship, the self-supporting women did as well academically as their nonworking counterparts (Self supporting students, 1910, p. 11).

Comstock took it on herself to oversee the employment of women, making sure that it was safe and fairly paid. People who wanted to employ students came to the dean, who tried to match employers with students. She once said that "this aspect of the work of my office is of very great interest to me. It brings me in contact with many girls whom I am especially glad to know" (Comstock, 1908a, pp. 4–5). She used Shevlin Hall as a clearinghouse for job listings, but often the choices were limited. To increase employment opportunities, Comstock spent the Christmas vacation of 1911–1912 walking up and down the streets of the Twin Cities trying to convince department stores of the sagacity of hiring women. She found that they "were particularly impregnable to the suggestion" (Blanshard, 1974, p. 11). By the 1920s, however, societal attitudes toward women working in retail shops changed. Women were sought as store clerks, but this change of heart and mind came too late to solve Comstock's immediate problem.

Other ways to assist financially needy students included scholarships and loans. During her tenure, Comstock helped establish three scholarships and one loan fund. Again it was the local women's college clubs that provided the necessary gifts (Comstock, 1913). In her last year at Minnesota, Comstock pushed for a vocational bureau. Such bureaus acted as separate organizations on campuses and were devoted exclusively to funding and supervising student employment. They also helped students discover their future calling for a profession. Her idea received the endorsement of the university's new president, George Vincent, who replaced Northrup in 1910. However, the bureau was not established until after she left Minnesota (Dean Comstock discussed vocation, 1912; Vincent, 1913).

An overwhelming number of women who entered a paid profession after graduation entered teaching. The reason was usually the lack of other viable options, rather than a commitment to or talent for classroom instruction. For Comstock (1925b), the "disadvantages of this situation for the teacher and the taught were obvious" (p. 430). Like her colleagues, she explored other-than-teaching career choices for women, but much of this work began in her last year at Minnesota.

Vocational concerns were frequent subjects of conversation at professional meetings, and several deans addressed the lack of vocational opportunities on their campuses. At the University of Chicago in 1910, for example, Marion Talbot investigated the vocational needs of students and the financial aid situation (Haddock, 1952). In fact, the Chicago vocational bureau that was established became one of the more successful examples in the country for women. Lucy Sprague was appalled by the lack of vocational choices for women at Berkeley and experimented with new curricular offerings that put students in contact with real-world work experiences (Antler, 1987).

OPENING HEARTS

In her "Report of the Dean of Women," Comstock (1913) informed the president that her work, as a rule, fell into four categories, including building a community for women on campus:

In dealing with so large a body of women, it seemed necessary to bring about as much unity of feeling as possible, so that public opinion might aid in the spread of good influences. To this end the large organizations which are open to all, such as the Women's League and the Young Women's Christian Association, have been utilized as much as possible and have been encouraged to concern themselves with undertakings in behalf of the University. (p. 158)

Creating community eventually became the sine qua non of the professional deans. Finally, they could envision fashioning something beyond the important but all-too-tangible needs of housing and jobs. For Lucy Sprague at Berkeley, Comstock's colleague and close friend, it was the inauguration of a "heart culture" that was central to her mission of creating a sense of community for the young women. For many deans, the desire for community obligated the university to provide a "place." Talbot created the Women's Union. For Comstock, it was Alice Shevlin Hall, and she described it as her most effective "tool" (Johnson, 1910, p. 194). She recognized that universities were organizations created and run by men "and however kindly the individual members of the faculty may show themselves . . . the close discipleships which the young men may enjoy . . . are not so easily attainable to the young women" (Comstock, 1929, p. 413). She realized that women students needed a physical place on campus to rest, study, eat, and associate with one another to ease the loneliness and feelings of isolation. Comstock succeeded in bringing all activities for women to one site on campus and estimated that Shevlin Hall performed an "incalculable service in bringing women together" (Comstock, 1913, p. 157). In several respects, Shevlin Hall was not unlike the women's centers that appeared on campuses in the 1970s.

The building itself was quite attractive and nicely appointed, full of polished woodwork, stained-glass windows, and Oriental carpets. Most of the furniture and appointments were donations from the YWCA, the Women's League, and private benefactors. The basement accommodated a dining room, which provided a low-cost lunch to over 400 women per day. It was so overly subscribed and crowded that the students referred to it as the "Bread Line." The basement had 1,000 lockers for women to stow their possessions and modern toilet facilities with hot and cold water. Comstock's office was on the first floor in the Jean Martin Brown Parlor, resplendent with mahogany furniture and colorful carpets. There was also an assembly room, a living room with a fireplace, a Bible study room, and offices for the YWCA and Women's League. The second floor housed the rest room with 15 couches and sick beds. There were meeting rooms for various organizations and an office for the building matron, Jessie Ladd, who earned $800 per year for her services. In addition, there was a study room that contained several reference books and other academic material (Comstock, 1906a, 1907d; Johnson, 1910; *Minnesota Daily*, 1906, November 21, p. 1; 1907, January, 10, p. 1, September 25, p. 1; 1908, December 18, p. 1).

The student newspaper once referred to Comstock as the Queen of Shevlin Hall because of all the activities she sponsored. Indeed, the list was considerable. There were Women's League Parties, the YWCA's Christmas Bazaar, Professor Maria Sanford's 70th birthday party, musical recitals, glee club concerts, meetings, speeches, and occasional receptions for Comstock herself (Shevlin Hall open to all, 1907, p. 1).

Ideas such as Comstock's were being implemented on several campuses. Dean Lucy Sprague had one of the more ambitious programs. Sprague was on Berkeley's campus from 1903 until 1911, but officially the dean only after 1906. Like Marion Talbot, Sprague was a protégée of Alice Freeman Palmer. In fact, she lived with the Palmers in their Cambridge home before and briefly after Alice's untimely death in 1903. George Herbert Palmer's increasing interest in and dependence on Sprague after Alice's death led Lucy to seriously consider President Benjamin Wheeler's offer of a teaching post as a "Reader" in English. Wheeler became a close friend and later promoted Sprague (Antler, 1987). Eventually, she became an assistant professor, but even then dared not attend faculty meetings. "Certainly we [she and the only other female faculty member] could have gone, but I know that would have prejudiced the men against us, and we already have enough prejudice to live down," she commented (quoted in Gordon, 1990, p. 62).

It disquieted Sprague to see women on coeducational campuses surrender their interests and aspirations to those of men (Sprague, 1908). Like other deans, she was worried about the isolation and ridicule that women faced as well as the dearth of cultural and intellectual stimulation. The women were taunted with the nickname "pelican" because they were perceived as "skinny, ugly, serious creatures destined to become old maids" (Antler, 1987, p. 96). She therefore dedicated much of her energy to creating what she called a "heart culture," a program of enriching activities that connected the women students to one another and to the outside world.

The outside world touched the Berkeley campus in other ways that affected Sprague's work with women students. Women's sexuality and the protection and regulation thereof always played a role in hiring deans of women or the matrons before them. Whether it was overtly stated or (usually) more subtly implied, deans knew that their task was to ensure sexual propriety. However, in the Progressive Era, deans became responsible for the sexual health of women students as well. Social reformers and women's rights advocates engaged in a "social purity" campaign designed to wipe out venereal disease and prostitution. Sprague felt that these trends "stormed the campus with hysterical intensity" (Antler, 1987, p. 116). Working closely with the only other professional women on campus—Dr. Eleanor Bancroft, the women's physician; Dr. Mary Ritter, in charge of physical education; and two women faculty—Sprague found herself attending to the "queerest" of all her duties. She dealt with the "seamy side of sex"—unplanned pregnancies, abortion, and sexually transmitted diseases. The physicians lectured on physiology, menstruation, and other women's health concerns under the guise of "hygiene" courses (Antler, 1987). Sprague's experience epitomized what happened to other deans as once again universities sought to control student sexuality by controlling the women (Bailey, 1988).

Sprague's myriad efforts were well received. The students commented, "The best thing that ever happened to the women of this University was the creation of the office of Dean of Women, and the best thing that ever happened to the office of Dean of Women was the appointment of Miss Sprague to fill it" (Gordon, 1990, p. 65).

Comstock and Sprague were driven by the belief that bringing all the young women into contact with one another fostered the high ideals of conduct and character about which they cared so deeply. A community nourished "dignity and graciousness" and allowed the women with the highest ideals, rather than merely the noisiest, to become the leaders of the community (Comstock, 1906a, pp. 10–12). In Comstock's (1907a) dedication of Shevlin Hall, she stated:

> There is an idea back of the Woman's Building. It has to do not only with physical comfort or even with health, though the building is designed for both health and comfort. It is an idea—or ideal—of education for women as including more than mere training of the mind. Refinement in personal habits is part of the ideal; a taste for beauty in surroundings is another part; but the greatest element of all—next to mental training—is hard to name. Let us call it a sort of personal cultivation which women students derive from free, happy, helpful intercourse with one another and which manifests itself in tact and sympathy and comprehension and the open heart. (p. 6)

Comstock's efforts at building a community were furthered by the creation of the *Shevlin Record*, a publication by and for the women of the university. The *Record* announced meetings and events and Comstock used it to explain policies and procedures. She also posted job opportunities for students near the Brown Parlor where she worked.

In short, Shevlin Hall was designed to meet many of the health, comfort, academic, religious, and social needs of women students. Comstock believed that it was more valuable than either a dormitory or gymnasium, although she continued her work to secure those buildings for women as well. In 1909, Mr. Shevlin was persuaded to donate an additional $20,000 for improvements, including a larger dining area in order to eliminate the Bread Line (Addition to Shevlin begun, 1909). In some ways, Shevlin Hall was similar to the Women's Union (which began in 1901) run by Marion Talbot at the University of Chicago, but there were a few key differences. The Women's Union did require a modest fee ($1 per year) to belong and had fewer physical amenities than Shevlin Hall. Talbot made much stronger links with the faculty and the larger community, however, while Comstock concentrated on bringing all on-campus activities to a single location.

Once Shevlin Hall was in place, Comstock wanted the women to learn to run it and take responsibility for the numerous activities and problems associated with the hall. The mechanism Comstock used to develop these skills was the Student-Government Association (SGA). SGA was first voted in by students in December 1906 for the purpose of aiding in the care and conduct of Alice Shevlin Hall. Such associations originated in the women's colleges and Comstock herself had been part of an SGA at Smith College. In fact, during the first decade of the 20th century, self-government groups became increasingly common on coeducational campuses, more likely than not at the instigation of deans of women who had experience with them from their own undergraduate days at women's colleges. Lucy Sprague on Berkeley's campus was convinced of their efficacy in building leadership skills and the urgent need for them on a coeducational campus. As she said in her 1908 article, "It is unquestionable that in a coeducational college, where the responsibility of social activities . . . falls in a lesser degree to the women, that the women develop self-possession less markedly than in a separate college" (p. 51; also quoted in Antler, 1987, p. 103).

Comstock believed that student-developed and student-enforced policies achieved more positive outcomes than those dictated by administrators and, in the meantime, the process taught students about leadership, consensus, law and order, and good citizenship (Comstock, 1909, p. 4; Ladd, 1910, pp. 7–8).

Every woman student in the university was regarded as a member of the SGA and there were no dues. The SGA made rules for the guidance of those using Shevlin Hall, provided committees to enforce the rules, gave permission for holding social functions in the building, and controlled the expenditure of any surplus receipts from the lunch room (University of Minnesota, 1908).

The association quickly expanded its scope beyond Shevlin Hall and considered all aspects of campus-conduct policy potentially under its purview. In due time, it took up the issue of stopping the petty theft that was plaguing Shevlin Hall and other campus buildings and the problem of cheating on examinations, known as cribbing. Both issues were brought to the attention of students at large mass meetings held in the chapel. These gatherings were full of speeches and testimonials by faculty, staff, and students. Comstock inevitably spoke at these meetings, and so did President Northrup. The women students eventually decided to sign pledge cards that promised they would behave honorably during exams and not crib. A cartoon soon appeared in the campus humor magazine depicting a man during an examination, gleefully consulting his crib notes. The woman next to him, obviously having trouble with her test, looked exasperated and sighed, "Oh, Darn, I wish I'd never heard of that no-cribbing pledge" (Cartoon, 1910; Comstock, 1908a, pp. 6–7).

One innovation Comstock brought to campus from the biennial deans' conferences was the notion of a point system to regulate student leaders. Many on campus felt that there was often a small core of women who monopolized leadership positions on campus. This frequently led to overwork and exhaustion for a few, and a lack of management opportunities for the majority. Under Comstock's direction, the SGA developed a system that assigned points to each office of a student organization based on the prestige and amount of responsibility expected of each post. No woman could exceed the agreed-on point limit.

It is difficult to estimate fully the value of self-government. In 1910, student Jesse Ladd said it created a "stronger feeling of unity and power as a force in university life" (p. 8). That was a powerful statement and a tribute to the success of the various initiatives by Comstock. The model was so successful that in 1910 a university-wide student council was created.

PROFESSIONAL CIRCLES

The deans gathered again in Chicago in December 1907 for the third Conference of Deans and Advisors of Women in State Universities.[1] Myra Jordan of Michigan was the chair and Ada Comstock, attending her first conference, was the secretary (Potter, 1927). For the first time, Marion Talbot did not attend but her reasons for missing the meeting are unknown. They met for 2 days in long sessions, talked over meals in between, and kept a complete set of minutes of the formal discussions. They spent time preparing and voting on a list of official resolutions. It was clear from the minutes that an important purpose to the meeting was informing each other about life on other campuses and the state of deans of women around the Midwest. They spent an afternoon session sharing information on salaries and duties, and the variation was considerable. Salaries ranged from $1,200 to $2,000, but the actual discrepancies were greater. For some women, their salary was on top of room and board, while others were obligated to pay the postage and entertainment expenses. Not surprisingly, the collective opinion was that salaries were too low and the university should pay the office expenses (CDAWSU, 1907).

They discussed housing, excesses in social life, athletics, and regulation of sororities. Those topics were the subjects of the final resolutions, but almost one-third of the 30 pages of substantive minutes was devoted to various aspects of women's education and the nature of the dean's role. Each dean told the group about the curricular requirements at her college and the nature of any concerns regarding women. They spoke about the problems of electives in the curriculum and the issue of younger students remaining too unfocused. They discussed academic deficiency and its causes and appropriate remedies. In terms of specific subjects in the curriculum, they were most concerned with pedagogy courses and home economics. There was a general feeling that home economics courses should be divided into two levels—a lower-level course that taught a skill, for example, cooking, and higher-level courses that emphasized science and research. The deans believed that no credit should be awarded for the lower level. They knew that the predominantly male faculty on their campus held the discipline in low regard and believed that a renewed commitment to make it more research intensive was necessary. Cora Woodward from Wisconsin stated that home economics was proving useful in serving the state and its status was improving (CDAWSU, 1907).

The deans also talked about general problems of coeducation and the increasing public reaction against it. One dean stated that women at coeducational institutions were harmed by the feeling that women were only a "side issue." Some deans, notably Breed, believed problems were caused by the lack of seriousness among the students. Still others thought the lack of seriousness came from the pressure on women in coeducational campuses to socialize too much. They believed that the environment was not as serious as that found on single-sex campuses. A few lamented the lack of opportunities for leadership and executive experience that arose when all the student organizations were controlled by men. Yet when women's organizations were formed, "the same people are constantly called upon and others are constantly left out" (CDAWSU, 1907, p. 17), leaving the very active with too little time to study. This sentiment was precisely the rationale Comstock used to support the creation of her point system.

Self-government was enthusiastically endorsed, and there was a brief discussion, at Comstock's instigation, on the problem of finding work for self-supporting women. The group decided that the 1907 meeting had been more substantive and therefore more enjoyable than the previous conference. It was determined that they would meet again in December 1909. On her return to Minneapolis, Comstock published a list of the conference resolutions in the *Minnesota Alumni Weekly* (Deans of women at Chicago, 1908).

In February 1909, Marion Talbot issued a call to deans to attend an informal conference in conjunction with the Religious Education Association, recognizing the need to "forge another link in the chain of the education of women" (Potter, 1927, p. 219). No minutes of the meeting survive, but one topic that received considerable attention was housing (Dean Comstock returns from deans' conference, 1909). The meeting was significant both for its link with another higher education association and the relative prestige afforded the deans by the company they kept. Comstock, Talbot, Breed, and 10 other deans attended. The Religious Education Association drew some of higher education's luminaries, including two nationally prominent men from Harvard University: President Charles Eliot and Plummer Professor of Christian Morals Francis Greenwood Peabody. Seventeen talks from that meeting were reprinted in the association's *Journal* in April 1909, including those by Breed and Talbot.

The fourth official Conference of Deans and Advisors of Women in State Universities met from December 20 to 22, 1909, again in Chicago. The trend of addressing consequential issues of women's education as well as housing and social life continued. The first two of the dean's eight resolutions pertained to curricular matters. The first called for closer faculty supervision of the academic progress for freshman women. The second resolution was dearer to Comstock's heart, "that technical courses of interest to women, such as courses in home economics, dairying, poultry, husbandry, journalism, philanthropy, library work, business management, etc., be increased in number and variety and that women be encouraged to take them with a view to entering other professions than that of teaching" ("Dean discusses co-ed problems at Chicago," 1910, p. 1; Potter, 1927, p. 220). Their final recommendation asserted the conviction that deans should hold academic posts and serve on important committees and councils of the faculty. Comstock was elected president of the 1911 meeting.

Interestingly, the deans from public universities held a few joint sessions with a newly constituted group of deans from private institutions. This second "conference" was also convened by Marion Talbot and held in Chicago. At the end of both conferences, the two groups agreed that they held many concerns in common and that broad, rather than narrow, representation was desirable.

The minutes and resolutions of the biennial Conference of Deans and Advisors of Women in State Universities over which Comstock presided

(1911) have not survived. All that was recorded was that in addition to what were by then routine topics of housing and sorority management, an entire session was devoted to vocational concerns for women. Such a discussion probably took place at Comstock's suggestion, because the chair of each meeting was typically responsible for setting the agenda (Potter, 1927).

The spread of ideas through the deans' conferences was critical for the development of the profession. Like most professional meetings, as much was accomplished in the unstructured time as in the formal sessions. Mary Breed reported to her president that she gained "much from informal intercourse, at meals, etc." (Breed, 1908b, n.p.). Comstock found the informal idea sharing particularly enjoyable (Blanshard, 1974). She and Lucy Sprague had time for lengthy casual conversations while rooming together at the hotels.

A similar phenomenon was happening at the annual ACA conventions. Many deans were also member of the ACA. In fact, Comstock (1950) once credited the ACA with helping push her agenda as dean of women. "I know what it meant," she said, "to have the Association, with its very definite standards as to conditions that should exist in a coeducational college, behind me" (p. 78). The ACA had many concerns in common with deans of women, but broader issues pertaining to women's education were also within its purview. In 1907, believing that there was sufficient evidence to refute the claim that university life ruined the health of women, the ACA turned to issues of professional opportunities and fair compensation for women (Fish, 1985). By 1911, there were several articles on vocational subjects in the ACA *Journal* (Holmes, 1939).

While traveling together on the train in 1910 en route to an ACA meeting in Denver, various deans decided to hold a special conference of deans in conjunction with the convention. They asked Gertrude Martin, Advisor to Women at Cornell University, to give a presentation, "The Position of Dean of Women" (Potter, 1927).

Martin was eager to learn of the experiences of other deans. Her enthusiasm for information drove her to conduct the first-ever survey of deans of women and she was preparing the results for publication when asked to speak to the ACA (Martin, 1911b). Her views on the deans' work were influenced by the data in her survey, but she was also very much affected by her own circumstances. At Cornell, the Advisor to Women position was formerly known as the Warden (housemother) of Sage College, the residence for women. Benefactor Henry W. Sage grew increasingly conservative with respect to women's education and demanded oversight of women's deportment and morals (Conable, 1977). Martin's position encompassed the full range of a dean's responsibilities, but she was acutely conscious of the Sage legacy. Yet Martin was also an astute observer of the inequities confronted by Cornell's women and grew angrier at this state of affairs. Her dean's reports are a fascinating example of deans articulating both traditional and feminist views.

Martin's 1910–1911 dean's report discussed the need for women to learn the social graces and the obligation to always be a "lady." She wanted the dorms to replicate the training received in "the excellent private home" and provide the knowledge and skills of "courtesies and social usage" (Conable, 1977, p. 110). In a subsequent dean's report, Martin challenged the university and its posture toward women. She wrote that "an unwillingness to admit that the institution is really and permanently committed to the policy of coeducation; the feeling that the presence of women somehow renders it inferior to the other great eastern universities . . . a determination to keep it in curriculum and atmosphere as distinctly a man's institution as possible" were deleterious to the full integration of women in university life (Conable, 1977, p. 130; Martin, 1911a).

The deans' enclave of the 1910 ACA convention discussed many of the same topics as the meetings of deans of state universities, and also the issue of whether deans should teach and the importance of home economics. The 1910 Conference of Deans of Women was unofficial, but the women decided to meet each year at the annual conventions of the ACA regardless. In 1911, the Executive Committee of the ACA gave the deans floor privileges, and the Conference of Deans became an official feature of ACA conventions with a report in the *Journal.* Thus deans began meeting every year at the ACA and biennially at the Conference of Deans and Advisors of Women in State Universities. There was some overlap in attendees (for example, Lucy Sprague was the secretary of the 1910 session at ACA), but the deans at the ACA conventions represented both large and small, public and private institutions (Conference of Deans of Women, 1910).

It was clear by the 1911 meeting that deans of women still had to address basic problems, but they were augmenting that aspect of their job with a new sense of expertise. Gertrude Martin (1911b) eloquently summed up the situation at the 1910 ACA convention when describing the new role for deans of women:

> Can she make it more than merely ornamental? . . . Can she do work more directly educational than that of housing and feeding her charges comfortably and of safeguarding their health and morals? Do not misunderstand me. These services are necessary and important. . . . But they are after all only preliminary; and if she stops here she stops short of her performance of her primary function as dean of women. . . . Why call her a dean at all unless her function is at least comparable with that of other officers bearing the same title? What is the function of a dean of the college? What is

the ground for his appointment? Is it not based on the supposition that he knows better than his colleagues the educational needs of the particular class of students?. . . . He is expected to know at all times the trend of education in his special field. . . .

It seems clear to me that in the great coeducational universities today there is urgent need of deans of women—truly such—who shall perform on behalf of women students—a special class with special educational need—a function closely parallel to the deans of the colleges. . . .

Here, if anywhere, it seems to me, the dean of women finds her true function—a function which, adequately performed, justifies both her title and high academic position generally accorded her. She must not be merely a scholar, but an educator with expert knowledge of her particular educational field. (pp. 74–76)

In 1912, Ada Comstock was approached by the president of Smith College to become its first dean. While she was fond of Minnesota and her position, she realized that she was ready for a new set of challenges and opportunities. She was also in the midst of a personal crisis. She was in love with a young history professor who wanted to marry her, but Comstock was unsure about marriage, fearing that it would stifle her professional career. Her suitor, Wallace Notestein, was understandably distressed. Staying near him and his hurt feelings was difficult for her; moving to Massachusetts felt like a reprieve. Notestein was obviously a patient man. They married 31 years later after Comstock had retired as the president of Radcliffe College (Solomon, 1993).

President Vincent and the women students expressed their regret at her leaving. The students published their tribute in the April 1, 1912, issue of the *Shevlin Record*. Comstock must have been moved by their remarks, which revealed that she had accomplished many of her goals:

Under her we have gained a more dignified and less casual position as part of the University. . . . Women students have been familiarly known as "co-eds" and there is a general lack of realization of the serious purpose and worth of university women. It is towards lessening this prejudice, the establishment of fixed and recognized standards and conventions, that Miss Comstock devoted her energy. She has been working with a large vision and great purpose. . . . This has been her great work—the establishment of woman, in all her dignity and reserve, as a recognized and revered member of the University of Minnesota. (pp. 1–2)

Lois Kimball Mathews, circa 1915. Associate Professor of History,
Dean of Women, 1911–1918, University of Wisconsin.
(Courtesy University of Wisconsin Archives)

Chapter 6

MORE THAN WISE
AND PIOUS MATRONS

The collective contributions of Marion Talbot, Mary Bidwell Breed, Lucy Sprague, Ada Comstock, and their like-minded peers successfully enlarged the scope of the position of dean of women. By 1911, the deans were well beyond chaperones and regularly concerned themselves with curriculum, community, and women's employment. They had proven their usefulness, overcome resistance, and carved out an appropriate field of expertise, but theirs was not quite yet a recognized profession. The final steps in the process of professionalization included the development of a professional literature, graduate training to prepare women for entry to the field, and a full-fledged professional organization. These steps were achieved before the end of World War I.

When Lois Mathews entered the University of Wisconsin as dean of women and associate professor of history in 1911, she was able to stand on the shoulders of her predecessors and draw on the knowledge from the previous Conferences of Deans. She also benefited, however, from circumstances unique to Wisconsin. First, the university had already had two previous deans of women, so the campus was familiar with the title, if not yet familiar with the potential of the office. Second, Charles Van Hise, Wisconsin's president, wanted a strong dean of women to demonstrate his commitment to women's education and to address a political problem he had on campus regarding coeducation (Curti & Carstensen, 1949). As a consequence, Van Hise was quite supportive of Mathews and her work.

By 1911, Wisconsin had adequate housing for women and Van Hise had promised Mathews a new women's building, Lathrop Hall. Lathrop, which had sufficient space for meetings, dining, and social gatherings, immediately became the center of life for women on campus under Mathews's leadership (Mathews, 1912, 1914b). Thus Mathews's contributions were of a different nature than those of other deans—those associated with the more tangible attributes of professionalization.

Mathews was a serious scholar by training and temperament and brought an intellectuality to the profession that was needed during her era to support a perceived loss of status for the position. Her strong views on the profession were informed by her beliefs in the nature of women's education, and she communicated those to numerous other deans through her speeches at professional meetings, her journal articles, her teaching, and especially her book, *The Dean of Women* (1915).

FROM GIRLHOOD TO WIDOWHOOD

Lois Carter Kimball[1] was born in Cresco, Iowa, in 1873, only a few miles from the Minnesota border. She was a direct descendant of Richard Kimball, who migrated from England to Puritan Massachusetts in the 1640s (Fley, 1980; Mathews, 1905; Rosenberry, 1942). The first White settlers in the area arrived in 1853, and Lois's father, Aaron Kimball, migrated in 1856. The next year, Mr. Kimball opened and taught in the first school of the county (Amundson, 1905). Like many midwestern towns in the mid-19th century, Cresco prospered because it was situated on the railroad. In the 1860s, several towns were squabbling over the location of the county seat—a designation that typically brought with it state funds for buildings and expansion. When Cresco won the honor in 1867, it was due in part to its proximity to the railroad, but credit was also given to the efforts of the town clerk, Aaron Kimball, who successfully wooed the selection committee (Fairbairn, 1919).

Much like Ada Comstock, Lois Mathews grew up with a father who was a pillar of the community and passed along to his daughter a sense of duty and a penchant for leadership. Aaron Kimball was the town's first real estate agent and also founded, with a partner, the first bank in Cresco, Kimball & Farnsworth, in 1869. He was successful in his banking, active in the church, and interested in schools. He held numerous leadership positions within the community, varying from president of both the county fair and the State Temperance Alliance, to state senator from 1877 to 1881. He stayed in banking until 1880, when he was bought out by his partner, and the firm dissolved in 1885 (Kimball, 1966).

Kimball married Irene Hatch, a sea captain's widow from Massachusetts, in August 1858, and they had one daughter, Mary, 10 years later. While childless, Irene Kimball was the co-proprietess of a millinery company, Cole & Kimball, and won prizes at the county fair for her bread and horses. Sadly, she died suddenly in 1870, leaving Kimball with their young daughter. Kimball remarried in 1872 to Emma Wilhelmina Laird, who gave birth to Lois 10 months later.

The second Mrs. Kimball had a deep commitment to education that she passed on to her oldest daughter. Kimball estimated his worth as over $10,000 dollars in 1870 so Lois grew up in quite comfortable circumstances. The household consisted of her parents, Lois, two younger sisters, Mary, her older half-sister (the Kimballs lost both of their sons in infancy), and a live-in servant. Lois seemed close to her family and, although she never lived there past the age of 15, she considered Cresco, of which she was quite fond, her home town and she chose to be buried there. She once remarked, "I am so glad I was brought up in a little town in Iowa . . . [where] my father and mother were good citizens who felt the obligations to the working out of democracy" (Rosenberry, 1942, n.p.).

Bright and interested in learning, young Lois graduated from high school in 1888, only 15 years old. Her class of 10 students was only the 10th high school class in the region. Lois gave a commencement oration entitled "The Three Caskets," referring to the choices made by Portia's potential suitors in Shakespeare's *The Merchant of Venice*. She gave some inkling of her future aspirations in her talk when she discussed the importance of both education and career (Graduation, 1888).

By this time the family had moved to their farm in nearby Austin, Minnesota. Lois began her college career at the State Normal School in Winona, Minnesota. After she earned her diploma in 1890, she taught public school for 4 years in two different towns in Minnesota and then moved to Utah for health reasons. Salt Lake City offered a warmer climate and her new job presented her with a fresh challenge as both an eighth-grade teacher and the assistant principal. While teaching, she took a year of study at the University of Utah and there she met a modern language professor, George R. Mathews. The 37-year-old George was a studious, religious man interested in broad culture and philosophy (Chamberlin, 1960). He was financially secure, having inherited a comfortable amount on the death of his parents when he was only 15. Lois and George married in 1897, but tragically he died of consumption (tuberculosis), leaving her a widow after only 18 months of marriage.

At the time of her husband's death she lived in Redlands, California, where the couple had moved in what turned out to be a failed effort to cure George's ailment. Redlands was a resort town of sorts on the edge of the Mojave Desert known for its wealthy, cultured, and intellectual inhabitants. It was settled by members of moneyed society seeking relaxation or relief in the desert air from chronic lung disorders (*Ingersoll's Century Annals*, 1904). Lois decided not to stay and instead chose to further her own education.

From Protégé to Professor

Mathews moved north and enrolled at Leland Stanford, Jr., University, where she studied history, concentrating in constitutional history and colonial expansion. In the summer of 1902, one of her professors, Max Farrand, encouraged her to mosey over to Berkeley and meet Professor Frederick Jackson Turner, who was teaching summer school at the state university. Lois's interest in her own Puritan ancestry, Colonial America, and the movement of New England's institutions westward intrigued Turner, who was already well known for his frontier thesis (Turner, 1894). Turner said to her, "You believe in those New England institutions, don't you? There has been much vague talk of the influence of New England in this country. Why don't you make a careful study of it" (quoted in Rosenberry, 1942).

Mathews graduated from Stanford in 1903 with Phi Beta Kappa honors, a distinction she attained while also earning her living teaching school. She chose to stay at Stanford and completed a master's degree in history in 1904. Her interest in a career in higher education, rather than schools, began during her time at Stanford as she set her sights on further graduate study.

A network of scholars guided Mathews to Cambridge, Massachusetts, in 1904 to pursue a Ph.D. Max Farrand of Stanford, Edward Channing and A. B. Hart of Harvard, and Frederick Jackson Turner at the University of Wisconsin were all friends and colleagues and urged Mathews to apply to Harvard or, actually, Radcliffe (Channing, 1906, 1907, 1919; "Frederick Jackson Turner," 1936). She was accepted to Radcliffe's Graduate School to pursue her interest in the westward spread of New England population and settlement.

Radcliffe College was originally formed as the Harvard Annex to afford young women the opportunity to learn from Harvard's faculty, and segregated undergraduate education was strictly maintained until 1943 (Schwager, 1982). Graduate training was another matter, however. Radcliffe, as a college, was not entitled to confer doctoral degrees. During the 1890s, several important American graduate schools voted to admit women, but Harvard remained recalcitrant. Even as late as 1898, the university denied degrees to women who had already passed the Ph.D. examinations. In response to pressure from women's groups and other interested parties, the Harvard Corporation created, in 1902, an entity on paper known as the Radcliffe Graduate School (Rossiter, 1982).

Students at Radcliffe studied under the same professors as the Harvard men and took the same qualifying examinations, but they were not given Harvard degrees. This policy did not change until 1963. Mathews's second-class citizenship manifested itself in myriad ways. For example, in Harvard's 1905–1906 catalog, the male students scheduled to take their qualifying examinations at the same time as Lois were listed as "instructors," indicating that they were allowed to teach and hold rank within the department. She was not. Perhaps there was small compensation in the fact that Lois received three scholarships specifically designated for women including the Edward A. Austin, Agnes Irwin, and Elizabeth Cary Agassiz scholarships. It is not known, however, how women's scholarships compared to the men's in terms of monetary value or prestige, but parity was unlikely.

Mathews enjoyed a good relationship with both Hart and Channing, with the latter serving as her advisor. She felt politically aligned with Hart, who was a former classmate and friend of President Theodore Roosevelt and once hosted the president during a visit to Boston. He was devoted to progressive causes, including women's education and the higher education of African Americans. He served as a trustee of Howard University and, at Harvard, recommended W. E. B. DuBois for Phi Beta Kappa honors (Hart, n.d.). She also grew close to Channing and spent time during the summer months at his vacation home on Cape Cod. Channing (1907) once referred to Mathews in a letter to Farrand (who also remained a longtime friend to Lois) saying she was "as entertaining as ever." Several years later she was excluded from attending his retirement tribute at the all-male Cosmos Club in New York and made her protest to such a policy known (Channing, n.d.; Rosenberry, 1918).

During the summer of 1905, Mathews studied with Frederick Jackson Turner in Madison. There she met President Van Hise and members of the Wisconsin history department for the first time. She returned to Cambridge in September, and in May 1906 became the first women to pass the Harvard University examinations for the Ph.D. degree in the department of history, economics, and political science. Her thesis on New England expansion was highly regarded and she was offered an assistant professorship at Vassar. She taught undergraduate courses in history and continued publishing in her field. Her major scholarly work, *The Expansion of New England*, published in 1909 and based on her thesis, was considered a classic in the field (Solomon, 1985). Almost 80 years later the work was still mentioned in a history lecture at Dartmouth (N. Hoit, personal communication, April 12, 1993). For the remainder of her life, the bulk of her historical writing was on the theme of migration and westward expansion.

In 1910, Mathews was appointed to the position of associate professor at Wellesley. She taught courses on colonial history and a special seminar, The Advance of the Frontier (Wellesley, 1910). From this post at Wellesley, President Van Hise recruited her to Madison. Mathews's negotiation with Van Hise revealed both her perceptions regarding the status and appropriate place of the dean of women on a coeducational campus and her commitment to intellectual work. The process also illustrated the vital role of strong male mentors for women attempting to break into previously all-male enclaves.

ON WISCONSIN

Unlike her predecessors Talbot, Breed, and Comstock, or even Lucy Sprague of Berkeley and Gertrude Martin of Cornell, Mathews was not the first dean of women on her campus. When President Van Hise went looking for a new dean of women in 1911, he searched for a strong and especially capable woman to replace the outgoing advisor to women, Cora Woodward. Woodward was not a scholar, and Van Hise considered her neither dynamic nor particularly effective because of her demonstrated inability to make student self-government as strong as he preferred (Curti & Carstensen, 1949, vol. 2; Van Hise, 1910a, 1910b, 1918).

Before Mathews

Wisconsin's first dean was appointed in 1897. At that time, Wisconsin was unusual in the amount of matron-supervised housing provided for women, so President Charles Kendall Adams was less worried about that issue than were his peers at other institutions. The faculty were concerned, however, with student behavior, the shift in campus climate from the "serious to the social," rushing, and rowdiness, especially among the men (Hague, 1984; Pyre, 1920). Demonstrating what was a typical response of the era, Adams appointed Anne Crosby Emery dean of women and assistant professor of classical philology. Her appointment was at "the urgent recommendation of the board" (University of Wisconsin, 1898, p. 12). Like Breed, Emery held both an undergraduate and a doctoral degree from Bryn Mawr, and she created a self-government association in Madison patterned after her experiences at her alma mater. Student rowdiness persisted, however. In October 1899, Ladies Hall (the women's dormitory) was broken into and several personal articles of clothing were stolen in what was a very early "panty raid." The women were quite affronted and threatened not to socialize with male students until restitution was made. Their stand was the first collective action taken by the self-government association (*Daily Cardinal*, 1899).

Emery left Wisconsin to become the dean of the Women's College of Brown University (later Pembroke) in 1901. Her reasons for leaving are unknown, but it was true that her position at Brown was exclusively administrative and she did not teach (Eisenmann, 1991). Although Emery was highly regarded personally, Adams was not enthusiastic about the position per se, and it remained vacant until Cora Woodward was appointed advisor to women in 1907 by Charles Van Hise (Curti & Carstensen, 1949; Troxell, 1948a). Woodward's previous experience was that of sorority director and she held no academic rank (Rosenberry, 1948).

There is no record of why the position went unfilled or Van Hise's precise reasoning for reviving the office (with a downgraded title) in 1907 except his general desire for student self-government and the typical association between such groups and deans of women. By 1911, however, Van Hise wanted the job restored along lines more similar to the Emery model, especially with regard to the dean's role as a faculty member (Rosenberry, 1948; Van Hise, 1918).

Coaxing Mathews to Madison

Van Hise devoted considerable personal attention to the matter of recruiting Mathews. One influential factor for his change of mind was a recent controversy on the campus regarding his commitment to coeducation. Van Hise was anxious to illustrate to the women of the community that he was supportive of their needs. As much as any university president of the era, Van Hise was an advocate of coeducation. In 1908, however, his commitment to the issue of women's education was challenged.

The controversy began in November 1907, when in a statement before an Association of Collegiate Alumnae (ACA) meeting in Boston, Van Hise declared that it was perhaps desirable if certain courses be taught in two sections, one each for men and women. He was not suggesting that women be excluded from any particular line of study, but rather that class discussion and course selection might be facilitated if the course were taught to a single-sex audience. Van Hise was concerned, like countless other educators of the era, by the seeming abandonment of the humanities by male undergraduates and the consequent "feminization" of the liberal arts college of the university. Many female educational leaders were equally concerned with the corresponding exclusion of women from scientific, technological, and vocational subjects, but Van Hise was particularly worried that men were losing their liberal heritage (In regard to segregation, 1908; Van Hise, 1907; Van Hise for coeducation, 1908).

In the early spring of 1908, Van Hise put his notion in front of the Wisconsin Board of Regents. Helen Olin, a class of 1876 graduate and wife of university regent John Olin, seriously challenged Van Hise and made a public issue of his remarks. In a pamphlet she published entitled "Shall Wisconsin University Remain a Co-Educational Institution," Olin accused Van Hise of favoring segregation of the sexes:

> Will our present Board yield to the prejudice of men who personally object to teaching men and women in the same class-room? Will they be misled by the argument that young men are now seeking an education in law, engineering, commerce, and agriculture, rather than in the classics, in ethics, or the modern languages, because they prefer not to enter the classroom with women? We think they will not, but they have the matter under consideration. (1908, n.p.)

In correspondence between Van Hise and Olin, Van Hise (1908) argued that his sentiments were "taken out of proportion" and defended his role as an advocate of women's education. In a letter to Mrs. Olin he wrote, "thruout [sic] my connection with educational work, wherever I have been, I have been a steady adherent of coeducation" (n.p.). Van Hise was aware of the university's checkered history with respect to women students and the strong anti-coeducation beliefs of former president, Paul Chadbourne. Van Hise was interested in avoiding ill will, so he publicly backed down and never again advocated segregated classrooms. In a protest response, Helen Olin (1909) published *The Women of a State University: An Illustration of the Working of Coeducation in the Middle West*, hoping to embarrass the president.

Just 2 years after this controversy erupted, the current advisor to women announced her resignation, and Van Hise seized the opportunity to bring in a different type of dean of women. He began his search for a new dean by writing to several colleagues at various institutions and making inquiries. Interestingly, Breed, Comstock, and Sprague were all brought to his attention as potential candidates, but by 1911 they were known more for their expertise in the work of deans, not their disciplines (Manly, 1911; Van Hise, n.d. [circa 1911]). Van Hise seemed determined to hire someone who was principally known as a scholar. He wrote later that, when searching for Mathews, he wanted the person he selected as dean of women to "have standing as a scholar in her field of knowledge, precisely as a member of the faculty whose chief function is instruction and research" (Van Hise, 1918, n.p.).

Van Hise wrote his friend, Frederick Jackson Turner, who was by then teaching at Harvard. Van Hise and Turner shared an interest in solving social problems using the tools of the social scientist embodying the "Wisconsin Idea" of intellectual service to the state and society (Curti & Carstensen, 1949, 1975; McCarthy, 1912). Turner had been quite influential on the Madison campus and was referred to as the "king-maker" for the role he played securing the presidency for Van Hise in 1903 (Veysey, 1965, p. 303).

Van Hise asked Turner about Mathews and said he wanted the new dean to teach at least one course so that she would have scholastic footing, but that her main work "would be as leader of the young women of the institution along all lines, scholastic, social, etc." (Van Hise, 1911c, n.p.). In a long letter, Turner discussed Mathews's scholarly record and once again revealed the reason an "Eastern" pedigree played such a significant role in the choice of a dean for a midwestern institution. In glowing terms, Turner recommended her as

> a woman of exceptional power and scholarship combined with real womanliness, sanity and poise. She has definit [sic] ideas and ideals, and would be likely to stand for them; but she is sensible. I know of no one whom I would prefer to her for the position of dean or adviser of women with work in the university class room, if she were willing to undertake it. I would be glad to have her in a history department with which I was connected. . . .
>
> She has social experience; . . . Mrs. Mathews is related, I believe, to the Boston Quincy family, but . . . she is not at all put out of sympathetic feeling for the middle west where she grew up. . . . She is essentially western with an eastern experience. . . . She is sufficiently good looking, well dressed, not dashing, talks easily and well and is a good listener. She has a keen sense of humor, is loyal, courageous, cool-tempered. She would not be a gentle figurehead, but rather an active force, but would do her work with tact and diplomacy, knowing how to get around an obstacle as well as how to face it squarely when necessary. (Van Hise, 1911a, n.p.)

Van Hise's original intention was to hire Mathews as Advisor to Women and Instructor in history at a salary of $2,500, but Mathews would not accept his offer unless the titles were changed to Dean of Women and Associate Professor. Changing her title from "advisor" to "dean" seemed to cause no consternation and Van Hise acquiesced on that point quickly. However, no woman had ever been an associate professor at the institution, and the history department was quite reluctant to agree to that title (Van Hise, 1911b). Van Hise was committed to the idea that the dean of women should have a joint appointment in an academic department, however, so he began to assuage the concerns of the history department, enlisting Turner as an ally. The department's initial response was that Mathews was qualified to be a dean of women, but they did not wish her to be an equal colleague or have her appointment interfere with the potential advancement of any man in the department. Dana Munro, chair of the history department, wrote to Van Hise:

> At the meeting of the Department on Monday it was voted that we desire to co-operate with the administration in every way possible, but that we felt that if Mrs. Matthews [sic] came here, she ought not to be in any way an incumbent upon the budget of the history department. Secondly, that while, of course, we should invite her to departmental meetings just as we do all of the members of the Department, including the instructors, that she ought not to have a vote in departmental affairs where instructors would not have a vote. In the third place, that the work that she might give should be arranged so as not to interfere with the work given by any of the other members of the Department. We would suggest that her title in the History Department should be that of Lecturer. (Van Hise, 1911b, n.p.)

Van Hise offered Mathews the title of Dean of Women and Instructor, but she persisted, demonstrating a keen awareness of the importance of title and status to achieving her goals. She argued that an associate professorship carried more weight with students and faculty and contributed to the dignity of her office. She pointed out that she had been an associate professor at Wellesley and did not want a position that represented a lower rank. She also noted that she might only spend a few years in administration and might choose to resume a full-time academic career and would need the rank of associate professor to secure her own future. When explaining why she did not relent she said, "If I were to undertake so great and serious a task as the deanship of women in the University of Wisconsin, it seemed to me it would be my first duty to make it in stature what it is in opportunity; and at the same time to try to make it an example to other universities in that regard" (Van Hise, 1911d, n.p.).

Frederick Jackson Turner once again went to bat for his friend and former student. With Van Hise's promise that Mathews's salary would not be taken out of the history departmental budget, Turner wrote to the chair of the history department offering advice and persuading him to give in to Mathews's demand with respect to title. Turner at first assured the history department chair that he had no intention of formally interfering, but wanted only to "offer a word or two" (Turner, 1911). He described Mathews as an "exceptional woman in the solidity and masculine quality of her judgment and ability to envisage a question; while she has the essentially womanly qualities that one demands of a woman." He went on to point out that the department would be politically savvy to accept her:

The case stands in my mind about like this—she would make the best dean of women that I personally know of and she is the most acceptable woman for a place in a history department of which I know. If I were in Wisconsin and had any right to advise—(which I haven't, of course), I should be impressed by the fact that if the president, and those regents interested, are convinced of the desirability of getting her for the administrative work, the department would gain, at no essential cost to itself, an additional member of the staff who would be exceptionally acceptable, when one considers what other women might be brought into a department. On the other hand, reluctance to accept the gift might not be wholly to the department's advantage—the matter of the good will and hearty support of the authorities if it were too sensitive in matters of detail.

I should also be impressed with this fact. The number of women's clubs, woman influence in the regents, and sentiment of the state, make it reasonably probable the pressure will continue upon the department to include a woman in a subject so generally interesting to the women of the state, and to the women in the university as history. I believe that sometime you will either take in a woman or continually resist pressure to that end, with resultant friction and departmental disadvantage. (Turner, 1911, n.p.)

Turner argued that acquiescing on the larger issue (a woman in the department) yet remaining recalcitrant on the smaller issue (title) only damaged the department. By late April 1911, with Turner's help in mollifying the history department, Mathews was hired as Dean of Women and Associate Professor, earning $2,750.

The history department that Mathews joined had a strong reputation despite the recent losses of Turner and Charles Homer Haskins to Harvard (Curti & Carstensen, 1949). George Sellery (1960), a former department chair of history, remembered Mathews as a good teacher and a contributor to the department, despite the limiting conditions they placed on her. She attended department meetings although her right to vote was restricted to issues that pertained exclusively to her courses.

Mathews believed that her teaching strengthened her position as dean because it provided her with a different view of students and students with a different view of her. She also believed that she gained a larger vision of the university by being part of the intellectual life and that this expanded vision made her a better administrator (Mathews, 1912). She taught on average 6 to 9 hours per week and supervised several senior theses each year for both men and women, but she probably did not supervise graduate students. The department obliged her to offer her version of the introductory survey course in history in reverse order (e.g., offering part two in the fall, part one in the spring) to serve out-of-sequence students and avoid conflict with the section of the survey course taught by a male professor. She taught in her general area of expertise, but the department also required her to develop a course on the history of the South despite her lack of desire to do so (Mathews, 1914b).

The Intellectual Dean

Between the time she earned her Ph.D. in 1906 and accepted her position at Wisconsin in 1911, her scholarly contributions were impressive, including one book, three journal articles, and an essay in a volume dedicated to Frederick Jackson Turner (Mathews, 1909, 1910a, b, c). The respected *Expansion of New England*, her 1909 book, was reprinted in 1936 and again in 1962. Despite her extraordinary promise as a professor, once again being a dean of women dimmed the scholarly potential of the woman who held the post. The combination of the toll taken by her administrative duties and the relative lack of status and support by the department slowed her scholarly pace in history after 1911. During her 6 years as dean of women, she published only three articles in her discipline (Mathews, 1913a, 1914a, 1918b). She never abandoned history completely, however. Almost 20 years after resigning from Wisconsin she published two additional articles, but the majority of her written work after 1912 was on the subject of women's education and deaning (Rosenberry, 1926, 1927, 1934, 1936).

Lois Mathews's intellectual bent made her quite comfortable with the sentiment of her peers, that deans should be experts on the education of women. For Mathews, however, that was a dean's "other" expert field; her first was her own academic discipline. One of her first efforts on campus coupled her skill as a historian with her desire to make female students feel they were an integral component of the university's intellectual community. She published an article in the campuswide *Wisconsin Magazine* on the history and purpose of women's education (Mathews, 1911). She went beyond a mere historical account, however, and declared in passionate terms the usefulness of women's higher education. For Mathews "usefulness" was connected to the social and political agenda of the Progressive Era and its emphasis on widespread social reform.

Mathews (1911) recognized the social ills of her era and believed that it would require the skills of both men and women to solve them. She wrote:

> Today, these problems are so great, so numerous and so intricate that men find themselves appalled before them. Women must lend their aid

whether they wish to do so or not. . . . This passion for service is not a monopoly by any means of the college-bred woman; but the college-bred woman has incurred the larger obligation by virtue of her larger opportunity. (pp. 7–8)

She concluded her article with her interpretation of the evolution of women's education up to her era of 1911:

The half-century of higher education of women has, then, brought forth out of dire necessity for self-support, out of sheer eagerness for intellectual food, out of sharp craving for individual expression, a loftier purpose of service for human folk of all kinds, a passion for learning as the means to that service, an ideal compromising the right of self-expression, a loyalty to every uplifting cause combined with an absolute devotion to some one specific task. (p. 9)

If service to the larger society was the goal of the woman graduate, the best preparation to fulfill that goal was a sound, rigorous, education (Mathews, 1916b). Mathews unequivocally believed that intellectual achievement was the *raison d'être* of college life. She wrote in a 1916 article:

No matter from what angle we view the college problem it will be found that the ultimate reason for having colleges and universities is the work of the classroom and the laboratory. From those centers must radiate the spiritual and intellectual ideals with which we trust our student bodies will be imbued; and in the last analysis all other interests must yield before the necessity on the part of the college or university to produce mental power in the student. (1916a, p. 69)

Therefore, women's education had to prepare women intellectually and, in so doing, equip them to be useful—in the home or work place—to themselves and society. But as dean she also included a nod to civility and propriety and the need to cultivate the right tastes (Mathews, 1915, pp. 160–161).

Mathews articulated some of her views in her dean's reports, thus formally sharing them with Van Hise and the board of regents. She wrote in 1912 that women's education was not merely a "duplication of men's education" (p. 209) and challenged the university to use its resources for the full development of women's possibilities. She recorded her goals more fully in her dean's report of 1914. She stated that there were three principles that guided her work: (1) to do all she could to develop the potential of women's education; (2) to secure for women the highest possible individual development; and (3) to develop in women the highest social responsibility (1914b, pp. 208–216).

In terms of activities for women, much of Mathews's work involved honing programs that already existed on campus or importing initiatives from elsewhere (Mathews, 1912; Rosenberry, 1948). Her skill was in refining or embellishing the programs and making them run efficiently. The two issues most closely related to her views on the purposes of women's education were the Women's Self-Government Association (WSGA) and the vocational conferences, and she devoted considerable energy to both endeavors (Allen, n.d.; Self-government is best training, 1911; Troxell, 1948b).

It was incumbent on Mathews to invigorate the WSGA, which actually began under Wisconsin's first dean of women but had been quiescent for several years (Rosenberry, 1948). She wanted women to evaluate themselves in terms of professional or intellectual accomplishments and was quite concerned that women students judged themselves according to a male standard that Mathews labeled "social availability," meaning sexual attractiveness (Mathews, 1915, p. 133).

Mathews (1913b) broadened the WSGA, however, in a way that was not typical of other deans. To further enhance organizational and leadership skills, Mathews encouraged the Wisconsin women to plan a midwestern conference of other university self-government associations. The heads of the WSGA wrote to all the deans who had participated in the 1911 Conference of Deans and Advisors of Women in State Universities and asked each woman to notify the head of self-government on her campus. The goal of the conference was for students to meet with and learn from each other and gain experience in cooperation and public speaking (Mathews, 1912; Rosenberry, 1948).

Establishing the annual vocational conferences was Mathews's second major initiative. Concern about vocational opportunities for women was rampant by 1912. Marion Talbot had introduced vocational conferences at the University of Chicago in 1910. Historian Margaret Dollar (1992) cites 1909 as the beginning of the vocational guidance movement when the ACA created their Committee on Vocational Opportunities Other Than Teaching. It was further spurred when the Women's Educational and Industrial Union in Boston began concentrating on college women in 1910. By 1913, there were occupational bureaus in Boston, Chicago, New York, and Philadelphia.

Mathews's contribution was bringing the issue to Wisconsin. The conferences began in the spring of 1912 to offer women alternatives to teaching careers—a problem Ada Comstock brought to her attention. As Mathews (1915) said, "College women have for at least half a century . . . gone almost without exception into teaching. . . . The enormous expansion of business has left teaching to the feminine part of the community because of the greater rewards offered men through professional life and mercantile enterprises" (p. 109). Her philosophy behind establishing the conference was outlined in her annual report to President Van Hise:

> The teaching profession for women is so "overstocked" that salaries are kept down to a mere living wage, save in rare instances where teaching is combined with administration. The opportunities for women in business, welfare work, in play-ground work, in charities and correction associations, and in all lines opened up by household economics and its allied subjects are almost numberless and as yet there are not enough trained women to fill them. (1912, p. 207)

The conferences were large undertakings involving 2 or 3 days of speakers, presentations, and social events (*Daily Cardinal*, 1912a, b, 1913a, 1914). Mathews brought in women professionals from a variety of fields including journalism, medicine, and library work, and famous social workers from nearby Chicago, following the lead of Marion Talbot. Mathews was especially interested in directing women into social service, which she defined as "Christianity applied to everyday living" (*Daily Cardinal*, 1915b).

President Van Hise agreed to open the first conference and, although he praised Mathews's efforts, he was a bit cautious and stressed that teaching was indeed a worthwhile profession and should not be totally abandoned by women (Chervenik, 1948). Helping women find appropriate and remunerative careers was a cherished goal for Mathews, perhaps because of her own experience of being widowed at a young age and therefore dependent on her professional skills for a livelihood. She successfully petitioned the university to hire a permanent vocational counselor for the women students. She also worked with alumnae in the Chicago area to form the Occupational Bureau to assist women in finding jobs. Mathews's initiatives at Wisconsin were so well received that in 1918 she was invited to be a keynote speaker at a vocational conference at the University of South Dakota (*Daily Cardinal*, 1918). The conferences were also popular on campus and male students soon agitated for the right to hold one of their own. While it is not clear if a men's conference came to pass, the vocational conferences for women lasted over 35 years (Chervenik, 1948). The conferences did not include teaching until 1917, when there were widespread teacher shortages. Not surprisingly, the 1918 conference focused on war-related work for women (Vocational Conference, 1918).

The entry of the United States in to the First World War in April 1917 brought about significant changes in Mathews's work. Predictably, women were left to fill posts vacated by men, who had "evaporated" from campus.[2] Mathews (1918a) immediately met with the head of the home economics department and organized summer school to teach women what they needed to be on a "war basis." Over 250 young women enrolled in the special courses; most of them studied first aid techniques, but many learned the professional skills necessary to do jobs now open to them on campus. The women ran the campus publications and business offices. They also rolled bandages, adopted French orphans, and organized a parade. Mathews posted the letters sent to her by women who volunteered for work in armed services or the Red Cross in Europe so that their friends in Madison could keep track of their whereabouts.

Between October 1917 and May 1918, Mathews gave 100 speeches and addresses throughout the Midwest on topics ranging from the history of Europe to what her office was doing for the war. She formed the Women's War Work Council and helped channel women into new types of professional opportunities in the larger society. She discovered that college women were in great demand, and she used her office as an employment agency to match students with employers. She encouraged women to resist their impulses and stay in college and complete their educations. In this regard, Mathews and Van Hise (1917) were in agreement. He spoke about encouraging young men to finish college and warned that if the United States sent all the college men to war, it would make the same mistake that cost England so dearly when the ranks of Oxford and Cambridge were depleted. In her last dean's report (1918a), she commented on the experience of the women during the war, stating that now that they had tasted the real world, they would demand even more from their university. They also demanded, and soon received, the vote.

Many of Mathews's other obligations were typical, not lending themselves to much innovation. She was responsible for women's housing and student discipline. She sat on numerous campuswide committees, where she often had authority only when issues before the committee pertained to women (Mathews, 1914b). Like Comstock, she was angered by the "humor" (which she thought should be more aptly described as "ridicule") aimed at the "coeds" in the campus yearbook. With permission from Van Hise she censured the *Badger* (the yearbook) for its derision of women and was criticized by the campus newspaper for her intervention (Dean of women censors Badger, 1912). She also helped set campus dance policy including, at one time, banning the notorious "Boston Dip" (Dean tabooes [*sic*] "Dip," 1912).

Mathews's approach to her routine duties was different from that of her predecessors, however, and in many respects she more closely resembled a modern student affairs administrator. She had a small paid staff and did not have to do everything herself, as Breed had, nor depend heavily on volunteers. Earlier, Comstock reported that she disliked the "mechanistic" duties and believed they could be shifted onto a secretary or assistant, but was never provided with one (Johnson, 1910). Mathews was more fortunate. She secured a staff consisting of an assistant to the dean, a stenographer during the academic year, a half-time assistant, and the mistress of both Chadbourne Hall (women's residence) and Lathrop Hall (women's building). She delegated the routine work to her staff and focused her attention on larger issues (Mathews, 1914b, 1916b, n.d.). While attending the deans' conferences, she noted that her situation in Wisconsin was admired, especially in terms of how much she was able to accomplish, by other deans who hoped to emulate her practice. Her office also became a training ground. By 1916, four of her assistants had resigned to become deans of women elsewhere. The practice of established deans placing staff in other dean positions was widely copied. Myra Jordan of the University of Michigan did it so regularly she was referred to as the "dean-maker" (Jordan, 1946).

BECOMING A FULL-FLEDGED PROFESSION

Mathews served as a model of a professional manager and a mentor to aspiring deans, both in Wisconsin and around the country. She invited aspiring deans to visit her on the Madison campus to learn about the job, the first dean of women to initiate such a program. One visitor was Agnes Wells, who entered the profession in 1918 at Mathews's urging and became an influential dean of women at Indiana University. Mathews also organized a statewide conference for all women deans in Wisconsin, including those from small colleges and normal schools, to coincide with the 1915 vocational conference on her campus. The meeting was so popular among the deans that Mathews organized two subsequent conferences as well (*Daily Cardinal*, 1915a, 1917).

Always the teacher, in the summer of 1915 she taught the course College Administration for Women for those wishing to enter the profession. The course, which she repeated in the summer of 1917, was the first of its kind taught in a public university and was offered concurrently with some of the first courses taught on the subject at Teachers College, Columbia University. Teachers College was the premier institution training women deans in a program that was a forerunner of modern student personnel programs. Under the leadership of Sarah M. Sturtevant, most of the research on deans of women during the 1920s and 1930s was generated from Teachers College.

Throughout her deanship Mathews had numerous public-speaking engagements, several of which were on the topic of women's education and the position of dean (*Daily Cardinal*, 1913b; Dean of women folder, n.d.). She published articles in local Wisconsin magazines and in the *Journal of the Association of Collegiate Alumnae* (Mathews, 1911, 1913b, 1916a). She was also a regular speaker at the conferences of the ACA and the biennial deans' meetings.

Her most lasting contribution, however, was her 1915 book, *The Dean of Women*, the first book ever written on the profession that eventually became known as student affairs. A second was not written until 1926 (Merrill & Bragdon). Mathews's view of the profession called for deans who were scholars, experts on women's education, and general advocates for women who expanded the social, vocational, and intellectual opportunities available to them. This book represented the collective wisdom of Mathews and her like-minded peers.

The book began with a lament about the lack of standardization in the profession and the fact that each woman was forced to create her position from scratch. Mathews's reason for writing was to address this issue and to stem the tide of what she believed was wasted energy by the constant reinvention of the wheel. Her book provided the type of information that the midwestern deans were sharing at the conferences.

The Dean of Women was essentially a primer in which Mathews recorded her views about the importance of title and scholarly achievement for deans as well as her practical advice on most aspects of the job. She provided a brief history of the position and, occasionally, discussed the difficulties and hardships of women students and faculty members in coeducational settings. For example, she discussed the antipathy of men, "open or veiled," toward women faculty (pp. 10–11).

Some of the text was taken from her previously written articles and reports, particularly those in which she discussed the value of the programs she was associated with at Wisconsin. She explained in close detail how one might establish a self-government association or a vocational conference. She also addressed issues of student discipline, social life, employment, and living conditions.

At more than 250 pages, the book was amazingly detailed. She said that a dean's duties fell into three categories: administrative, academic, and social. She often gave definitive and declarative advice. Of student government associations she said: "The relation of the dean of women to the association must be intimate but not dictatorial, advisory rather than mandatory, cordial but not familiar" (p. 139). As another example of the level of her specificity, when discussing the ideal size of a women's residence hall, she stated: "There is no question over this fact—that the hall must accommodate seventy-five girls if it is to be the ideal economic unit" (p. 47). She acknowledged that state universities must often house as many as 125 to 150 women in each hall out of sheer economic necessity. Under those conditions, however, "it is a good plan to have two dining-rooms in each hall, with accommodations in each for girls who shall come in from the outside lodging-houses for their meals" (pp. 47–48). She also stipulated that each dining room should be designed to serve 100 students.

She provided specific examples of by-laws and constitutions of women's organizations as well as sample forms and program announcements. It was not surprising that the book became the standard for the profession for many years and reportedly sat on the bookshelf of almost every dean in the country (Fley, 1979).

The Dean of Women was hardly a polemic. The only point on which there was even much discussion among her colleagues was the issue of deans as faculty members. Mathews's ardent belief in the needed intellectual competence of deans was perhaps the mostly strongly worded section of her book. She wrote:

> If the position of dean of women is to be of intellectual significance—that is, if a part of her fitness as a candidate is to be determined on the basis of the intellectual training and power of which she may be possessed; if she is to have professorial rank and offer courses of such quality as are offered by her colleagues; if, by virtue of her training, her ability, and her position, she is to be the leader in developing the intellectual life of the women students,—then she must properly diagnose the present condition of affairs and be ready to offer remedies, both immediate and far-reaching. A dean of women ought to be, as has been said earlier, so far as possible an expert on women's education in a coeducational institution. . . . If she has "arrived" in her profession as a teacher, by virtue of excellence in the actual work of teaching and of directing students in research, as well as by having put forth a piece of work which has won the respect of her colleagues, she is more nearly ready to take this place of intellectual leadership which it is important for the women student and for the institution she assume. . . . No glorified chaperon is able to fulfill this function. (1915, pp. 190–191)

Most early deans of women entered their jobs with academic credentials, but a few were questioning the idea that it was necessary to be both a faculty member and a dean. In reporting the results of her survey, Gertrude Martin (1911b), Advisor to Women at Cornell University, asserted that some women found "no inherent connection between their work as teachers and their work as deans" (p. 72). Martin believed that assigning deans faculty status was merely an attempt to raise the status of the dean's position rather than an essential ingredient to her work and it was difficult for women who felt they were only barely tolerated by the almost all-male faculties of their institutions (Rossiter, 1982). Even Mathews acknowledged the antagonism of male faculty members toward women, but she held firm that teaching was necessary. Martin (1911b), on the other hand, thought the proper role for a dean was as an expert in women's education. She wrote that a dean "must not be merely a scholar, but an educator with expert knowledge of her particular educational field" (p. 76). In fact, as was illustrated by the declining academic productivity of most deans, the dual role of faculty/dean proved too difficult to sustain. By the 1920s, only a minority of new deans of women entering the field had faculty jobs, a trend that presumably did not please Mathews.

A NEW ORGANIZATION

After 1910, deans of women had two organizations that regularly addressed issues of concern to them. Deans in midwestern state universities continued to meet at their biennial conferences and deans from all types of institutions were welcomed at the Conference of Deans held in conjunction with the now annual conventions of the ACA. During the years that Mathews was a dean, two important developments in the professional organizations occurred. The ACA exerted its influence to help increase the number and status of deans, and the National Association of Deans of Women (NADW) was formed. By 1920 it was evident that the ACA and NADW were serving two different types of women professionals.

When Gertrude Martin reported her research results at the 1910 Conference of Deans at the ACA convention, her findings on the waning interest in the dual faculty role worried Marion Talbot (Rossiter, 1982). Talbot realized that the strategy she had envisaged many years before—of women entering the professional world via sex-typical fields—had not paid the high dividends she had hoped for. While the job of dean of women had opened the door for women as a position inside the academy, it had not led to the further widening of opportunities. As Margaret Rossiter (1982) maintained, by 1911 "'women's work' no longer seemed as progressive a step as it had in the 1880s and 1890s" (pp. 71–72).

In 1913, Talbot presented the executive committee of the ACA with a list of suggestions on how they might pressure colleges and universities to improve the conditions for women on campus, especially fac-

ulty women, which included deans. Talbot suggested that the association toughen its own accreditation and membership policies to include
the presence of women on the board of trustees, the guarantee of housing for women, and—the most radical notion they put forth—the requirement that women faculty earn approximately the same salary as men of
the same rank.

Talbot also included the provision that institutions desiring membership must have a dean of women with rank above instructor, who gave
instruction and who counted as a regular member of the faculty (Holmes,
1939; Rossiter, 1982). This resolution met with resistance as the ambiva-
lence noted by Martin manifested itself more ardently. The deans at the
ACA meeting voted to strike the "give instruction" provision of Talbot's
proposal (Potter, 1927).

Even the resolutions agreed on by the deans posed problems. Such
edicts were difficult to enforce. Further, applying them rigidly would
have disqualified institutions that already belonged to the ACA, reported
Ada Comstock as the chair of the Committee on Recognition of Colleges
and Universities. The ambiguous wording of the resolutions raised
another quandary. For example, what does "presence" on a board of
trustees actually mean? However, the nature of the association itself
was the most vexing problem. It was an organization of alumnae and
not a full-accreditation body, so it had little leverage over institutions
(Rossiter, 1982).

In the end, the more meaningrful issues of equity for women faculty
were not resolved, but the resolutions Talbot put forth were nevertheless important. Many members of the ACA thought that their old mission
of opening college doors to women had been accomplished (Rossiter,
1982). It was time for a change of direction and the resolutions represented a new charge for the association—equity for women faculty. The
revised mission galvanized membership for the ACA and its successor,
the American Association of University Women (AAUW), for generations
afterward.

Also in 1913 Mathews attended her second Conference of Deans and
Advisors of Women in State Universities. Vocational guidance was a
prevalent topic of discussion, but so were academic matters. The deans
discussed curricular issues, including how to stimulate academic commitment among women students. The deans passed a resolution that
made their strongest case to date for deans as educational experts. They
wanted deans with academic backgrounds, but not necessarily disciplinary scholars. Like the deans at the ACA meeting, those who attended this
conference did not stress the teaching component of a dean's job despite
their insistence on intellectual attainment:

> That, recognizing the important responsibilities proper to the office of the dean of women, the Conference recommends that the universities select for this office, women, not only of fine character and personality, but also of high intellectual attainments; that they accord to this office the fullest possible recognition of its academic as well as its administrative functions; that to this end the dean of women be appointed to serve on such faculty committees as regulate the educational policies of the universities as well as those that deal only with the moral and social problems of women students. (Potter, 1927, p. 225)

The meetings continued. At the 1915 ACA convention, Mathews (1916a) gave the keynote talk, "Raising the Standards of Intellectual Life," in which she encouraged faculty to engage in more research and urged presidents to act swiftly to weed out weak courses. Her talk also focused on pedagogy and the appropriate use of lectures, introductory courses, and so forth.

It was clear that Mathews's interests were more in keeping with the ACA and in 1917 she was elected president, a post she held for 4 years and even after she retired from the University of Wisconsin. She was the first dean of women to serve as president since Marion Talbot resigned in 1897. At the 1917 ACA convention, the association voted to hold a joint meeting with still another group, the Conference on College Professors, Deans, and Women Trustees. The ACA continued to have its Conference of Deans and met jointly with professors and women trustees until well into the 1920s. The emphasis on faculty issues continued when the ACA became the AAUW in 1921, with Ada Comstock as its first president (Talbot & Rosenberry, 1931).

In addition to the meeting of deans at ACA conventions and the Conference of Deans and Advisors of Women in State Universities, another group of deans gathered in New York City. While attending summer school at Teachers College, this third group formed a new professional organization whose focus remained exclusively on deans.

In 1913, Anne Dudley Blitz, one of Comstock's successors at Minnesota, was feeling the need for formal training in the work of deans. She approached Dean James Russell of Teachers College in 1913, who looked "aghast" at her suggestion (Tuttle, 1996). However, by 1914 Teachers College began offering a professional diploma entitled "Dean of Women in Colleges and Normal Schools," which could be earned during consecutive summers in conjunction with a master's degree. Kathryn Sisson McLean (later, Phillips) was one of 26 women studying at Teachers College learning the "techniques of deaning" during the summer of 1915. McLean talked informally with four other women in the summer program, and they asked professor Paul Monroe to speak to them on the topic "The

Place in the Educational Scheme for Deans and Advisors for Women" (Phillips, Kerr, & Wells, 1927). They enjoyed the small discussion groups and decided to make the opportunities for conversation more formal. The students in the program were scheduled to return to New York the following summer to resume their study, and they began making plans (Schetlin, 1939).

McLean's ambition to hold a meeting of women with similar interests was spurred by her belief that deans had few opportunities to converse with one another (Past Presidents Association, 1941). Apparently she had never attended the Conference of Deans at ACA meetings or the conferences frequented by Mathews and her associates. McLean's absence from the conferences was illustrative of the geographical and institutional biases of the conferences and the women who ran them. In general, new deans in smaller, private, less-prestigious, or normal institutions were excluded. There were very few from outside the Midwest or Northeast and almost no women from the South (Bashaw, 1992).

As it happened, the National Education Association (NEA) was scheduled to hold its annual conference in summer of 1916, also in New York, so McLean wrote and eventually secured permission for her group to meet under the auspices of the NEA. The women held their first meeting in July 1916 and 200 people attended. The topics under consideration were not unlike issues discussed by the other groups of deans and included chaperoning, residence life, and the control of social life. The keynote speaker was Gertrude Martin of Cornell. Fifty of the women attending decided to form a new organization and elected McLean their first president (Phillips, 1953). This was the beginning of the National Association of Deans of Women (NADW).

In 1917, the NADW became a department of the NEA and held its second meeting that summer. The emphasis of the new organization was somewhat different from that of the other two gatherings of deans. The new focus for the NADW was on the appropriate training for deans. Its members no longer assumed that academic credentials were necessary and the movement toward deans' entering the profession with degrees in education (rather than in academic disciplines) began. By 1918 the NADW had adopted a charter and was a full-fledged working organization with various sections and branches. Plans for a journal began in 1919, but did not come to fruition until 1923 when the first *NDAW Yearbook* was published (Phillips et al., 1927). By 1926 it had a national office in Washington, DC, at the AAUW headquarters.

Between 1917 and 1921 the NADW met annually and the Conference of Deans and Advisors of Women in State Universities met biennially. It was not clear what overlaps in membership occurred between the two groups, but there must have been some. The records indicate, for example, that Comstock, Martin, and Talbot at least were speakers at NADW meetings. In 1921, the women attending the last Conference of Deans and Advisors of Women in State Universities voted for their organization to become officially part of the NADW, which thus became the exclusive professional organization for women deans (Phillips et al., 1927).

The ACA-cum-AAUW and the NADW were serving different women, although they maintained a cooperative relationship. Members of the NADW argued that they belonged to a "professional" organization concerned with standards and training for the profession. They believed the AAUW was essentially a lay organization open to any woman with a university degree (Morris, 1939).

The nature of what was appropriate expertise for the profession had changed. It was no longer necessary, they believed, to be an expert in the special needs of coeducation. Instead, the NADW advocated that deans should be counselors and experts in vocational guidance (Catton, 1956). Mathews had contributed to the status of deans and the literature on which the new profession was based. It was ironic that her vision of a dean who was also a scholar lost out to the newer vision of the profession, but she was certainly not opposed to the idea of deans acting as vocational advisors or academic counselors. Her articles and book assisted this new generation of deans in performing their tasks. Mathews probably would have thought, however, that the new role for deans as carved out by the NADW was limiting and not sufficiently intellectually challenging for her tastes.

Lois Mathews resigned from her post as dean of women in June 1918, although she remained on campus to teach in the history department for the 1918–1919 academic year while two of her male colleagues continued their war-related service to the government in Washington DC (Rosenberry, 1948). Her resignation was prompted by her marriage to Marvin Rosenberry, a Progressive Republican like herself, who later became the Chief Justice of the State Supreme Court of Wisconsin and was noted for enforcing pro-labor initiatives such as the 8-hour work day ("Marvin Rosenberry," 1960).

Mathews was remembered as both a good teacher and a leader among the women. Professor George Sellery (1960) commented in his memoir, *Some Ferments at Wisconsin*, that Mathews was one of the outstanding *men* in the department (p. 4). Like Talbot, Breed, Sprague, and Comstock, Mathews meant a great deal to the women students personally. As a member of the class of 1917 said, students felt as if Dean Mathews were their own "personal property" (*Wisconsin State Journal*, 1942). Not quite 2 years after she arrived, the students published a tribute to her:

In the short time that she has been at Wisconsin, Dean Mathews has accomplished wonders in making life more worthwhile for the women here.
For in addition to the intellectual and social benefits which every woman
should receive at an institution of this sort, she should also have the spiritual and moral stimulus which can come from contact with an older woman
who brings to her task the results of her wider experience of joy, of grief,
and of usefulness. (Dean L. K. Mathews, 1913)

Students remembered her as understanding, charming, humane,
friendly, and elegant. She was also recalled as a disciplinarian, but always
fair, in contrast with the less favorable memories of Mathews's successor, Louise Nardin (Teicher, n.d.). Students appreciated the fact that she
did not go about her work in a heavy-handed way, although she was
obligated to be a watchdog of propriety. "She was a modern woman of
the time. . . . She wanted us to be proper, but she was never silly about
it," commented a surviving member of the class of 1917 (H. Stephens
[née Reed], personal communication, July 20, 1992).

At a testimonial dinner in 1942, Mathews was remembered as giving
"the women a sense of importance" (Personal and educational contributions, 1942). Shortly after her death, the university named a dormitory
in her honor. The plaque read:

Mathews' instruction in history meant an incisive, stimulating exploration
of the New England past. For thousands of Wisconsin coeds, the Mathews
deanship signified new understanding and skillful, effective guidance. For
all young women reaching toward their birthright through education, Lois
Mathews represented intelligent leadership and high devotion to a high
cause.

She would have been honored to be remembered first as a faculty member, but would have hated that the inscription included the word *coed*.
Probably even more important to Mathews than such praise was the
realization that by the time she had resigned, the position had emerged
into a "definite administrative and academic office" (Mathews, 1915,
p. 28).

Chapter 7

A LEGACY ASSESSED

It was important to Lois Mathews that her office be viewed as a permanent part of the university's administrative structure. She did not want to see it disappear at the end of her tenure. Her fear was mostly unfounded, although "disappear" is precisely what happened to Marion Talbot's position at Chicago. However, by 1920 dean of women offices were *de rigueur* on coeducational college campuses. The quest for professionalization and permanence was complete, but to what end? What is the ultimate significance of this first cohort of deans for their students and for higher education? Assessing their impact requires an examination of their strategies, accomplishments, motivations, limitations, and perhaps most important, what happened after they passed the torch to the next generation of deans.

PROFESSIONAL DEANS OF WOMEN

What the first cohort of deans strove for provides a priori evidence of what they deemed important. In terms of the tangible manifestations of a profession, they sought paid work (rather than volunteer efforts) of sufficient amount so that the practitioner was able to derive her full income from her job. They developed a theoretical and intellectual basis, a defined area of expertise, sufficient status within home institutions to complete the required work, a knowledge base that was shared among practitioners and aspirants through published literature and professional meetings, and a professional organization. In addition, entry to the profession required graduate training. In the years prior to 1920, the educational preparation needed was the same as that required of aspiring faculty members—an advanced degree in an academic discipline. After 1920, however, the professional association recommended graduate training in specific disciplines (such as counseling or psychology) thought more in keeping with the growing emphasis on personnel work and encouraged participation in preparation programs such as those offered at Teachers College, Columbia University.

Appraising the motivations of the deans is a bit more speculative. Scholars such as Burton Bledstein (1976) have analyzed various groups of workers who sought professional status at the beginning of the century. However, Bledstein (and other examples of this literature) examined only male-dominated professions. He ascribed career mobility, the pursuit of authority, and the desire for middle-class status as primary motivating forces among those who strove to turn their occupations into professions. This catalogue of motivators has recently come under scrutiny recently by studies (especially feminist analyses) that focus on the growth of professions dominated by women (Dzuback, 1993).

The motivations of the deans of women resemble those in other feminized professions, not the more typical male-dominated ones. It is unlikely that this cohort of deans advocated professionalism solely as a means of entry to the middle class with an emphasis on individual financial gain. Available evidence suggests that the active participants in the process were already middle (if not upper) class in terms of family background. Nor could a convincing case be made that deans aspired to professional status exclusively for career mobility because there was very little career mobility *within* coeducational institutions. Deans who remained deans had little hope for advancement, and the position did not become a ready route to faculty status. Opportunities for interesting post-dean careers existed only outside the university, and it was not clear what role the former dean's experience played in securing subsequent employment. Ada Comstock moved from a dean's position to a presidency of a women's college, and Marion Talbot had a brief stint abroad as a women's college president after retirement. Lois Mathews and Mary Breed assumed leadership positions within secondary education for girls, but each for only 1 year. Lucy Sprague started her own college. Only Breed resumed a dean's role.

Rather, this cadre of deans wanted professionalization for different reasons, including, simply, personal fulfillment. These women were highly educated, ambitious, and talented, trained to enter a profession that they held in high esteem—university professor. Yet prevailing conditions prevented all but a very few women from having significant academic careers. Elevating the position of dean made the most of a second choice and eased the disappointment that accompanied the compromise of an unfulfilled academic life.

A second important motivation for deans was a sense of altruism and service, common in other women-dominated professions. One of the earliest historians of student affairs, William Cowley (1940), acknowledged that deans entered the profession out of "humanitarian impulses" (p. 158). Like other groups seeking professional status, the deans were interested in exercising authority over their "clients," the women students, but for reasons that went beyond mere status seeking. As Estelle Freedman (1979) noted, "the new female professionals often served women and children clients, in part because of the discrimination against their encroachment on men's domains, but also because they sincerely wanted to work with the traditional objects of their concern" (p. 518).

Perhaps their motivations, therefore, invite little criticism, but did these women accomplish what they hoped they might? Assessing the visions of Talbot, Breed, Comstock, and Mathews and their like-minded peers is at one level easy. The position of dean of women became a profession. Yet, on another level, their particular vision for the profession never fully came about. By as early as 1918, the new leadership of the NADW was backing away from a key ingredient—the simultaneous faculty role, which proved impossibly difficult to sustain.

Lois Mathews was an articulate and forceful advocate for deans of women to hold faculty rank. She argued in her book *The Dean of Women* (1915), that in an environment "where the measure of a professor's power and effectiveness both inside and outside the classroom came most largely through his [sic] intellectual attainments combined with his [sic] personality, it would be necessary for an adviser of women to hold a position on the faculty" (p. 10). She acknowledged that some university presidents (including her own president, Charles Van Hise) also looked for women of high intellectual caliber when appointing a dean. Mathews noted that if a woman held a faculty position in addition to her administrative responsibilities, her title was more likely to be "dean" than "advisor." In terms of professionalization, "the difference in nomenclature was most significant" (p. 11).

Yet, as a historian, Mathews was keenly aware, like her modern counterparts, of the vicissitudes women faced in obtaining faculty posts or securing promotion if employed. Women, if hired at all, languished on the lower rungs of the faculty hierarchy. This made the professorial life of a dean of women quite difficult. Mathews (1915) summed up the dilemma:

> But an obstacle was then encountered in the antipathy, open or veiled, to the appointment of women on faculties composed almost exclusively of men. Many institutions which deny stoutly any theoretical objections to women *per se* on faculties, when they go a-seeking new incumbents for positions do not make strenuous endeavors to have laid before their impartial eyes full lists of available candidates drawn from both sexes. The consequence is that men seem to be the only persons eligible and the ranks of new instructors are filled overwhelmingly from the male sex. Appointed under such circumstances, the new dean and professor had to make good

against tremendous odds in which personality and charm, valuable as these assets are, weighed out of all proportion to their real importance. (p. 11)

In fact, the discrimination against hiring women faculty at coeducational institutions was pervasive. Ironically, the very institutions that opened up graduate training for women allowed them to learn, but rarely hired them to teach. While on-paper qualifications (degrees earned, publications cited) entitled many women to faculty jobs, the "internal market"—referring to estimations about how she might "fit in"—disqualified her (Clifford, 1989). Only in women's departments might this not be true. For example, for those who were hired, home economics departments became a ghetto of sorts. Even women who had advanced degrees in other subject areas such as chemistry were relegated to home economics departments. By 1911, over 60% of all female professors at coeducational institutions were housed in one discipline—domestic science (Solomon, 1985). Otherwise, women were not perceived as colleagues by male academics fearful of loosing the prized same-sex solidarity within a department. Women candidates were avoided, not because "they had low prestige, but because they were outside the prestige system entirely" (Clifford, 1989, p. 8) and for this reason they could do nothing to help the department secure good new recruits.

Margaret Rossiter (1982) illustrated in her study of academic scientists that the Great Depression of the 1930s was especially taxing for women faculty, who had more difficulty securing a position and were laid off in greater numbers than their male counterparts. The proliferation of antinepotism policies made it nearly impossible for women married to faculty men to be hired by the same institution. As a result, there was still a stream of women entering deans' positions who had been trained as, but could not find employment as, faculty members. Even for those who continued to teach, such as Agnes Wells, who was both a mathematician and dean at Indiana University, the effect of an administrative job on a scholarly career during the 1920s and 1930s was just as deleterious as it had been for the early deans.

The history of the position of dean of women therefore leaves an ambiguous legacy for academic women. The dean/faculty dual appointment provided an entrée to the university for talented women, many of whom were unlikely to have been hired exclusively as faculty. That the early-20th-century deans had faculty credentials, and the accompanying cachet, contributed to professionalization. But in reality, the dean/faculty appointment amounted to a "subfaculty" position lacking both the prestige and the opportunity for genuine scholarly contribution that a full-time faculty appointment would have afforded. As a consequence of deans' not holding academic appointments, the distance between faculty and deans increased and eventually the faculty, even women faculty, "lost sympathy" (Sayre, 1950, p. 78) with the work of deans, just as Lois Mathews predicted.

Yet evaluating the first deans based on their failure to become the "entering wedge" for women into academia ignores their attainments as administrators. The deans themselves articulated their primary goal as improving the intellectual, social, and material life of women students. From 1892 to 1918 and within the limits of turn-of-the-century attitudes toward women in general and coeducation in particular, these deans of women did accomplish a great deal of that agenda. Their intellectuality and commitment saved the professional from, as Lucy Sprague's successor at Berkeley said, the "bog of discipline and decorum" (Antler, 1987, p. 111). It was their strategy, however, that is perhaps most troubling to their contemporary descendants—deans of students. The early deans built a separate, parallel women's community within the coeducational campus that began what is now a century-old debate: Do women thrive better in a single-sex environment, even a single-sex enclave within a coeducational setting? In such settings, will integration with men mean the loss of a power base for women and leadership opportunities? Or does a single-sex situation set up a separate (and perhaps not-so-equal or even artificial) environment that implies that women must be treated differently from men, protected and/or guarded? Does this ultimately inhibit women's successful integration into the larger society after graduation and contribute to their infantilization?

THE GREAT DEBATE

If the deans explicitly engaged the merits of this debate, they left no written record. Clearly the deans followed what Freedman (1979) identified as "separatism as strategy," almost as if there were no need to question what seemed so obvious. The separatism impulse was evident in the women's club movement as well as the founding of many women's colleges. Recognizing that women's needs could not be met in the male-run dominant campus culture, deans instinctively embarked on a plan to replicate male advantages in a correspondent system of clubs, activities, offices, and programs. They even created environments for women that did not have counterparts for men, such as Talbot's Women's Union and Comstock's Shevlin Hall. The parallel structure was consciously designed and desired; it was not viewed by the deans or the students as a default position or the lesser choice.

Separating the sexes calmed the uneasiness of critics regarding the unsupervised fraternization of young men and women. However, deans believed that women truly benefited from the sense of community that was created and the opportunities for leadership that extracurricular activities offered. Mathews (1915) explained her support of segregated activities: "The young men's standard of judging their fellow students among the young women is commonly that of social availability [sexual attractiveness], and that only. Young women judge one another by a quite different measure," one that encourages academic achievement and socially worthy activities (p. 160).

In response to the deans' encouragement, women students sought their own company. They joined local women's clubs and, where possible, made connections with professional women in the larger community. They spent a great deal of time cultivating female friends. Many women also worked in settlement houses or for other charitable organizations near the campus. They created women's pages for the newspapers and women's literary and dramatic societies, and developed their own rituals (Gordon, 1990; Solomon, 1985). They also created a culture entirely different from that of their male peers. Women's undergraduate culture had an "exuberance and independence," but not "the hostile edge of its masculine counterpart. . . . Women had not participated in the conflicts of the previous centuries and did not see themselves at war with their professors. . . . They took their studies seriously, and they did not cheat" (Horowitz, 1987, p. 197).

The Student-Government Associations (SGAs) were a significant component of the separate women's culture because they encouraged independent political activity among students. They taught students important lessons, including "negotiating, almost bargaining, with the college on behalf of their peer constituencies. On many issues—drinking, dancing, motoring, leaving campus, and other restrictions—such associations served as agents through which compromises could be reached" (Solomon, 1985, pp. 106–107).

Most deans of women and female faculty supported the practice of segregated activities, "believing that women brought special gifts to the university and had, in turn, special needs to be fulfilled" (Gordon, 1990, p. 43). It is important to note the distinction that several women educators made between forming separate women's communities and encouraging separate curricular opportunities, however. Women educators did not want a separate curriculum for fear that it would be deemed inferior. In this respect the argument the deans mounted played both sides of the gender issue, not unlike other women entering previously all-male professions in the same era. Analogously, female doctors lobbied unrelentingly for coeducational medical schools to ensure that their training was on a par with that for men. However, they also maintained that women should be allowed in medicine because of the special and unique gifts that women could offer. After 1920 or so, some educators began to soften their views about the curriculum and believed that women were indeed served by such women-oriented courses of study as domestic science (Freedman, 1979). Differences in employment possibilities and future social roles caused both male and female educators to agree that some forms of separate education might be desirable. Certain trends within the university, including departmentalization, specialization, and the growth of professional schools, made the task of compartmentalizing specific courses for women easier (Rosenberg, 1982).

The strategy of creating a separate women's community was generally not taken up by deans of women appointed after 1920. By then, America was on the precipice of becoming a very different society for most citizens, but particularly the White middle class. Victorianism waned and new social mores gradually dominated. Higher education changed as well. Normal schools became state teachers colleges, community colleges increased in number, and universities emerged as large, bureaucratic institutions enmeshed in the political and economic affairs of the nation. College life changed profoundly with the times, too. Historian Helen Horowitz (1987) demonstrated in her book *Campus Life* that the "world that undergraduates made" (p. 3) had cast off many of the vestiges of the separate spheres. The young men no longer resisted dating the college women. Both women and men enjoyed college for the extracurricular life and the social contacts. Dating, dancing, and rooting for the team were all the rage. As time passed, women found that some men were also open to accepting them as friends and classmates. Correspondingly, several women savored friendships and working relationships with men, which heretofore had not been a typical female experience. Such friendship or dating could lead to serious relationships and among the college women who married, several married classmates (Rosenberg, 1988).

For undergraduate women, the chilly climate warmed a smidgen. Most campuses had residence halls, sororities, and gymnasiums for women by the 1920s. Women were permitted to attend athletic events and before the 1920s were over, women were allowed to assume the quintessential role of women on the sidelines—cheerleader. For the most part, attempts to segregate women from men in the classroom were relegated to the past. The parallel female campus culture that earlier generations had created faded and the women students did not agitate for its return.

A form of postsuffrage acquiescence and lassitude pervaded among students and the women's community in general. The culture encouraged men to become more masculine and aggressive. The new feminism encouraged sexuality in women, and college women became more interested in exploring the possibilities. On campuses, men and women shared few intellectual or practical interests and did not participate in the same campus groups and clubs. However, men and women did enjoy each other's company at social occasions. So the double standard prevailed—men fought to keep women out of clubs, but coaxed them into rumble seats. Many women enjoyed the ride. For them, it was a significant step up from the days when men shunned college women altogether (Gordon, 1990).

Dating and heterosexual coupling became an essential aspect of college life for women. Horowitz (1987) asserted that between 1920 and 1960, the majority of college women seemed content to "glow in reflected light" (p. 208)—they sought not to be valued because of their own accomplishments, but rather to be judged by the achievements of the men they dated. Sadly, this posture among undergraduates is perhaps still more prevalent than many post-1960s feminist educators wish to believe (Holland & Eisenhart, 1990).

The relative lack of feminist agitation, however, should not mask the realities of inequity. Many of the concerns of the first professional deans were also issues for their successors. As some of the precious few professional women on campus, the deans of the 1920s through the 1950s continued the battles for educational and occupational equity for women students (Tuttle, 1996). They did not, however, choose separatism as a strategy, nor was their work couched in strong, explicitly feminist rhetoric.

Another reason for the rather dramatically rapid decline of the strong same-sex culture among women was an increasing social uneasiness with the sexual appropriateness of the situation. Concern with lesbianism was hinted at, although rarely stated explicitly.

The sexuality of women students has been of great concern to both critics and proponents of women's education. For critics of the first generation, the target was the lack of sexuality—measured in terms of low marriage and birth rates. Many women of that generation who did not marry lived in women's communities or same-sex relationships without stigma. Because unsupervised contact between men and women was so frowned on, young women lived in very homosocial environments during the Victorian era (Faderman, 1991). Women's colleges especially, but coeducational colleges as well, tolerated the practice of smashing—in which female students formally courted, dated, and established a romantic friendships with one another. College-educated professional women, believing that marriage and career were mutually exclusive, married less and had fewer children than their noneducated, nonworking peers. Often, such women lived in same-sex households, so common in the East that they were referred to as "Boston marriages." Turn-of-the-century society saw little wrong with the arrangements per se, and expressed concern only about the lack of progeny generated by these women (Nidiffer, 1998).

The personal lives of the early deans reflect the marriage-and-career dilemma typical of women of the Progressive Era. Marion Talbot and Mary Breed never married. Neither did Dr. Eliza Mosher, the first dean of the University of Michigan. Talbot had several close women friends and a deep relationship with Sophinisba Breckenridge. There was a brief mention in the Indiana University student newspaper of Breed's engagement, but she never married and it is unknown if she lived the remainder of her life alone or with friends or family (Breed-Brooks, 1903). Mosher seems to have lived most of her life alone.

Ada Comstock broke an engagement while she was at Minnesota and subsequently discouraged Wallace Notestein's attentions as well. While dean of Smith College, Comstock lived with a female companion, Florence Gilman, who moved with her when Comstock became president of Radcliffe College. The two lived together for almost 25 years in an emotionally and professionally supportive relationship. Comstock did eventually marry Notestein, however, in 1943 after her retirement from Radcliffe (Solomon, 1993).

Similar to Comstock, Lucy Sprague fell in love early in her professional life and agonized whether she could marry and fulfill her professional goals in education. She married later, but only after her husband-to-be, Wesley Mitchell, agreed to support her aspirations and dreams (Antler, 1987). Sprague was the only one among the women mentioned in this study to have children. Lois Mathews was the only one to have been married before she assumed her job. During her career at Wisconsin she lived as a widow but, on her marriage to Marvin Rosenberry, she resigned her deanship.

Collectively, the deans' lives offer evidence about women's beliefs regarding the incompatibility of professional aspirations and marriage to men. Primary relationships with women were possible, however. These same-sex relationships did provide companionship and intellectual camaraderie and emotional sustenance. Whether such relationships were lesbian in the strict physical or sexual sense of the term is unknown and possibly unknowable. Yet, because of prevailing social constructs regarding women, work, and marriage, these professional women imagined that the demands placed on them by men, the expectations of conventional marriage, and the possibility of motherhood were incongruous with their aspirations.

This situation changed markedly after World War I as social attitudes shifted, and women began to believe that marriage and career, at least prior to child-rearing, was possible. More and more deans of women were married while working. Lillian Faderman (1991), however, believes that this social change was not caused by the success of feminist arguments regarding the professional possibilities for women as much as it was due to strong antispinster attitudes that flourished beginning in the 1920s. The way society came to view Boston marriages changed. Educated Americans became aware of the work of Sigmund Freud and various sexologists who began to label same-sex relationships deviant, inverted, perverse, and even pathological. The innocence with which Boston marriages and smashing had been viewed was lost (Nidiffer, 1998).

Thus, for a variety of reasons, discrete women's communities on coeducational campuses receded, only to have the issue resurface in late 1960s and early 1970s. Some of the early scholarship on women's higher education history was critical of the deans of women and the separate campus structure they created (Conable, 1977; McGuigan, 1970). In addition to vague accusations of lesbian tendencies, it was believed that the separate communities established under the early deans led the university down the path of making policy "based on sex difference and different social roles" (Conable, p. 105). It was charged that the parietal rules and policies that limited the movement and freedom of women, but not men, were the ultimate outcome of the dean's initial strategy. Ironically, agitation to abolish parietal rules and different behavior standards for men and women occurred in the same era as women's studies programs and women's centers were opening on campuses, giving students and faculty members all-women enclaves once again.

In terms of enrollment patterns since 1920, the admission numbers indicate that women students preferred coeducation. Since the late 1960s, when the admission of women to all the elite universities was finally achieved, enrollment in women's colleges has slowed considerably (Touchton & Davis, 1991). Yet despite students' predilection for coeducation, several studies in recent years indicate that, at least in terms of future professional success, single-sex environments are more advantageous (Smith, 1988; Tidball, 1973, 1980, 1991; Tidball & Kistiakowsky, 1976). Psychologist Elizabeth Tidball (1980) demonstrated that women's colleges produced more "achievers"—those who demonstrated success in their chosen professions. She argued that the presence of women faculty and administrators and the lack of hostile climates allowed women to gain the experience and confidence they needed to succeed—and renewed the debate. Although aspects of Tidball's results have been challenged on both substantive and methodological grounds (Oates & Williamson, 1978; Rice & Hemmings, 1988; Stoecker & Pascarella, 1991), the cumulative evidence of all the studies suggests that single-sex environments are beneficial to women.

In terms of the benefits of the separate women's communities, two historical analyses have been sympathetic. Joyce Antler (1987) noted that creating an essentially separate-but-equal social life for women often reinforced the sexual status quo by making the separate spheres seem immutable. Perhaps that limited the choices for women even further. Yet the creation of a discrete "social structure . . . was a positive response to the pervasive sexism on campus" (pp. 98–99). Linda Kerber (1988) found that the separate spheres had a "double character" that both restrained *and* empowered women. Kerber said they were both "instrumental and prescriptive" (p. 26). In fact, the relative autonomy and fulfillment that the college experience provided prompted a more poignant question: "After college, what?" (Antler, 1980). The fiction written by women college graduates in which they describe their feelings is revealing. Often the tone of the "commencement chapter" is bittersweet, as if they know that life after college will be more limited and constrained (Marchalonis, 1995).

In the final analysis, the strategy the deans used was appropriate for the era and beneficial to the women students. It is perhaps understandable, however, why the next generations of deans did not follow the strategy of creating separate, parallel communities. While it is typical in patriarchal societies for male authority over sexuality and women's bodies to be used as a tool that controls and limits women's behavior, in America in the 1920s a new dimension was added—homophobia. A powerful weapon, it is used again in the modern era to discourage or frighten women students from majoring in women's studies, joining women's centers, or participating in women's athletics (Griffin, 1998). For the next generation of deans of women, a powerful stigma was now attached to female homosocial activity and a new, vibrant heterosexuality was encouraged. As a result, college life became more integrated for men and women and dating became an all-important activity. Unfortunately for women, they often had second-class citizenship on the gender-integrated campus. The sense of belonging that existed within the parallel communities at the turn of the century, as well as the leadership opportunities and the effective power base from which to operate within a coeducational environment, was lost.

PASSING THE TORCH

By 1918 and the formal incorporation of the NADW, most of the early deans had gone on to other things. Their "post-dean" lives included a variety of activities, primarily in the field of education. Only Eliza Mosher, whose first love was medicine, left the field altogether. With the exception of Alice Freeman Palmer (who was briefly the dean of women at the University of Chicago and who died quite unexpectedly in 1902), the other deans lived a relatively long time and continued contributing to women's education.

Marion Talbot retired from the University of Chicago in 1925 after 33 years as dean. She twice served as president of Constantinople Women's College in Turkey (1927–1928 and 1931–1932). Post retirement, she published her autobiography, *More Than Love*, and occasional journal articles in the field (Talbot, 1939). She died in Chicago at the age of 90 in 1948. Mary Bidwell Breed left Indiana University and served as adviser to women at the University of Missouri until 1912, when she accepted a one-year appointment as Associate Head of St. Timothy School in Cantonsville, Maryland. She then became the director of the Margaret Morrison College of the Carnegie Institute of Technology in Pittsburgh, where she was credited with elevating the institution from a trade school to a college. She retired in 1929, traveled extensively until 1935, and then made her home in New Jersey until her death in 1949 at the age of 79. Lucy Sprague grew interested in children's literature and the progressive education movements of her day. She founded the innovative Bureau of Educational Experiments in 1916, which became the Bank Street College of Education in New York City. She lived the last 19 years of her life as a widow and died in 1967 at the age of 89.

Ada Comstock became the first dean of Smith College in 1912 and became the president of Radcliffe College in 1923. She was credited with transforming Radcliffe into a nationally recognized institution and forcing Harvard to offer academic parity to its undergraduate women. She resigned in 1943 after Radcliffe was formally integrated into the Harvard community. She was also the first president of the newly formed AAUW, serving from 1921 to 1923, where she concentrated on improving academic standards for admission to the organization and creating the AAUW national headquarters in Washington, DC. She served on two important national committees. She was the only female member of the National Commission of Law Observance and Enforcement (Wickersham Commission) in 1929 and the National Committee for Planned Parenthood in 1941. After her marriage, she lived in New Haven, Connecticut, and continued to work for Radcliffe and Smith Colleges. She died at the age of 97 in 1973.

Lois Mathews married Marvin Rosenberry in 1918 and resigned as dean, although she taught at Wisconsin for one additional year. She was the last president of the ACA, from 1917 to 1921, and oversaw the merger with the Southern Association of College Women, which resulted in the AAUW. She was the director of the Madison YWCA from 1923 to 1925, a founder of the International Association of University Women, and, during the 1928–1929 academic year, the acting principal of the National Cathedral School for Girls in Washington, DC. In 1931, she co-authored a history of the AAUW with Marion Talbot. She also continued to publish in her discipline of history, albeit in a limited fashion. She lived the rest of her life in Madison, active in many civic organizations. At one time she was president of the Madison Civics Club and the Madison College Club, and the director of the Neighborhood House. She died only few months after her husband in 1958 at the age of 85. (See Chapter 6, Note 1.)

After their tenure as dean, most of the original cohort were not active in the National Association of Deans of Women, only giving occasional talks. Instead, the original cohort participated in the AAUW. Most of their successors, however, preferred to belong to the NADW. While the post-1920 deans had to wage many of the same battles as the early deans, they mounted their fights as administrators and personnel workers, rather than from the dual post of faculty member/dean. Deans who did not have faculty appointments found the AAUW less relevant. Most saw the AAUW as a lay organization open to all college-educated women, while the NADW was their true professional organization (Tuttle, 1996).

THE NADW

By the 1920s, deans of women not only had the trappings of a profession but also had a critical mass of practitioners. The *Educational Directory* of 1925 indicated that 302 deans of women were employed in colleges and universities (Hatcher, 1927). The number of courses of study dedicated to training deans was growing. In addition to Mathews's course at Wisconsin and the program Teachers College, Agnes Wells was teaching two courses at Indiana University by 1923, and Thyrsa Amos taught at the University of Pittsburgh (Haddock, 1952). Other universities followed suit soon thereafter.

Interestingly, two books were published in the 1920s that listed "dean of women" as an available professional option: Catherine Filene's (1920) *Careers for Women* and O. Latham Hatcher's *Occupations for Women* (1927). Filene's book listed Mathews's *The Dean of Women* (1915) as required reading and echoed Mathews's view on the importance of teaching. By 1927, however, Hatcher's description of the position made no mention of teaching duties.

After the end of World War I, the leadership of the new profession was firmly in the hands of the NADW, which for the first 25 years was led almost exclusively by women whose background included a degree from an eastern women's college, a position in a prestigious midwestern university, a diploma from the Teachers College preparation program, or, most often, some combination of the three (Bashaw, 1992). Race was an additional characteristic they held in common, reflecting the racism of almost all professional organizations of the era. The leadership of the NADW was comprised solely of White women. The early history of the NADW with respect to African American deans is both demoralizing and all too typical. The organization displayed a formal disregard of and insensitivity toward its African American members, despite the efforts of individual White women to bring about change (Brett, Calhoun, Piggott, Davis, & Bell-Scott, 1979).

Exclusion of African American Professionals

A relatively small number of African American students during the late 19th and early 20th centuries were educated in northern institutions, but the majority attended what are now regarded as the Historically Black Colleges and Universities (HBCUS). Professional opportunities for African American women were virtually nonexistent at predominantly White institutions until well into the 20th century (Noble, 1988; Perkins, 1988). So it was not surprising that the first African American dean of women, Lucy Diggs Slowe, worked at Howard University (Anderson, 1989). Slowe assumed her position in 1922 and from the beginning of her career she defined herself not as a matron, but as an expert in women's education. Like her pioneering White counterparts, Slowe was concerned about the effect of the curriculum on women, the paucity of vocational options, the undesirable living conditions, and the particularly restrictive social rules placed on women that were typical of historically Black institutions during the 1920s and 1930s. She was dedicated to making a viable women's community on Howard's campus. Unlike many other deans, however, Slowe was also an activist and an "instinctive" feminist (Anderson, 1989).

Slowe was a firm believer in the power of women's organizations and the importance of communities of women. As an undergraduate at Howard, from 1904 to 1908, Slowe founded Alpha Kappa Alpha, the first Greek-letter sorority for African American women. In 1924, she became the first president of the National Association of College Women (NACW), an organization for African American women that closely paralleled the

AAUW, whose restrictive practices made most African American women ineligible for membership. In 1922, Slowe became the first African American woman to join NADW. Eventually, the NACW became the National Association of University Women and merged in 1954 with the National Association of Personnel Deans of Negro Educational Institutions, an organization for both men and women (Davis & Bell-Scott, 1989).

While the NADW did not formally exclude African American women from membership, their practices effectively eliminated participation. It was customary of the NADW to hold their annual meetings in restrictive hotels, which meant that African American women were neither accommodated nor served meals (Brett et al., 1979). Slowe constantly protested this policy, but it did not change. In response, she gathered her peers at a Conference of Deans and Advisors of Women on Howard's campus in 1929. The conference was run under the auspices of the Standards Committee of the NACW until 1935, when it became an organization in its own right, the Association of Deans of Women and Advisers to Girls in Negro Schools (ADWAGNS). Slowe provided vital leadership from the first conference in 1929 until her death in 1937 (Brett et al, 1979).

The purposes and goals of ADWAGNS were quite similar to those of the NADW. It sought better conditions for women students and more professional opportunities for women deans. Slowe's death left a leadership vacuum that was filled by Hilda Davis, who had joined the NADW in 1932, possibly only the second African American women to do so (Brett et al., 1979). Davis also felt affronted by the NADW practice of holding meetings in restricted hotels and organized a protest by African American deans, of which there was a growing number by 1938. However, it was not until after 1954 (when the Supreme Court ruled in *Brown* v. *The Board of Education of Topeka Kansas*) that the NADW voted formally to meet only in hotels that complied fully with integration laws. By the late 1960s and early 1970s, African American women had administrative positions in predominantly White institutions in slightly greater numbers; they also gained, for the first time, leadership positions within NADW, which had changed its name to the National Association of Women Deans, Administrators, and Counselors (NAWDAC) (Brett et al., 1979).

Marginalization

Although by 1920 the NADW was a full-fledged professional organization led by women with impressive credentials, because it represented a women-dominated profession, attending to issues typically ignored by men, it suffered from a lack of prestige. As a consequence of this phenomenon, the leaders of the NADW concentrated much of their work during the 1920s and 1930s on further defining the profession and improving the public's perception of the work that deans accomplished. The new organization's commitment to defining the parameters of the profession began with the master's thesis of Kathryn Sisson (McLean) Phillips, the first president of NADW (Phillips, 1919; Sayre, 1950).

The primary vehicles for public education, as well as professional development for members, were the NADW-sponsored publications. In 1923 the organization began publishing the *NADW Yearbook*, which recorded the business of the organization and contained copies of papers delivered at annual meetings. In 1926, the NADW supplemented the *Yearbook* with the *Bulletin*, a monthly publication that reprinted research reports commissioned by the association. While the preponderance of the material in the two publications was the findings of research projects, one quarter of the space was dedicated to the issue of improved public perception (Bashaw, 1992).

Much of the early research on the profession was at the instigation of Professor Sarah Sturtevant of Teachers College and her colleague, Ruth Strang, and focused on defining the qualifications and duties of a dean. Sturtevant, Strang, and the leadership of NADW commissioned, sponsored, published, or wrote numerous publications between 1925 and 1940. One of their first efforts, published by the Press and Publicity Committee of the NADW, was *The Vocation of Dean* by Ruth Merrill and Helen Bragdon (1926) of the Harvard Graduate School of Education. The authors conducted survey research, identified the categories of duties for a dean, and compiled a list of desirable qualifications. The list of 64 characteristics was remarkable in its expectations. For instance, the ideal dean needed sound administrative skills (insight, resourcefulness, logical habit, judgment, analytic ability), impeccable personal qualities (tact, patience, honesty, courage), and attributes appropriate to women (sympathy, amiability, motherly interest, good Christian character, refinement). The list also recommended that she have a graduate degree, teaching experience, expertise in women's education, a driver's license, and the ability to play golf (Merrill & Bragdon, 1926).

Two years later, the NADW president, Dorothy Stimson, appointed a committee to construct a formal statement of qualifications. This list of qualifications was more reasonable than that of the Merrill and Bragdon (1926) study, and it reflected the shift of the profession toward counseling and what was termed "personnel work." The 1928 committee believed the most important qualifications were graduate study in the philosophy of education, sociology, psychology, and human physiology (Bashaw,

1992; Sayre, 1950). Subsequent publications came regularly after 1928, all on the same theme of defining the duties, qualifications, and roles of deans (Acheson, 1932; Jones, 1928; NADW, 1950; Pierce, 1928; Stimson, 1930; Sturtevant & Hayes, 1930; Sturtevant & Strang, 1928; Sturtevant, Strang, & Kim, 1940; Wells, 1930). One exception to the trend was the first book on the history of the position, published in 1939 by Lulu Holmes.

The content of the books in this spate of publications had much in common and it was clear that *student personnel* had been substituted for the term *deaning* to describe the work. Deans were still expected to be experts in women's education, but the desired expertise was generally in counseling and guidance. In 1938 the *Yearbook* and *Bulletin* were combined into the *Journal of the NADW*, which became the official publication of the association. A new theme that appeared in the NADW literature was an awareness of the increasing numbers of other professionals on campus involved in student personnel work, including deans of men.

THE DISAPPEARANCE OF THE DEAN OF WOMEN

The beginning of the end of the position of dean of women was the creation of the position of dean of men. On most coeducational campuses, a dean of men was appointed after the position of dean of women (Clark, 1922), occasionally as the result of her prompting. Both Comstock (1910) and Mathews (1915), for example, believed that their work in managing the social life of women students would benefit from having someone controlling the men. Thomas Arkle Clark, who served as an administrator at the University of Illinois from 1901 to 1931 (from 1909 onward as the official dean of men), was considered the father of the movement (Fley, 1979).

The duties of the dean of men were not unlike those of a dean of women, although there was rarely the same moral overtone to their responsibilities. The men were also less inclined to professionalize as quickly as the deans of women (Tuttle, 1996). Deans of men met informally for the first time in 1919 when Scott Goodnight, who worked at the University of Wisconsin from 1916 to 1945, invited his peers to Madison for a meeting, much as his colleague Lois Mathews had done earlier. Clark invited the group to the University of Illinois for a meeting the subsequent year, and the National Association of Deans of Men (NADAM) met regularly thereafter but formally incorporated only in 1929 (Tuttle, 1996). NADAM, like NADW, was concerned that faculty did not understand or respect their work. In 1931 they established a committee to define the duties and characteristics of deans of men (Gardner, 1934).

As early as 1940, the various professional groups attempted to band together under one professional organization, but in many respects the practitioners came from different points of view and integration was unlikely. William Cowley (1940) described the three traditions working in student affairs by 1940: the humanitarians, who were often academicians and served as advocates for students; the administrators, dedicated to greater efficiency and a business ethos; and the psychologists, using the techniques of testing and guidance (see also Tuttle, 1996). In many respects the same three strands are observable today in student affairs. The early deans of women and men were absolutely of the humanitarian tradition, while the post-1920s deans of both genders were just as likely to be trained as counselors and guidance experts. However, deans of men gradually incorporated the business/efficiency aspects of the profession to a greater extent than did women.

The name changes of the organizations for both deans of women and men reflect their history. From the humanitarian and advocate-for-women tradition of NADW, the increasing emphasis on counseling was reflected in a name change in 1956 to the National Association of Women Deans and Counselors. There was a slight change again in 1973 to the National Association of Women Deans, Administrators, and Counselors and finally to the National Association of Women in Education (NAWE) in 1991. The shift in the men's organization is even more telling. With a focus on senior administration, NADAM became the National Association of Student Personnel Administrators (NASPA) in 1951. The psychological and counseling tradition is best represented in the American College Personnel Association (ACPA) (Tuttle, 1996).

By the mid-1940s, there was a growing concern that deans of women were being eased or forced out of their positions while deans of men were being promoted. In 1946, Sarah Blanding noticed that colleges were increasingly placing men, often the dean of men, in charge of counseling and guidance and reducing the dean of women to a "secondary officer" (p. 148). Typically, deans of women who were dismissed or demoted were told that such an action was in the name of efficiency. Ruth McCarn of Northwestern University spoke at the 1948 NADW convention about why she was fired: "I am one of the disappearing deans," she said, and it was done "for the good of the administrative set up" (Tuttle, 1996, p. 1). Alice C. Lloyd (1946), dean of women at the University of Michigan, summed up the problem succinctly. Not only were deans of women losing their jobs, or at minimum their power within the institution, but women students were losing their advocates:

Still more disquieting has been a trend on many coeducational campuses
to abolish the office of the dean of women in favor of a dean of students
(always a man) with a counselor of women under him. In every instance
where this has occurred, and there have been many, the position of women
has diminished in salary and in prestige. There are not many women on
university faculties and in university administration to defend the position
of women. (p. 133; see also, Tuttle, 1996, p. 1)

The tremendous growth in personnel administration exacerbated the
phenomenon that Deans Blanding, McCarn, and Lloyd noticed. The proliferation of specialties within the field of student affairs meant that
universities hired separate professionals to administer the housing programs, look after Greek-letter societies, provide academic or career
counseling, and manage a host of other areas. The situation looked unwieldy to many. Deans of men made the case to university presidents that
a reorganization should be completed in the name of efficiency. The
change in campus organizational structure as a result was noticeable.
Early deans of women and men typically held equivalent positions on the
organizational chart and both reported directly to the president. A survey conducted in 1936 found that 86% of deans of women still reported
to the president (Whitney, 1964). A 1962 survey found that less than 30%
of deans of women continued to report to the president (Whitney, 1964).
For almost 20 years the dean's position was demoted or eliminated on
campuses all over the country. In 1968, Elizabeth Greenleaf, one of the
first women presidents of the American College Personnel Association,
summed up the situation: "During the past few years, there has been a
major reorganization of student personnel positions on campus after
campus. When this takes place, most often a major problem is how to
reassign the Dean of Women. She is left either as Director of Women's
Education . . . or she is given an undefined job as a general administrator. Rarely are women in our profession given a real functional responsibility" (p. 225).

Within the professional literature arguments went back and forth
about the future of the deans. At their core, the arguments both for and
against were rewordings of the continuing debate within women's education. Opponents of the position maintained that it set women apart
and prevented their full integration into the life of the campus. Others,
responding primarily to stereotypical ideas about deans as morality
monitors and disciplinarians, thought the title and position archaic.
Those in favor cited evidence that women students continued to avail
themselves of the services of the dean. Still others were worried about
the absence from campus of anyone particularly looking after the interests of women and expressed concern that, if this position were elimi-

nated, there would be no women in senior administrative positions on the campus (Gillies, 1975; Kinnane, 1967; Offenberg, 1967; Whitney, 1964). Only in veiled terms did anyone suggest that efficiency was perhaps a smoke screen behind which deans of men wrested power away from deans of women.

The clarion call of efficiency proved quite powerful and by the mid-1970s there were relatively few deans of women on public coeducational campuses. The prevailing model became the Dean of Students, now often titled the Chief Student Affairs Officer (CSAO). The CSAOs were in charge of a staff of various subspecialists and they were overwhelmingly male. By the early 1990s, less than 20% of the most senior administrators in student affairs were women (Touchton & Davis, 1991).

ANACHRONISM OR UNMET NEED

In contemporary higher education the term *dean of women* seems anachronistic. The title certainly sounds antiquated and conjures up images of older, matronly, cantankerous women, determined to keep college students from fully enjoying campus life. The type of student for whom the dean's position was originally created—the traditionally aged, full-time, female student—accounts for less than 20% of all postsecondary students in America. The growing student populations are the older, increasingly urban part-timers with significant family and work responsibilities. They depend less on campus-run activities than in the past and seek different types of services to meet their changing needs (C. Forrest, personal communication, July 1997). Only on the more traditional and frequently elite campuses does the popular image of campus life maintain a significant presence.

Is there a place in a modern coeducational university for a dean of women? It is true that many of the functions historically performed by deans of women, such as housing, career advising, discipline, and health care, are executed by various student affairs professionals of both genders. But to assume that such functions were the sine qua non of the work of pioneers such as Palmer, Talbot, Breed, Comstock, Sprague, Martin, Jordan, and Mathews is to ignore the historical evidence. What drove the pioneering deans to create a new model for the role was a desire to address the inequities in coeducational environments, build communities, and attend to the intellectual development of women students. While deans did attend to the basic needs and acted as disciplinarians, they did so because it was necessary to build a foundation upon which they could work toward their higher goals.

There is no shortage of evidence to suggest that while the coeducational campus may be more welcoming than it was in 1900, it is still a "chilly climate" for women (Hall & Sandler, 1982; Sandler, Silverberg, & Hall, 1996). By way of illustration that caustic attitudes are not completely relegated to the past, a recent compendium of quotes concerning women included a 1985 quip by Kurt Vonnegut: "Educating women is like pouring honey over a fine Swiss watch. It stops working" (Vonnegut, 1991, p. 200). There is still a need to help women combat the effects of sexism, achieve intellectual parity, and find a community on campus. If the work of a dean, in the tradition of the pioneers, is needed, perhaps it is being accomplished today by new types of professionals such as the heads of women's studies programs and the directors of women's centers.

When deans of women left their positions, a void was created. As one director of a women's center noted, "Lost in this shuffle was a sense of identity for women students, someone with whom they could talk about issues directly affecting them and not generally affecting their male peers" (Brooks, 1988, p. 18). Women's centers generally came about as a "natural response to the . . . unmet needs of women. Acknowledging the extent and the depth of discrimination against all women, campus women's centers were created to raise and examine new questions about women's lives, roles, and expectations; to help women develop a feminist consciousness; to combat feelings of isolation; and to establish a sense of community among women" (Gould, 1989, p. 219).

The published mission statements of both women's centers and women's studies programs illustrate that, at their core, they are not dissimilar to the vision of the early deans. For example, the University of Michigan's Center for the Education of Women states that the center was established "to help women enter and stay in the mainstream of education and professional preparation, to lower institutional barriers to the equal participation of women, and to conduct and disseminate research about women's lives" (see http://www.Umich.edu/~ceul). In a similar vein, the women's center at the University of Pennsylvania, "unlike most university offices, provides services for . . . students, faculty, staff and community women . . . and has an explicitly advocacy function" (see http://pobox.upen.edu~/pwc). These centers are also the physical location on campus where women gather, not unlike the Women's Union at the University of Chicago, Shevlin Hall at the University of Minnesota, or Lathrop Hall at the University of Wisconsin.

Women's studies departments and programs also speak to women's needs, especially their need for full intellectual equity with men on campus. As Peggy McIntosh (1989) of the Wellesley Center for Research on

Women stated, "Further institutionalization of women's studies is our best present hope for meaningful education of women as well as men, for it is the only area of the curriculum in which women's existence is fully registered" (p. 402). If neither women's centers nor women's studies departments existed on campus, it is difficult to imagine who would attend to women's special needs.

Concurrent with the establishment of women's centers and women's studies programs was the explosion of the modern women's movement onto American campuses for faculty, students, and administrators alike. As a result, modern women's center directors and programs heads are usually unabashedly feminist, while the early deans were much more cautious. The absence of feminist discourse among the deans must be considered within the context of their era and positions within the university. The political reality for deans of women in the early 20th century was that they were marginalized as both women faculty members and administrators on male-dominated campuses. Their personal marginalization was compounded by the fact that their constituency was female students, a group not especially prized by the administration or the faculty or even other (male) students. Although these deans grappled with issues that today would be labeled "feminist," most were reluctant to use that word to describe themselves.

The term *feminist* implied participation in public discourse, an aggressive demeanor, or radical beliefs (Antler, 1987; Mathews, 1915). Also, feminists were thought to be the outspoken champions of women's rights, especially the right to vote. Despite the fact that the deans were advocates for women during an era when suffrage was clearly on the national agenda and on the minds of many college women, they were remarkably and maddeningly silent. Many women educators were afraid that if the "vote came too soon it might jeopardize the newly won gains of women within higher education" (Antler, 1987, p. 111). They believed they had a great deal to lose if, by being identified with a controversial political issue, they or their "clients" were further marginalized or subjected to even greater amounts of antagonism. The deans remained taciturn.

Despite the reluctance of the early deans to label themselves feminist, their ideas, goals, vision, and even some of their strategies, long ago rebuffed, are now seen as important by the feminist constituencies within higher education. Today, while a person with the title of dean may not be needed, someone with her agenda most assuredly is. Perhaps no more evidence is needed than noting that within days of being obligated to coeducation, the Citadel appointed its first dean of women (First dean of women, 1997).

We can and should learn from the remarkable women who, nearly a century ago, pioneered an essential role on coeducational campuses. Lois Mathews Rosenberry (1927) provided a compelling justification for a dean and her work:

> First of all, let us answer the question, Why have a dean of women at all? The answer is, to give to the women students individually and collectively the leadership and inspiration which the best kind of woman alone can give; to give to women students the example and guidance the best sort of president of the college or university gives to the men students. Young women do not look to a man for personal leadership, they look to a woman who not only represents in every way what they most admire, but is capable of leading them on to higher levels of achievement in their personal lives, to rousing in them ambitions which were latent or only half-developed. The women's college provides such leadership in women like Presidents Pendleton, Wooley and Thomas. The state universities must depend upon the dean of women for such leadership if their body of women students is to have it at all. The capacity for outstanding leadership is then the first and greatest qualification of the woman you select for the position of dean of women. The next thing is to make possible the conditions for such leadership. (p. 206)

NOTES

CHAPTER 2

1. Prior to the Civil War, the study of some sciences and engineering was considered less demanding and rigorous than the more formal classical curriculum. At Harvard and Yale, students who studied science—in scientific schools only tangential to the campus, not central—were awarded the lesser Bachelor of Science degree in lieu of the Bachelor of Arts.

2. Barbara Miller Solomon (1985) identified the initial three generations of students: the first generation attended from 1870 to 1889; the second from 1890 to 1909; and the third from 1910 to 1930. She argued that there were important distinctions among the three generations, but especially between the first and second. Lynn D. Gordon (1990), on the other hand, stated that there were only two generations, one from 1870 to 1890 and a second one from 1890 to 1920. She argued that there were fewer distinctions between the two groups than had been depicted by other historians. In either case, the first generation was characterized similarly by both historians.

3. Charles Van Hise of Wisconsin received massive criticism, including the public anger of the wife of a prominent regent, for his suggestion of gender-segregated classrooms; William Rainey Harper and the faculty of Chicago discovered that operating separate facilities was too costly; Stanford imposed a quota on the number of women admitted, which lasted for a few decades but was eventually overturned; and the decision at Wesleyan to return to an all-male college was not sustained for long.

4. Future President of the United States and Williams College graduate James A. Garfield apparently uttered this aphorism in 1871 at a meeting of Williams College alumni during the last years of Mark Hopkins's presidency of the college. For how this utterance came to be a symbol for the American liberal arts college, see Rudolph (1956).

CHAPTER 4

1. Breed's letter to Swain is lost, but his reply refers to her letter, "In answer to your letter of June 24th permit me to say that it is designed that the Dean of Women shall be a member of the faculty" (Swain, 1901a, July 1).

CHAPTER 5

1. The conference in 1905 was labeled the First Conference and the meeting in 1907 was billed as the Third, implying that a meeting was held in the interim. The minutes of 1905 indicate that Myra Jordan of Michigan was asked to call the deans to Ann Arbor in 1906, but no record of the meeting survives.

CHAPTER 6

1. Biographical facts about Lois Kimball were taken from the following: Rosenberry, 1960, p. 271; "Lois Rosenberry," 1973a, p. 774; and "Lois Rosenberry," 1973b, p. 620. She spoke of Richard Kimball in a speech she gave in Madison, WI, in April 1942 on the occasion of the dedication of her portrait to be hung in Lathrop Hall. The text of the speech was among the collection of Lois's papers found at the home of her stepgranddaughter, Nancy Hoit (Rosenberry, 1942). I refer to material found among these papers as the Hoit Collection although it is a personal, informal, and nonindexed collection. Other information was gathered from informal publications and newsletters of the Winneshiek County Genealogical Society, which acts as the local historical association in Cresco, IA. Information on Lois Mathews's parents was gathered from various newspaper articles including: Death of Aaron Kimball (1899); *Iowa Plain Dealer* (1867, June 7), p. 1; *Iowa Plain Dealer* (1868, November 13), p. 2; Mrs. Aaron Kimball (1923).

2. When asked "what happened when you heard the news of our entry to the war?" a surviving member of the class of 1917 simply said of the men, "they evaporated!" (H. Stephens [née Reed], class of 1917, personal communication, July 20, 1992).

REFERENCES

Abbot, A. (1988). *The system of professions: An essay on the division of expert labor.* Chicago: University of Chicago Press.

Acheson, E. M. (1932). *The effective dean of women.* Chicago: University of Chicago Press.

Addition to Shevlin begun. (1909). *Minnesota Alumni Weekly, 9,* 12.

Allen, N. (n.d.). A half century of progress, a future of promise. Madison: University of Wisconsin Archives. [WGSA commemorative booklet]

Amundson, A. O. (1905). *History of Howard County Iowa.* Cresco, IA: Business Directory.

Anderson, K. (1989). Brickbats and roses: Lucy Diggs Slowe, 1883–1937. In G. J. Clifford (Ed.), *Lone voyagers: Academic women in coeducational universities, 1870–1937* (pp. 281–307). New York: The Feminist Press.

Anderson, O. S. L. (1878). *An American girl and her four years in a boy's college.* New York: D. Appleton and Company.

Antler, J. (1977). *The educated woman and professionalization: The struggle for a new feminine identity, 1890–1920.* Unpublished doctoral dissertation, State University of New York at Stony Brook.

Antler, J. (1980). "After College, What?": New graduates and the family claim. *American Quarterly, 32,* 409–434.

Antler, J. (1987). *Lucy Sprague Mitchell: The making of a modern woman.* New Haven: Yale University Press.

Bailey, B. L. (1988). *From front porch to back seat: Courtship in twentieth-century America.* Baltimore: The Johns Hopkins University Press.

Bashaw, C. T. (1992). *We who live "off on the edges": Deans of women at southern coeducational institutions and access to the community of higher education, 1907–1960.* Unpublished doctoral dissertation, University of Georgia, Athens, GA.

Blanding, S. (1946). The dean's contribution to the life of our times. *Journal of the National Association of Deans of Women, 9,* 147–150.

Blanshard, R. Y. (1974). Ada Louise Comstock: Some of her memories of her life up to 1943, collected for reading to the Saturday Morning Club, March 16, 1974. Cambridge, MA: Radcliffe College Archives, Schlesinger Library.

Bledstein, B. J. (1976). *The culture of professionalism: The middle class and the development of higher education in America.* New York: Norton.

Bogue, A. G., & Taylor, R. (1975). *The University of Wisconsin: One hundred and twenty-five years.* Madison: University of Wisconsin Press.

Breed, M. B. (1901, November 20). Correspondence to registrar of Berkeley. Bloomington, IN: Indiana University Archives.

Breed, M. B. (1903a, October). Dean's report. Bloomington, IN: Indiana University Archives.

Breed, M. B. (1903b, October 10). Dean Breed wishes Indiana to obtain A.C.A. membership. *Daily Student*, 1.

Breed, M. B. (1904a, June 14). Dean's report. Bloomington, IN: Indiana University Archives.

Breed, M. B. (1904b, November 14). Dean's report. Bloomington, IN: Indiana University Archives.

Breed, M. B. (1905a, June 13). Correspondence to Mrs. S. T. Smith. Bloomington, IN: Indiana University Archives.

Breed, M. B. (1905b, June 15). Dean's report. Bloomington, IN: Indiana University Archives.

Breed, M. B. (1906a, January 4). Dean's report. Bloomington, IN: Indiana University Archives.

Breed, M. B. (1906b, May 25). Correspondence to "Madam" [form letter]. Bloomington, IN: Indiana University Archives.

Breed, M. B. (1906c, May 26). Correspondence to William Lowe Bryan. Bloomington, IN: Indiana University Archives.

Breed, M. B. (1906d, June 14). Dean's report. Bloomington, IN: Indiana University Archives.

Breed, M. B. (1907). Women and the academic curriculum. *The Missouri Alumna Quarterly, 2*(4), 214–219.

Breed, M. B. (1908a). The control of student life. *Journal of the Association of Collegiate Alumnae, Series III, 18,* 60–73.

Breed, M. B. (1908b, January 4). Correspondence to President Jesse. Columbia, MO: University of Missouri Archives.

Breed, M. B. (1909). The private boarding-house for women students. *The Journal of the Religious Education Association, 4,* 60–64.

Breed, M. B. (1949, September 16). Miss Mary Breed, retired educator—Obituary. *New York Times*, 28(N).

Breed-Brooks. (1903, Sept. 22). *Daily Student*, 2.

Brett, R., Calhoun, E. M., Piggott, L. J., Davis, H. A., & Bell-Scott, P. (1979). A symposium—our living history: Reminiscences of Black participation in NAWDAC. *Journal of the National Association of Women Deans, Administrators, and Counselors, 43,* 3–13.

Brint, S., & Karabel, J. (1989). *The diverted dream: Community colleges and the promise of educational opportunity in America, 1900–1985.* New York: Oxford University Press.

Brooks, K. H. (1988). The women's center: The new dean of women. *Initiatives, 5,* 17–21.

Bryan, W. L. (1903a, March). Report of the president. Bloomington, IN: Indiana University Archives.

Bryan, W. L. (1903b, June). Report of the president. Bloomington, IN: Indiana University Archives.

Bryan, W. L. (1904, March 28). Report of the president. Bloomington, IN: Indiana University Archives.

Cartoon. (1910, January). *Minne-Ha-Ha!*, *3*, 11.

Catton, B. (1956). Our association in review. *Journal of the National Association of Deans of Women, 10*, 3–9.

Chamberlin, R. V. (1960). *The University of Utah: A history of its first hundred years, 1850 to 1950*. Salt Lake City: University of Utah Press.

Channing, E. (1906, October 21). Correspondence to Max Farrand. Cambridge, MA: Harvard University Archives.

Channing, E. (1907, December 18). Correspondence to Max Farrand. Cambridge, MA: Harvard University Archives.

Channing, E. (1919, April 22). Correspondence to Max Farrand. Cambridge, MA: Harvard University Archives.

Channing, E. (n.d.). Personal File, HUG 300. Cambridge, MA: Harvard University Archives.

Chervenik, E. (1948). Thirty-five years of careers conferences. *Journal of the National Association of Deans of Women, 11*, 145–148.

Cheyney, M. (1905). Will nature eliminate the college woman? *Association of Collegiate Alumnae, 3rd Series*, 1–9.

Clark, T. (1970–1973). *Indiana University: Midwestern pioneer* (*Vols. 1–2*). Bloomington: Indiana University Press.

Clark, T. A. (1922). History and development of the office of dean of men. *School and Society, 16*, 65–70.

Clarke, E. H. (1873). *Sex in education: Or, a fair chance for the girls*. Boston: James R. Osgood and Co.

Claxton, P. P. (1912). *Report of the Commissioner of Education for the Year Ended June 30, 1911*. Washington, DC: Government Printing Office, 1912.

Clifford, G. J. (1988). Women's liberation and women's professions: Reconsidering the past, present, and future. In J. M. Faragher & F. Howe (Eds.), *Women and higher education in American history* (pp. 165–182). New York: Norton.

Clifford, G. J. (Ed.). (1989). *Lone voyagers: Academic women in coeducational institutions, 1870–1937*. New York: The Feminist Press.

Co-ed dean has plans. (1907). *Minnesota Alumni Weekly, 6*, 7–8.

Comstock, A. L. (1906a, May 14). The Alice Shevlin Hall. *Minnesota Alumni Weekly, 5*, 10–12.

Comstock, A. L. (1906b). What Alice Shevlin Hall stands for. *Minnesota Alumni Weekly, 6*, 17–18.

Comstock, A. L. (1907a). The Alice A. Shevlin Hall. *Gopher*, p. 6.

Comstock, A. L. (1907b). Plead for a dormitory. *Minnesota Alumni Weekly, 6*, 10.

Comstock, A. L. (1907c). A spring reckoning. *Minnesota Magazine, 13*, 275–277.

Comstock, A. L. (1907d, June 8). Correspondence to Board of Regents. Records of the Comptroller, AB6.1, Folder 320. Minneapolis, MN: University of Minnesota Archives.

Comstock, A. L. (1908a, March 16). The office of dean of women. *Minnesota Alumni Weekly, 8*, 4–5.

Comstock, A. L. (1908b). The question of a dormitory. *Minnesota Magazine, 14*, 259–263.

Comstock, A. L. (1909). What student government means. *Minnesota Alumni Weekly, 8*, 4.

Comstock, A. L. (1910). What the building means. *Minnesota Alumni Weekly, 9*, 4–5.

Comstock, A. L. (1911). Report of the dean of women. In *Sixteenth Biennial Report of the Board of Regents of the University of Minnesota* (pp. 40–41). Minneapolis: University of Minnesota.

Comstock, A. L. (1913). Report of the dean of women. *The President's Report, 1911–1912, Bulletin of the University of Minnesota, 6*, 157–162.

Comstock, A. L. (1925a). The new demand: Commencement address at Smith College. *Smith Alumnae Quarterly, 16*, 448–454.

Comstock, A. L. (1925b). New devices and desires in colleges for women. *Addresses and Proceedings of the Sixty-Third Meeting, National Education Association of the United States, 63*, 426–434.

Comstock, A. L. (1929). The fourth R for women. *Century Magazine, 117*, 411–417.

Comstock, A. L. (1940). Memories of Minnesota. *Minnesota Alumni Weekly, 39*, 191–192.

Comstock, A. L. (1950). Aims and policies of the AAUW. *Journal of the American Association of University Women, 43*, 76–80.

Conable, C. W. (1977). *Women at Cornell: The myth of equal education.* Ithaca: Cornell University Press.

Conference of Deans and Advisors of Women in State Universities. (1905). *Minutes of the conference of deans and advisors of women in state universities.* Bowling Green, OH: Bowling Green State University, Center for Archival Collections.

Conference of Deans and Advisors of Women in State Universities. (1907). *Minutes of the third conference of deans and advisors of women in state universities.* Bowling Green, OH: Bowling Green State University, Center for Archival Collections.

Conference of Deans of Women. (1910). *Minutes of the conferences of deans of women held in Bemis Hall, Colorado College, Colorado Springs.* Bowling Green, OH: Bowling Green State University, Center for Archival Collections.

Conference of Deans of Women of the Middle West. (1903). *Minutes of the conference of deans of women of the Middle West.* Bowling Green, OH: Bowling Green State University, Center for Archival Collections.

Cott, N. (1987). *The grounding of modern feminism.* New Haven: Yale University Press.

Cowley, W. H. (1934a). The history of student residential housing. *School and Society, 40*, 705–712.

Cowley, W. H. (1934b). The history of student residential housing II. *School and Society, 40*, 758–764.

Cowley, W. H. (1940). The history and philosophy of student personnel work. *Journal of the National Association of Deans of Women, 3*, 153–162.

Curti, M., & Carstensen, V. (1949). *The University of Wisconsin: A history, 1848–1925* (*Vols. 1–2*). Madison: University of Wisconsin Press.

Curti, M., & Carstensen, V. (1975). The University of Wisconsin: To 1925. In A. G. Bogue & R. Taylor (Eds.), *The University of Wisconsin: One hundred and twenty-five years* (pp. 3–38). Madison: University of Wisconsin Press.

Daily Cardinal, (1899, October 31, November 2), p. 1.

Daily Cardinal, (1912a, April, 1, 10, 11, 12, 13), p. 1.

Daily Cardinal, (1913a, May 2), p. 4.

Daily Cardinal, (1913b, November 19), p. 4.

Daily Cardinal, (1914, December 2), p. 4.

Daily Cardinal, (1915a, February 10, 11), p. 6.

Daily Cardinal, (1915b, November 5), p. 4.

Daily Cardinal, (1917, March 7, 9), p. 6.

Daily Cardinal, (1918, May 1), p. 4.

Daily Student, (1903a, December 7, 8, 12), p. 1.

Daily Student, (1903b, September 29, October 3, 5, November 12). No title, no author, all p. 1.

Daily Student, (1904, June 6, September 24). No title, no author, both p. 1.

Daily Student, (1906, April 12). No title, no author, p. 1.

Davis, H. A., & Bell-Scott, P. (1989). The Association of Deans of Women and Advisers to Girls in Negro Schools, 1929–1954: A brief oral history. *Sage*, *6*, 40–44.

Dean Breed resigns. (1906, May 6). *Daily Student*, p. 1.

Dean Comstock desires approved boarding houses. (1908, September 19). *Minnesota Daily*, p. 1.

Dean Comstock discussed vocation. (1912). *Minnesota Alumni Weekly*, *11*, 29–30.

Dean Comstock praises. (1910, May 11). *Minnesota Daily*, p. 1.

Dean Comstock praises first number. (1908, April 2). *Minnesota Daily*, p. 1.

Dean Comstock returns from dean's conference. (1909, February 17). *Minnesota Daily*, p. 1.

Dean discusses co-ed problems at Chicago. (1910, January 10). *Minnesota Daily*, p. 1.

Dean L. K. Mathews. (1913, May 29). *The Daily Cardinal*, p. 4.

Dean of women. (1906a, September 22). *Minnesota Daily*, p. 2.

Dean of women. (1906b). *Minnesota Alumni Weekly*, *6*, 1.

A dean of women. (1906). *Minnesota Alumni Weekly*, *6*, 1.

Dean of women censors Badger. (1912, May 2). *The Daily Cardinal*, p. 1.

Dean of women folder. (n.d.). Artifacts of the Office of Dean of Women. Madison, WI: University of Wisconsin Archives.

Dean tabooes [*sic*] "Dip" at naval ball. (1912, April 20). *The Daily Cardinal*, p. 1.

Deans of women at Chicago. (1908). *Minnesota Alumni Weekly*, *8*, 4.

Death of Aaron Kimball—Obituary. (1899, January 19). *Howard County* [*Cresco, IA*] *Times*, p. 1.

Dollar, M. C. (1992). *The beginnings of vocational guidance for college women: The Women's Educational and Industrial Union, the Association of Collegiate*

Alumnae, and women's colleges. Unpublished doctoral dissertation, Harvard University Graduate School of Education, Cambridge, MA.

Downs, W. S. (Ed.). (1934). Ada Louise Comstock. *Encyclopedia of America biography* (pp. 178–179). New York: The American Historical Society.

Duffey, E. B. (1874). *No sex in education: Or, a fair chance for both boys and girls: Being a review of Dr. E. H. Clarke's: Sex in education.* Philadelphia: J. M. Stoddart & Co.

Dzuback, M. A. (1993). Professionalism, higher education, and American culture: Burton J. Bledstein's *The culture of professionalism. History of Education Quarterly, 33*, 375–385.

Eddy, E. D., Jr. (1956). *Colleges for our land and time: The land-grant idea in American education.* New York: Harper & Brothers.

Eisenmann, L. (1991). "Freedom to be womanly": The separate culture of the women's college. In P. W. Kaufman (Ed.), *The search for equity: Women at Brown University, 1891–1991* (pp. 54–85). Hanover: Brown University Press.

Eliot, G. (1872). *Middlemarch.* New York: US Book Co. (1992, Bantam Books edition).

Eschbach, E. S. (1993). *The higher education of women in England and America, 1865–1920.* New York: Garland.

Etzioni, A. (Ed.). (1969). *The semi-professions and their organization: Teachers, nurses, social workers.* New York: The Free Press.

Faderman, L. (1991). *Odd girls and twilight lovers: A history of lesbian life in twentieth-century America.* New York: Penguin.

Fairbairn, R. H. (1919). *History of Chicasaw and Howard Counties.* Chicago: S. J. Clarke.

Ferguson, A. (1988). Woman's moral voice: Superior, inferior, or just different? In J. M. Faragher & F. Howe (Eds.), *Women and higher education in American history* (pp. 183–197). New York: Norton.

Filene, C. (Ed.). (1920). *Careers for women.* Boston: Houghton Mifflin.

First dean of women appointed at Citadel. (1997, August 11). *Feminist News,* p. 1.

Fish, V. K. (1985). "More than lore": Marion Talbot and her role in the founding years of the University of Chicago. *International Journal of Women's Studies, 8*, 228–249.

Fitzpatrick, E. (1989). For the "women of the university": Marion Talbot, 1858–1948. In G. J. Clifford (Ed.), *Lone voyagers: Academic women in coeducational universities, 1870–1937* (pp. 85–124). New York: The Feminist Press.

Fitzpatrick, E. (1990). *Endless crusade: Women social scientists and progressive reform.* New York: Oxford University Press.

Flexner, A. (1915). Is social work a profession? *School and Society, 1*, 901–911.

Fley, J. A. (1979). Student personnel pioneers: Those who developed our profession, Part I. *National Association of Student Personnel Administrators Journal, 17*, 23–39.

Fley, J. A. (1980). Student personnel pioneers: Those who developed our profession, Part II. *National Association of Student Personnel Administrators Journal, 17*, 25–44.

Frankfort, R. (1977). *Collegiate women: Domesticity and career in turn-of-the-century America.* New York: New York University Press.

Fraser, N. (1989). *Unruly practices: Power, discourse and gender in contemporary social theory.* Minneapolis: University of Minnesota Press.

Frederick Jackson Turner. (1936). In *Dictionary of American biography, 19,* 62. New York: Charles Scribner's Sons.

Freedman, E. (1979). Separatism as strategy: Female institution building and American feminism, 1870–1930. *Feminist Studies, 5,* 512–529.

Friedson, E. (1986). *Professional powers: A study of the institutionalization of formal knowledge.* Chicago: University of Chicago Press.

Gardner, D. H. (1934). Duties of the dean of men. *Journal of Higher Education, 5,* 191–196.

Geison, G. L. (Ed.). (1983). *Professions and professional ideologies in America.* Chapel Hill: University of North Carolina Press.

Gillies, J. (1975). In defense of the dean of women: A new role for a new world. *Journal of the National Association of Deans of Women, 38,* 156–162.

Glazer, P. M., & Slater, M. (1987). *Unequal colleagues: The entrance of women into the professions, 1890–1940.* New Brunswick: Rutgers University Press.

Goodspeed, T. W. (1916). *A history of the University of Chicago: The first quarter century.* Chicago: University of Chicago Press.

Gordon, L. D. (1979). Co-education on two campuses: Berkeley and Chicago, 1890–1912. In M. Kelley (Ed.), *Woman's being, woman's place: Female identity and vocation in American history* (pp. 171–193). Boston: Hall.

Gordon, L. D. (1990). *Gender and higher education in the Progressive Era.* New Haven: Yale University Press.

Gould, J. S. (1989). Women's centers as agents of change. In C. S. Pearson, D. L. Shavlik, & J. Tochton (Eds.), *Educating the majority: Women challenge tradition in higher education* (pp. 219–229). New York: Macmillan.

Graduation. (1888, July 26). *Plain Dealer,* p. 2.

Gray, J. (1951). *The University of Minnesota, 1851–1951* (Vols. *1–2*). Minneapolis: University of Minnesota Press.

Greenleaf, E. (1968). How others see us: ACPA presidential address. *Journal of College Student Personnel, 9,* 225–231.

Griffin, P. (1998). *Strong women, deep closets: Lesbians and homophobia in sport.* Amherst, MA: University of Massachusetts Press.

Ha-Ha! Minne comes again. (1909, April 30). *Minnesota Daily,* p. 1.

Haber, S. (1974). The professions and higher education in America: A historical view. In M. Gordon (Ed.), *Higher education and the labor market* (pp. 237–280). New York: McGraw-Hill.

Haddock, R. (1952). *A study of five deans of women.* Unpublished doctoral dissertation, Syracuse University, Syracuse, NY.

Hague, A. (1984). "What if the power does lie within me?": Women students at the University of Wisconsin, 1875–1900. *History of Higher Education Annual, 4,* 78–100.

Hall, G. S. (1906). The question of coeducation. *Munsey's Magazine, 34,* 588–592.

Hall, R. H., & Sandler, B. R. (1982). *The classroom climate: A chilly one for women?* Washington, DC: Association of American Colleges.

Harding, S. B. (Ed.). (1904). *Indiana University, 1820–1904.* Bloomington: Indiana University Press.

Harper, W. R. (1900). The associates degree. *Educational Review, 18,* 412–415.

Harper, W. R. (1902, January 16). Correspondence from Marion Talbot. President's Papers, 1889–1925, box 60, folder 11. Chicago, IL: Department of Special Collections, The University of Chicago Library.

Harper, W. R. (n.d.). Correspondence from John Dewey. President's Papers, 1889–1925, box 60, folder 11. Chicago, IL: Department of Special Collections, The University of Chicago Library.

Harris, B. J. (1978). *Beyond her sphere: Women and the professions in American history.* Westport, CT: Greenwood Press.

Hart, A. B. (n.d.). Personal File, HUG 300. Cambridge, MA: Harvard University Archives.

Hatch, N. O. (Ed.). (1988). *The professions in American history.* Notre Dame, IN: University of Notre Dame Press.

Hatcher, O. L. (Ed.). (1927). *Occupations for women.* Atlanta: Southern Women's Educational Alliance.

Holland, D. C., & Eisenhart, M. A. (1990). *Educated in romance: Women, achievement, and college culture.* Chicago: University of Chicago Press.

Holmes, L. (1939). *A history of the position of dean of women in a selected group of co-educational colleges and universities in the United States.* New York: Teachers College, Columbia University, Bureau of Publications.

Honor Dean Comstock. (1907). *Minnesota Alumni Weekly, 7,* 5.

Horowitz, H. L. (1984). *Alma mater: Design and experience in the women's colleges from their nineteenth century beginnings to the 1950s.* New York: Knopf.

Horowitz, H. L. (1987). *Campus life: Undergraduate cultures from the end of the eighteenth century to the present.* New York: Knopf.

Howe, J. W. (Ed.) (1874). *Sex and education: A reply to Dr. E. H. Clarke's "Sex in education."* Boston: Roberts Brothers.

Howes, A. (1885). *Health statistics of women college graduates: Report of a special committee of the Association of Collegiate Alumnae.* Boston: Massachusetts Bureau of Statistics of Labor.

Hughes, E. C. (1965). Professions. In K. S. Lynn (Ed.), *The professions in America* (pp. 1–15). Boston: Houghton Mifflin.

Hutchinson, L. (1908). Student government association. *Minnesota Alumni Weekly, 8,* 6–7.

Hyde, I. (1938). Before women were human beings: Adventures of an American Fellow in German universities of the 90s. *Journal of the American Association of University Women, 31,* 226–236.

Ihle, E. L. (Ed.) (1992). *Black women in higher education: An anthology of essays, studies and documents.* New York: Garland.

In regard to segregation. (1908, April 2). *The Democrat,* p. 1.

Indiana University. (1897). *The 1897–8 student handbook,* Bloomington, IN.

Ingersoll's century annals of San Bernardino County, 1769 to 1904. (1904). Los Angeles: L. A. Ingersoll.

Is co-education a success? (1906). *Minnesota Alumni Weekly, 6,* 13–15.

Johnson, E. B. (Ed.). (1910). *Forty years of the University of Minnesota.* Minneapolis: The General Alumni Association.

Jones, J. L. (1928). *A personnel study of women deans in colleges and universities.* New York: Teachers College, Columbia University Bureau of Publications.

Jordan, M. (1946, October 23). Mrs. Myra Jordan dies at her home at age of 83—Obituary. *Ann Arbor News.*

Kehr, M. (1938). The pioneer days of the dean of women. *The Journal of the National Education Association, 27,* 6–7.

Kelley, M. (Ed.). (1979). *Woman's being, woman's place: Female identity and vocation in American history.* Boston: Hall.

Kerber, L. K. (1988). Separate spheres, female worlds, women's place: The rhetoric of women's history. *The Journal of American History, 75,* 9–39.

Kimball, A. (1966, June 15). Aaron Kimball—Obituary. *The Times Plain Dealer,* [Cresco, IA], p. 2.

Kinnane, M. (1967). From whom would college women seek assistance. *Journal of College Student Personnel, 8,* 80–84.

Kraditor, A. S. (1981). *The ideas of the woman suffrage movement, 1890–1920.* New York: Norton.

Ladd, J. (1910). What student government means to the girls. *Minnesota Alumni Weekly, 9,* 7–8

Lasser, C. (Ed.). (1987). *Educating men and women together: Coeducation in a changing world.* Urbana: University of Illinois Press.

Leonard, J. W. (Ed.). (1914). Breed, Mary Bidwell. *Woman's Who's Who of America: A Biographical Dictionary of Contemporary Women of the United States and Canada.* New York: The American Commonwealth Co.

Lloyd, A. C. (1946). Women in the postwar college. *Journal of the American Association of University Women, 39,* 131–134.

Lois Rosenberry. (1973a). *American women 1935–1940: A composite biographical dictionary.* Detroit: Gale Research Company.

Lois Rosenberry. (1973b). *Who was who in America, Vol. 5.* Chicago: The A. N. Marquies Company.

Manly, W. G. (1911, March 31). Correspondence to W. L. Westermann, University of Wisconsin, forwarded to Van Hise. Charles Van Hise Correspondence. Madison, WI: University of Wisconsin Archives.

Marchalonis, S. (1995). *College girls: A century in fiction.* New Brunswick: Rutgers University Press.

Martin, G. S. (1911a). Report of the advisor of women, 1910–1911. Ithaca, NY: Cornell University Department of Manuscripts and University Archives.

Martin, G. S. (1911b). The position of dean of women. *Journal of the Association of Collegiate Alumnae Series IV, 2,* 65–78.

Martin, G. S. (1912). Report of the advisor of women, 1911–1912. Ithaca, NY: Cornell University Department of Manuscripts and University Archives.

Marvin Rosenberry. (1960). *Encyclopedia of American biography*. New York: American Historical Company.

Maslow, A. H. (1954). *Motivation and personality*. New York: Harper & Row.

Mathews, L. K. (1905). Application for the Ph.D. at Harvard University. Cambridge, MA: Harvard University Archives.

Mathews, L. K. (1909). *The expansion of New England: The spread of New England settlement and institutions to the Mississippi River, 1620–1865*. Boston: Houghton Mifflin.

Mathews, L. K. (1910a). Some activities of the Congregational Church west of the Mississippi. In G. S. Ford (Ed.), *Essays in American history dedicated to Frederick Jackson Turner* (pp. 3–34). New York: Holt.

Mathews, L. K. (1910b). The American frontier. *Proceedings of Nantucket Historical Association sixteenth annual meeting*, 34–42.

Mathews, L. K. (1910c). The Erie Canal and the settlement of the West. *The Holland Land Company and Canal construction in western New York, 14*, 187–203.

Mathews, L. K. (1911). A half-century of higher education for women. *The Wisconsin Magazine, 9*, 5–9.

Mathews, L. K. (1912). Report of the dean of women. In *The University of Wisconsin, biennial report of the Board of Regents, 1910–11 and 1911–12* (pp. 201–210). Madison, WI: University of Wisconsin Archives.

Mathews, L. K. (1913a). The Mayflower Compact and its descendants. *Mississippi Valley Historical Association proceedings, 6*, 79–106.

Mathews, L. K. (1913b). Women's self-government association. *Wisconsin alumni magazine, 14*, 388–393.

Mathews, L. K. (1914a). Benjamin Franklin's plans for a colonial union, 1750–1775. *The American political science review, 8*, 393–412.

Mathews, L. K. (1914b). Report of the dean of women. In *The University of Wisconsin, biennial report of the Board of Regents, 1912–13 and 1913–14* (pp. 237–245). Madison, WI: University of Wisconsin Archives.

Mathews, L. K. (1915). *The dean of women*. Boston: Houghton Mifflin.

Mathews, L. K. (1916a). Raising the standards of intellectual life. *Journal of the Association of Collegiate Alumnae, 9*, 69–76.

Mathews, L. K. (1916b). Report of the dean of women. In *The University of Wisconsin, biennial report of the Board of Regents, 1914–15 and 1915–16* (pp. 215–221). Madison, WI: University of Wisconsin Archives.

Mathews, L. K. (1918a). Report of the dean of women. In *The University of Wisconsin, biennial report of the Board of Regents, 1916–17 and 1917–18* (pp. 226–233). Madison, WI: University of Wisconsin Archives.

Mathews, L. K. (1918b). The making of Americans. *Vassar Quarterly, 3*, 252–258.

Mathews, L. K. (n.d.). University of Wisconsin faculty employment cards. Madison, WI: University of Wisconsin Archives.

Mathews, L. K. (n.d.). Papers of Lois Kimball Mathews. Madison, WI: University of Wisconsin Archives.

McCarthy, C. (1912). *The Wisconsin idea*. New York: Macmillan.

McGrath, E. J. (1936). *The evolution of administrative offices in institutions of higher education in the United States from 1860 to 1933.* Unpublished doctoral dissertation, University of Chicago, Chicago, IL.

McGuigan, D. G. (1970). *A dangerous experiment: 100 years of women at the University of Michigan.* Ann Arbor: Center for the Continuing Education of Women.

McIntosh, P. M. (1989). Curricular re-vision: The new knowledge for a new age. In C. S. Pearson, D. L. Shavlik, & J. Touchton (Eds.), *Educating the majority: Women challenge tradition in higher education* (pp. 400–412). New York: Macmillan.

Merrill, R. A., & Bragdon, H. D. (1926). *The vocation of dean.* Washington, DC: Press and Publicity Committee of The National Association of Deans of Women.

Minnesota Daily. (1906, November 21), p. 1.

Minnesota Daily. (1907, January, 10, September 25). No title, no author, both p. 1.

Minnesota Daily. (1908, December 18), p. 1.

Möebius, P. J. (1991). *Concerning the physiological intellectual feebleness of women.* In Tama Starr (Comp.), *The "natural inferiority" of women: Outrageous pronouncements by misguided males* (p. 195). New York: Poseidon Press.

Moore, W. E. (1976). *The professions: Roles and rules.* New York: Sage.

Morpurgo, J. E. (1976). *Their Majesties' Royall Colledge: William and Mary in the seventeenth and eighteenth centuries.* Williamsburg, VA: The Endowment Association of the College of William and Mary.

Morris, M. S. (1939). Cooperation: A.A.U.W. and N.A.D.W. *Journal of the National Association of Deans of Women, 2,* 105–108.

Morrison, S. P. (1919). Some sidelights of fifty years ago. *Indiana University Alumni Quarterly, 6,* 529–535.

Mosher, E. (n.d.). Alumnae survey, University of Michigan Alumnae Council. Ann Arbor, MI: Bentley Historical Library, University of Michigan.

Mrs. Aaron Kimball—Obituary. (1923, January 31). *Howard County [Cresco, IA] Times,* p. 2.

Narrative of Bacon's rebellion. (1896). *The Virginia Magazine of History and Biography, 4,* 159–175.

National Association of Deans of Women (NADW). (1950). *The dean of women in institutions of higher learning.* Washington, DC: Author.

Newcomer, M. (1959). *A century of higher education for American women.* New York: Harper & Row.

Nidiffer, J. (1998). Boston marriages. In L. Eisenmann (Ed.), *Historical dictionary of women's education* (pp. 52–54). Westport, CT: Greenwood Press.

Noble, J. (1988). The higher education of Black women in the twentieth century. In J. M. Faragher & F. Howe (Eds.), *Women and higher education in American history* (pp. 87–106). New York: Norton.

Northrup, C. (1901, July 8). Correspondence from Ada Louise Comstock. Minneapolis, MN: University of Minnesota Archives.

Northrup, C. (1903, June 21). Correspondence from Ada Louise Comstock. Minneapolis, MN: University of Minnesota Archives.

Northrup, C. (1904, February 25). Correspondence from Ada Louise Comstock. Minneapolis, MN: University of Minnesota Archives.

Oates, M. J., & Williamson, S. (1978). Women's colleges and women achievers. *Signs: Journal of Women in Culture and Society, 3*, 795–806.

Offenberg, R. S. (1967). Are deans of women necessary? *Journal of College Student Personnel, 8*, 2.

Office of women's dean sought by many. (1907, March 23). *Minnesota Daily*, p. 1.

Olin, H. R. (1908). Shall Wisconsin University remain a co-educational institution? Madison, WI: University of Wisconsin Archives.

Olin, H. R. (1909). *The women of a state university: An illustration of the working of coeducation in the Middle West.* New York: G. P. Putnam's Sons.

Palmeri, P. A. (1987). From republican motherhood to race suicide. In C. Lasser (Ed.), *Educating men and women together: Coeducation in a changing world* (pp. 49–64). Urbana: University of Illinois Press.

Parsons, T. (1968). Professions. In *International encyclopedia of the social sciences, Vol. 12* (pp. 536–547). New York: Macmillan.

Past Presidents Association. (1941). Twenty-five years in review. *Journal of the National Association of Deans of Women, 4*, 117–120.

Perkins, L. M. (1988). The higher education of Black women in the nineteenth century. In J. M. Faragher & F. Howe (Eds.), *Women and higher education in American history* (pp. 64–86). New York: Norton.

Personal and educational contributions to UW of Mrs. Rosenberry lauded. (1942, April 22). *Capitol Times*, p. 12.

Phillips, K. S. M. (1919). *The work of a dean of women.* Unpublished master's thesis, Teachers College, Columbia University, New York.

Phillips, K. S. M. (1953). Beginnings. *Journal of the National Association of Deans of Women, 16*, 143–145.

Phillips, K. S. M., Kerr, M., & Wells, A. (1927). History of the National Association of Deans of Women. *National Association of Deans of Women yearbook, 1927*, 228–235.

Pierce, A. E. (1928). *Deans and advisors of women and girls.* New York: Chatham Press.

Platter, A. W. (1892, October 15). Correspondence from Platter, Secretary, Indiana Branch of the Association of Collegiate Alumnae, to President John Coulter. Bloomington, IN: Indiana University Archives.

Potter, M. R. (1927). Report of Committee on History of the National Association of Deans of Women. *National Association of Deans of Women yearbook, 1927*, 212–227.

Preston, J. A. (1991). Gender and the formation of a women's profession: The case of public school teaching (Working Paper No. 245). Wellesley, MA: Wellesley Center for Research on Women.

Pyre, J. F. A. (1920). *Wisconsin.* New York: Oxford University Press.

Report on the admission of females. (1915). In *Proceedings of the Board of Regents, University of Michigan, 1837–1864* (p. 791). Ann Arbor, MI: Bentley Historical Library, University of Michigan.

Rice, J. K., & Hemmings, A. (1988). Women's colleges and women achievers: An update. *Signs: Journal of Women in Culture and Society, 13,* 546–559.

Rosenberg, R. (1982). *Beyond separate spheres: The intellectual roots of modern feminism.* New Haven: Yale University Press.

Rosenberg, R. (1988). The limits of access: The history of coeducation in America. In J. M. Faragher & F. Howe (Eds.), *Women and higher education in American history* (pp. 107–129). New York: Norton.

Rosenberry, L. K. M. (1926). Have women students affected the standards of coeducational institutions? *Journal of the American Association of University Women, 20,* 37–40.

Rosenberry, L. K. M. (1927). The new Americanism and the dean. *National Association of Deans of Women yearbook, 1927,* 201–210.

Rosenberry, L. K. M. (1934). Migrations from Connecticut prior to 1800. In *Tercentenary Commission of the State of Connecticut* (pp. 1–36). New Haven: Yale University Press.

Rosenberry, L. K. M. (1936). Migrations from Connecticut after 1800. In *Tercentenary Commission of the State of Connecticut* (pp. 1–29). New Haven: Yale University Press.

Rosenberry, L. K. M. (1942, April 21). Speech at the University of Wisconsin.

Rosenberry, L. K. M. (1948). The deanship at Wisconsin, 1897–1918. *Journal of the National Association of Deans of Women, 11,* 130–131.

Rosenberry, Lois Carter Kimball Mathews. (1960). *Encyclopedia of American biography.* New York: The American Historical Company, 271.

Rosenberry, M. (1918, June 21). Correspondence to Max Farrand.

Rossiter, M. W. (1982). *Women scientists in America: Struggles and strategies to 1940.* Baltimore: Johns Hopkins University Press.

Rothenberger, K. (1942). *An historical study of the position of dean of women at Indiana University.* Unpublished master's thesis, Indiana University, Bloomington.

Rudolph, F. (1956). *Mark Hopkins and the log: Williams College, 1836–1872.* New Haven: Yale University Press.

Rudolph, F. (1962). *The American college and university: A history.* New York: Knopf.

Sandler, B. R., Silverberg, L. A., & Hall, R. M. (1996). *The chilly climate: A guide to improve the education of women.* Washington, DC: National Association for Women in Education.

Sayre, M. B. (1950). *Half a century: An historical analysis of the National Association of Deans of Women, 1900–1950.* Unpublished doctoral dissertation, Teachers College, Columbia University, New York.

Schetlin, E. M. (1939). Fifty years of association—Ninety years of dreams. *Journal of the National Association of Deans of Women, 2,* 111–115.

Schudson, M. (1980). On Larson's *The rise of professionalism. Theory and Society, 9,* 215–229.

Schwager, S. (1978). *Arguing for the higher education of women: Early experiences with coeducation.* Unpublished Qualifying Paper, Harvard University Graduate School of Education, Cambridge, MA.

Schwager, S. (1982). *"Harvard Women": A history of the founding of Radcliffe*

College. Unpublished doctoral dissertation, Harvard University Graduate School of Education, Cambridge, MA.

Schwager, S. (1987). Educating women in America. *Signs*, *12*, 333–372.

Self-government is best training for citizenship. (1911, September 29). *The Daily Cardinal*, p. 1.

Self supporting students. (1910). *Minnesota Alumni Weekly*, *9*, 11.

Sellery, G. C. (1960). *Some ferments at Wisconsin, 1901–1947: Memories and reflections*. Madison: University of Wisconsin Press.

Shay, J. E., Jr. (1966). *Residence halls in the age of the university: Their development at Harvard and Michigan, 1850–1930*. Unpublished doctoral dissertation, University of Michigan, Ann Arbor.

Shevlin Hall open to all. (1907, September 10). *Minnesota Daily*, p. 1.

Shevlin Record. April 1, 1912.

Smith, A. (1776). *An inquiry into the nature and causes of the wealth of nations*. Dublin: Whitestone.

Smith, A. T. (1903). Coeducation in the schools and colleges of the United States. In *Education Report 1903*. Publisher Unknown.

Smith, D. (1988). *Women's colleges and coed colleges: Is there a difference for women?* Unpublished manuscript, Claremont Graduate School, Claremont, CA.

Smith, S. M. (1977). Ada Comstock Notestein: Educator. In B. Stuhler & G. Kreuter (Eds.), *Women of Minnesota: Selected biographical essays* (pp. 208–225). St. Paul: Minnesota Historical Society Press.

Solomon, B. M. (1980). Ada Louise Comstock. In *Notable American women, the modern period: A biographical dictionary* (pp. 157–159). Cambridge: Harvard University Press.

Solomon, B. M. (1985). *In the company of educated women*. New Haven: Yale University Press.

Solomon, B. M. (Ed.). (1987). *The evolution of an educator: An anthology of published writings of Ada Louise Comstock*. New York: Garland.

Solomon, B. M. (1993). *From Western prairies to Eastern commons: A life in education, Ada Louise Comstock Notestein, 1876–1973*. Unpublished manuscript, Schlesinger Library, Radcliffe College. [Note: edited posthumously by Susan Ware]

Sprague, L. (1908). The forms and results of student social activities. *Journal of the Association of Collegiate Alumnae, Series III*, *18*, 50–55.

Sprague, R. J. (1915). Education and race suicide. *Journal of Heredity*, *6*, 158–162.

Stimson, D. (1930). Women deans. *Journal of the American Association of University Women*, *13*, 60–64.

Stoecker, J. L., & Pascarella, E. T. (1991). Women's colleges and women's career attainments revisited. *Journal of Higher Education*, *62*, 403–406.

Storr, R. (1966). *Harper's university: The beginnings*. Chicago: University of Chicago Press.

Storr, R. (1971). Marion Talbot. In *Notable American Women, 1607–1950: A biographical dictionary* (pp. 423–424). Cambridge: Harvard University Press.

Strom, S. H. (1992). *Beyond the typewriter: Gender, class, and the origins of modern office work, 1900–1930.* Urbana: University of Illinois Press.

Student Life and Interest Committee. (1913). Notes of the Student Life and Interest Committee. Madison, WI. University of Wisconsin Archives.

Students are doing noble work at settlements. (1910, October 12). *Minnesota Daily*, p. 1.

Sturtevant, S. M., & Hayes, H. (1930). *Deans at work.* New York: Harper & Brothers Publishers, 1930.

Sturtevant, S. M., & Strang, R. (1928). *A personnel study of deans of women in teachers colleges and normal schools.* New York: Teachers College, Columbia University Bureau of Publications.

Sturtevant, S. M., Strang, R., & Kim, M. (1940). *Trends in student personnel work as represented in the positions of dean of women and dean of girls in colleges and universities, normal schools, teachers colleges, and high schools.* New York: Teachers College, Columbia University Bureau of Publications.

Swain, J. (1899, November). Report of the president. Bloomington, IN: Indiana University Archives.

Swain, J. (1900, June). Report of the president. Bloomington, IN: Indiana University Archives.

Swain, J. (1901a, June 21, July 1, & July 21). Correspondence to Mary Bidwell Breed. Bloomington, IN: Indiana University Archives.

Swain, J. (1901b, June). Report of the president. Bloomington, IN: Indiana University Archives.

Swain, J. (1901c, November). Report of the president. Bloomington, IN: Indiana University Archives.

Swain, J. (1902, June). Report of the president. Bloomington, IN: Indiana University Archives.

Talbot, M. (1897, October). Present day problems in the education of women. *Educational Review, 14,* 248–258.

Talbot, M. (1898, December). Some further considerations. *Journal of the Association of Collegiate Alumnae, Series II, 1,* 25–28.

Talbot, M. (1903, April 7). Correspondence to William Rainey Harper. Marion Talbot Papers. Department of Special Collections, The University of Chicago Library.

Talbot, M. (1908). The women of the university. In W. R. Harper, *President's report, 1908–1909.* Chicago: University of Chicago Press.

Talbot, M. (1909, April). Moral and religious influences as related to the environment of student life. *The Journal of the Religious Education Association, 4,* 41–46.

Talbot, M. (1910). *The education of women.* Chicago: University of Chicago Press.

Talbot, M. (1936). *More than lore: Reminiscences of Marion Talbot.* Chicago: University of Chicago Press.

Talbot, M. (1939). Women in the university world: A story of a century's progress. *Journal of the American Association of University Women, 32,* 203–214.

Talbot, M., & Breckinridge, S. (1912). *The modern household.* Boston: Whitcomb and Barrows.

Talbot, M., & Rosenberry, L. K. M. (1931). *The history of the American Association of University Women.* Boston: Houghton Mifflin.

Teicher, B. (Director.) (n.d.). Oral history project—tape recorded interviews with various surviving members of the university's past. Madison, WI: University of Wisconsin Archives.

Teicher, B., & Jenkins, J. W. (1987). *A history of housing at the University of Wisconsin.* Madison: UW History Project.

Those regulations. (1903, October 3). *Daily Student,* p. 1.

Tidball, M. E. (1973). Perspective on academic women and affirmative action. *Educational Record, 54,* 130–135.

Tidball, M. E. (1980). Women's colleges and women achievers revisited. *Signs: Journal of Women in Culture and Society, 13,* 505–517.

Tidball, M. E. (1991). Comment on "Women's colleges and women's career attainments revisited." *Journal of Higher Education, 62,* 406–408.

Tidball, M. E., & Kistiakowsky, V. (1976). Baccalaureate origins of Americans scientists and scholars. *Science, 193,* 646–652.

Touchton, J. G., & Davis, L. (Comp.) (1991). *Fact book on women in higher education.* New York: Macmillan.

Treichler, P. A. (1985). Alma mater's sorority: Women and the University of Illinois, 1890–1925. In P. A. Treichler, C. Kramarae, & B. Stafford (Eds.), *For alma mater: Theory and practice in feminist scholarship* (pp. 5–61). Urbana: University of Illinois Press.

Troxell, L. (1948a). Is it self-government? *Journal of the National Association of Deans of Women, 11,* 132–135.

Troxell, L. (1948b). Looking back upon Wisconsin's women's self-government. *Journal of the National Association of Deans of Women, 11,* 136–138.

Turner, F. J. (1894). *Proceedings of the State Historical Society of Wisconsin, 1893.* Madison: State Historical Society of Wisconsin.

Turner. F. J. (1911, April 1). Correspondence to Dana C. Monroe. Charles Van Hise Correspondence. Madison, WI: University of Wisconsin Archives.

Tuttle, K. N. (1996). *What became of the dean of women?: Changing roles for women administrators in American higher education, 1940–1980.* Unpublished doctoral dissertation, University of Kansas, Lawrence, KS.

University of Minnesota. (1906, December 11). Minutes of the Board of Regents. In *University Board of Regents fourteenth biennial report, 1906.* Minneapolis, MN: University of Minnesota Archives.

University of Minnesota. (1908). *Bulletin. University of Minnesota college of science, literature, and the arts, 1908–09.* Minneapolis, MN: University of Minnesota Archives.

University of Wisconsin. (1898). *The University of Wisconsin, biennial report of the Board of Regents, 1896–97 and 1897–98.* Madison, WI: University of Wisconsin Archives.

Van Hise, C. (1907). Educational tendencies in state universities. *Educational Review, 24*, 504–520.

Van Hise, C. (1908, April 7). Correspondence to Helen Olin. Madison, WI: University of Wisconsin Archives.

Van Hise, C. (1910a, May 26). Correspondence from Cora Woodward. Madison, WI: University of Wisconsin Archives.

Van Hise, C. (1910b, May 28). Correspondence to Cora Woodward. Madison, WI: University of Wisconsin Archives.

Van Hise, C. (1911a, March 19). Correspondence from Frederick Jackson Turner. Madison, WI: University of Wisconsin Archives.

Van Hise, C. (1911b, March 22). Correspondence from Dana C. Munro. Madison, WI: University of Wisconsin Archives.

Van Hise, C. (1911c, March 22). Correspondence to Frederick Jackson Turner. Madison, WI: University of Wisconsin Archives.

Van Hise, C. (1911d, April 17). Correspondence from Lois K. Mathews. Madison, WI: University of Wisconsin Archives.

Van Hise, C. (1917). War measures in higher educational institutions. *Addresses and proceedings of the fifty-fifth meeting of the National Education Association of the United States, 55*, 293–296.

Van Hise, C. (1918, June 27). Correspondence to Nicholas Murray Butler. Madison, WI: University of Wisconsin Archives.

Van Hise, C. (n.d. [circa 1911, March]). Correspondence from Lida King. Madison, WI: University of Wisconsin Archives.

Van Hise for coeducation. (1908, April 7). *Fond du Lac Commonwealth*, p. 1.

Veysey, L. R. (1965). *The emergence of the American university*. Chicago: University of Chicago Press.

Veysey, L. R. (1988). Higher education as a profession: Changes and continuities. In N. O. Hatch (Ed.), *The professions in American history* (pp. 15–32). Notre Dame, IN: University of Notre Dame Press.

Vincent, G. (1913, January). The President's Report, 1911–1912. *Bulletin of the University of Minnesota*, 95–100.

Vocational Conference. (1918). *War-vocational conference* [Program for the 1918 vocational conference]. Madison, WI: University of Wisconsin Archives.

Vonnegut, K. (1991). In Tama Starr (Comp.), *The "natural inferiority" of women: Outrageous pronouncements by misguided males* (p. 200). New York: Poseidon Press.

Waite, A. G. (1904). Notebook. For *Economics 3, Principles of Sociology* with Professor Carver. Cambridge, MA: Harvard University Archives.

Walsh, M. R. (1977). *"Doctors wanted, no women need apply": Sexual barriers in the medical profession, 1835–1935*. New Haven: Yale University Press.

Wellesley College. (1910). *Courses of Instruction, 1910–11*. Wellesley, MA.

Wells, A. E. (1930). The changing order: The dean of women in a large university. *Journal of the American Association of University Women, 13*, 70–73.

Welter, B. (1976). *Dimity convictions: The American woman in the nineteenth century*. Athens, OH: Ohio University Press.

Whitney, M. (1964). Women student personnel administrators: The past and future. *Journal of College Student Personnel, 12,* 7–10.

Wilensky, H. L. (1964). The professionalization of everyone? *American Journal of Sociology, 70,* 137–158.

Wilson, W. (1896). Princeton in the nation's service. *Forum, 22,* 450–466.

Wisconsin State Journal. (1942, April 22).

Women's mag to feature need for dormitories. (1908, April 2). *Minnesota Daily,* p. 1.

Woody, T. (1929). *A history of women's education in the United States (Vols. 1–2).* New York: Science Press.

Words of thanks. (1905, May 26). *Daily Student,* p. 2.

Zschoche, S. (1989). Dr. Clarke revisited: Science, true womanhood, and female collegiate education. *History of Education Quarterly, 29,* 545–569.

INDEX

ABOUT THE AUTHOR

Jana Nidiffer is an assistant professor in the Center for the Study of Higher and Postsecondary Education at the University of Michigan, Ann Arbor. Her areas of specialization include both history and gender issues in higher education. Prior to this position, she taught the history of higher education at the Harvard Graduate School of Education and the University of Massachusetts at Amherst. She has also been the Assistant Dean of the College and Coordinator of Women's Studies at Brandeis University. Ms. Nidiffer holds an undergraduate and a master's degree from Indiana University and a doctorate from Harvard University.

Ms. Nidiffer's research interests focus on access, particularly how higher education serves previously underserved populations, especially women and the economically disadvantaged. Her first book, *Beating the Odds: How the Poor Get to College*, is co-authored with Arthur Levine, President of Teachers College, Columbia University. In addition to *More Than a Wise and Pious Matron*, she is the co-editor, along with Carolyn Bashaw, of *Women Administrators in Higher Education: Historical Contributions and Contemporary Challenges*, due out in 2000. She has presented papers on her work at conferences of the History of Education Society, the American Educational Research Association, and the Association for the Study of Higher Education. In 1992, Ms. Nidiffer was awarded the Alice E. Smith Fellowship for women in history.